POLITICAL PARTIES AND ELECTIONS

Election Law, Politics, and Theory

Series Editor: David Schultz

Election Law, Politics, and Theory broadly examines election law at the national, subnational, and international or comparative levels. Titles in the series provide both empirical and theoretical analysis of topics and issues that affect voting, campaigns, and elections, and as such offer coverage of political as well as legal concerns and controversies. Useful for scholars, researchers, and practitioners in the field, volumes address such subjects as voting rights, reapportionment, ballot access, campaign finance reform, the courts and election regulation, and the role of actors including political parties and the media. The series' ultimate goal is to build scholarship in this key area by seeking to understand how elections function in an increasingly complex, technological, and global community, and the ways in which election law impacts outcomes, disputes, and eventually governance in particular nations and societies.

Other titles in this series

Electoral College Reform
Challenges and Possibilities
Edited by Gary Bugh
ISBN 978 0 7546 7751 2

State Secretaries of State
Guardians of the Democratic Process
Jocelyn F. Benson
ISBN 978 0 7546 7745 1

The Battle Over Bilingual Ballots
Language Minorities and Political Access Under the Voting Rights Act
James Thomas Tucker
ISBN 978 0 7546 7572 3

Political Parties and Elections

Legislating for Representative Democracy

ANIKA GAUJA
University of Sydney, Australia

ASHGATE

Published by
Ashgate Publishing Limited
Wey Court East
Union Road
Farnham
Surrey, GU9 7PT
England

Ashgate Publishing Company
Suite 420
101 Cherry Street
Burlington
VT 05401-4405
USA

www.ashgate.com

British Library Cataloguing in Publication Data
Gauja, Anika.
Political parties and elections : legislating for representative democracy. -- (Election law, politics, and theory)
1. Political campaigns--Law and legislation. 2. Political parties--Law and legislation.
I. Title II. Series
342'.078-dc22

Library of Congress Cataloging-in-Publication Data
Gauja, Anika.
Political parties and elections : legislating for representative democracy / by Anika Gauja.
p. cm. -- (Election law, politics, and theory)
Includes bibliographical references and index.
ISBN 978-0-7546-7704-8 (hbk) -- ISBN 978-0-7546-9409-0 (ebk)
1. Political parties--Law and legislation. 2. Campaign funds--Law and legislation.
I. Title.
K3270.G38 2010
342'.07--dc22

2010022356

ISBN 9780754677048 (hbk)
ISBN 9780754694090 (ebk)

Printed and bound in Great Britain by
MPG Books Group, UK

Contents

List of Tables

Acknowledgements

First and foremost, I would like to acknowledge the contribution of my friends and colleagues in the Department of Government and International Relations, the University of Sydney, who have provided valuable intellectual support and mentorship throughout this past year. It is a pleasure to work in a department where early career researchers (such as myself) are welcomed and encouraged to pursue their own research agendas with the full support of their colleagues. I would also like to thank David Schultz for his comments on the manuscript, as well as others who provided feedback on the various chapters at the Australian Political Studies Association Conference at Macquarie University (2009), the Political Studies Association Conference in Edinburgh (2010) and the Electoral Regulation Workshop held by the Faculty of Law, The University of Melbourne, in November 2009. The University of Sydney through a Faculty of Arts Research Support Scheme Grant provided financial support for this research.

Chapter 1
Public Law, Political Parties and Representative Democracy: A Framework for Comparative Analysis

In this chapter, I argue the need for a comparative assessment of the way in which the law seeks to regulate the activities of political parties as actors in elections – an assessment that acknowledges the inherent relationship between politics and the law. My central contention is that any differences between legal regimes and the way in which they have changed over time can best be understood as the product of lawmakers' normative conceptions of representative democracy and the place of parties within it. The chapter will also briefly examine the symbiotic nature of the relationship between politics and the law, who are the key lawmakers in the regulation of political parties, and introduce the crucial debate on the public–private distinction in public law and how this has been applied to the legal regulation of political actors. Finally, I outline the book's research design and method, the selection of states for analysis, and provide a brief chapter outline.

Introduction: Political Parties and Representative Democracy

Political scientists have long recognized the importance of political parties in the functioning of modern representative democracy. For example, Giovanni Sartori (1968: 471) has claimed that 'citizens in Western democracies are represented *through* and *by* parties. This is inevitable', while Schattschneider (1942: 1) argued that 'modern democracy is unthinkable save in terms of political parties' (see also Kelsen 1929; Ware 1987; Rosenblum 2000; Pildes 2004: 101). Actual political practice suggests that political parties are crucial actors in democratic elections: in established democracies, it is typically the political parties that nominate candidates for public office, run highly visible and organized election campaigns, and whose names (alongside their nominated candidates) appear on the ballot paper. As voters, we are much more likely to identify with, and express a general preference for a political party than endorse the policies of an individual candidate. This general conception of the importance of parties is reiterated in public opinion – an analysis of survey data from 13 states revealed that three-quarters of respondents thought that political parties were necessary for democracy (Dalton and Weldon 2005: 933). Although the definition and exact function of political parties is a topic of constant contestation in political science scholarship, a common theme underlying all accounts of parties in modern liberal democratic systems (and one that distinguishes them from other political actors such as pressure or interest groups) is that they exist for the purpose of contesting elections for public office.[1]

While the significance of parties is often taken for granted in politics and society, there exists considerable variation between legal systems as to the nature and extent to which parties are regulated, or even formally recognized, as participants in electoral and democratic institutions and processes. In common law liberal democracies such as the United Kingdom, Australia, Canada and New Zealand, only recently has the law acknowledged political parties as anything more than mere 'voluntary associations', akin to social and sporting clubs. In these democracies, many electoral law provisions continue to be characterized in terms of individual candidates rather than battles between national political party organizations. This categorization of political parties has had important consequences for voters, for example, in the area of campaign financing where expenditure by political parties has for the most part of the twentieth century been unregulated and hence issues regarding transparency and fairness in the electoral contest have arisen. It has also had important ramifications for members of political parties by historically restricting their legal rights and opportunities to seek redress for any wrongs committed by a party against them. This absence of any substantial legal regulation of the financial and internal affairs of political parties has been portrayed by many commentators as a 'double standard' between the importance of political parties in modern systems of representative democracy and their status at law, and has been followed by calls for increased legal regulation.[2]

However, this *laissez-faire* treatment of political parties is not something that is common to all nations. Political parties in the United States are some of the most comprehensively regulated parties in the world, despite constitutional freedom of speech and association provisions that could conceivably be used as a shield to protect political parties and their members from interference by the state. The impact of First Amendment rights upon attempts to regulate the activities of political parties is a constant source of tension in American jurisprudence. Amongst European democracies, the legal position of parties in Germany is so strongly articulated in the country's Basic Law that they are regarded as 'institutions of constitutional law' (Müller and Sieberer 2006: 439). Parties also feature prominently in the constitutions of Portugal, Spain and many newly established democracies following the collapse of the Soviet Union. What these diverse experiences

1 For example, Epstein (1980: 9) defines a party as 'any group, however loosely organized, seeking to elect government office holders under a given label'; Aldrich (1995: 19) argues that 'political parties can be seen as coalitions of elites to capture and use public office'; whereas Smith (1997: 157) conceives parties as 'organisations which aim to influence public policy in favour of an ideology or set of interests, primarily by attempting to gain control of public office'.

2 See for example, Somes (1996); Bennett (2002); Gauja (2005), (2006a).

suggest is that political parties are viewed and regulated differently across nations according to historical experiences, political philosophies, social attitudes towards the normative role that political parties should play in representative democracies and how elections as processes are actually defined.

A difficulty with much of the existing literature on the legal status of political parties is a tendency to treat the political importance of parties and the fact that they have not been subject to a great deal of regulation in many liberal democracies as a curious paradox, without providing any sustained historical, political and legal analysis as to why this has occurred. Adequately explaining the current climate of legal regulation and predicting future developments not only requires a legal and political analysis of the body of case law and precedent relating to both the legal and political status of parties, but also a broader examination of the legislative and constitutional design of representative democracy in the various nations under consideration, and an appreciation of the political and historical context within which major reforms have occurred.

Political parties are particularly fascinating to explore as subjects of legal regulation not only because of their importance in the functioning of representative democracy as we currently know it, but their unique characteristics and dynamic nature. Parties are constantly evolving in their organizational forms, they are multi-levelled and multi-layered institutions with several centres of power and by their very nature as aggregators of citizen opinion they embody significant disagreements between and within members, supporters and party activists. However, the fact that political parties are not autonomous or unified actors poses a significant challenge for their legal regulation.

Given these interesting variations, a comparative analysis of the ways in which advanced industrial democracies seek to regulate (or refrain from regulating) the activities of political parties in electoral contests is timely. Furthermore, it is appropriate to adopt a theoretical perspective to rationalize and analyse these divergent legal regimes that acknowledges that the regulation of political parties through the public law is inherently connected to lawmakers' own normative visions of representative democracy and the place of parties within it. As lawmakers within the legislative arena are typically also party members, these normative visions might also embody a particular regard for partisan interests. There is an intimate relationship between politics, normative political theory and election law that reflects the diversity of electoral law provisions across the globe. Although this relationship between law and politics is readily acknowledged by constitutional law scholars, it needs to be more explicitly and systematically addressed in electoral law studies.

Political Parties and Elections analyses the electoral laws of five common law democracies with similar legislative and representative traditions, similar levels of economic and political development, yet with significantly different electoral provisions: the United States, the United Kingdom, Canada, Australia and New Zealand. The book specifically focuses on the ways in which these jurisdictions seek to regulate the behaviour of their political parties as the product of a broader normative vision of how representative democracy ought to function. Such visions are more often than not obscured or unacknowledged and identifying them requires a careful analysis of both legislative provisions and case law, informed by historical and contemporary political debates. Although the primary aspect of this study is elections, the way in which political parties contest government is regulated through more than simply a discrete body of electoral law. In this respect, I also examine the impact of ancillary legislation such as funding regulations, associations and corporations law, administrative law and constitutional provisions. The analysis incorporates both legislative sources and developments in case law – the latter source is most often missing from works published on parties in the political science tradition. It is an original synthesis of secondary material, new legal and empirical political research and critical commentary.

Existing Literature on the Legal Regulation of Political Parties

Compared to the burgeoning generalist literature on political parties, electoral and party systems, very few books have been written to date on election law in the democracies under consideration, let alone specifically on the role and regulation of political parties as electoral actors.[3] This is perhaps a consequence of the fact that the topic sits at the intersection of two interrelated, yet conceptually distinct disciplines (political science and law), that until recently have tended to talk past, rather than to, one another. Few manuscripts published in the legal tradition adequately acknowledge the importance of politics (and particularly parties) in shaping the contours of representative democracy. As Bogdanor (2004: 718) argues:

> It is perhaps because the law was so late in recognising political parties that constitutional lawyers and other writers on the constitution have taken insufficient notice of the fact that parties are so central to our constitutional arrangements and, more particularly, that these arrangements vary with the configuration of the party system.

Similarly, many politics books dealing with parties and democracy pay little attention to the substantial body of public law that regulates and shapes the activities of these organizations. This is surprising given that party politics essentially reflects society and is played out within a set of rules, which, although

3 However, Persily and Cain (2000: 775) note that the case law and legal scholarship in the last half decade in this area now constitutes 'a subdiscipline in American law'. Books dealing with electoral law in the other democracies under consideration in this research remain limited in number: see Lowenstein and Hasen (2004); Issacharoff, Karlan and Pildes (1998); Orr, Mercurio and Williams (2003); Geddis (2007a); Tham, Costar and Orr (2011).

changeable, inherently influence parties' conduct (Jupp 1968: 36). All party systems are characterized by a particular set of social, political, cultural, economic and legal circumstances. Although the first four of these influences have been analysed at great length by the political science community, the various legal frameworks governing the operation of political parties have received far less attention, particularly from a comparative perspective (van Biezen 2008a). This is a significant omission, as the potential for the law to influence the activities of political parties is considerable. Legal regulations are the most direct form of state intervention in party politics, requiring parties to fulfil conditions that relate to the content and form of their organizations (Müller 1993), in addition to indirectly influencing parties' priorities through the design of electoral systems.[4] In bringing together these two perspectives, I hope this book to be of use to both lawyers and those interested in studying politics.

Nevertheless, as the trend towards increased regulation is becoming more apparent, comparative party scholars have devoted more attention to the topic of legal regulation in recent years (see, for example, van Biezen 2008a; Karvonen 2007; Gauja 2008; Janda 2005; Casas-Zamora 2005; Johns 1999). Of particular concern is the potential impact that legal regulation may have on parties as organizations, and the character of the broader democratic system within which they operate. In this respect, discussion of the legal framework has centred upon the design of electoral systems, and hence the impact of the law on political parties tends to be evaluated predominantly to the extent that party activities intersect with the proper functioning of a competitive electoral system (see, for example, Rae 1967). The main areas of existing inquiry include the regulation of political campaigns (including party finance, broadcasting and advertising), the conduct of elections and disputed returns, the registration of parties and electoral administration. Excluding some more recent scholarship in the US (see, for example, Kang 2005; Magarian 2003; Garrett 2002; Persily and Cain 2000), there has been comparatively less analysis of the impact of the law on parties in their capacity as participatory organizations.

Studies of the legal regulation of political parties have been more numerous in the democracies of Western Europe. Many earlier writings centred on the experience of Germany, which provides explicit regulation for its political parties, but academic attentions are becoming increasingly comparative in scope, now focusing on other nation states of Europe (see, for example, van Biezen 2008a, 2008b; Müller and Sieberer 2006). American legal scholarship has also paid increasing attention in the last decade to what Issacharoff (2000: 596) refers to as 'the structural and institutional mechanisms necessary for participation in democratic politics', of which party law forms a crucial element (see, for example, Epperson 1986; Persily and Cain 2000; Magarian 2003). Apart from several recent

4 The scope of this volume is limited to examining the effects of legal provisions on the behaviour of political parties as electoral actors, excluding indirect provisions such as the form of voting and the distribution of electoral boundaries.

volumes that focus on campaign financing (Ewing and Issacharoff 2006; Ewing 2007), party regulation is remains relatively under-studied in the United Kingdom, Australia, Canada and New Zealand.[5]

The Relationship Between Politics and the Law

The research and analysis presented here is underpinned by the fundamental assumption that politics and the law are intertwined. Employing a legal-procedural perspective in evaluating comparative regulatory frameworks, I argue that the laws that regulate how elections are conducted are just as worthy of analysis as the outcomes that they produce (which is the predominant focus of the political science discipline).[6] As Geddis (2007a: 1) argues, 'on most occasions when the electoral process comes under scrutiny, the institutions and practices underpinning it are treated as given'. From a procedural perspective, how laws are made, who makes them and the purpose they are meant to serve are questions just as relevant as their specific content and their political consequences. In examining these questions, important policy issues and conflicts come to the fore, and the different norms and conceptions of politics that various actors might hold will inevitably lead to competing assessments and different prescriptions about the appropriate status and legal regulation of political parties (van Biezen 2008a: 14).

For a complete comparative picture, it is necessary not only to evaluate the current laws that regulate the behaviour of political parties as electoral actors, but also analyse the deeper policy and political issues that lie behind the decisions to adopt different legal regimes that are not always made explicit. The book demonstrates how debates over the rules, laws and regulations that are adopted and applied to political parties reflect historical developments, deeper notions of the nature and form of representative democracy, and how this might differ not only between political actors, but between jurisdictions and nation states.

I take a new institutionalist approach to law and the role of the courts in investigating the ways in which courts *are* political institutions and how they are connected to the larger framework of government and representative democracy. The underlying assumption of this approach is that law, political processes and institutions are symbiotic. Laws reflect prevailing political and socioeconomic forces, but they are also constitutive of these elements as they can 'privilege certain groups or ideas above others, can influence the strategies of actors in the political and socio-economic systems, and can also shape the attitudes and goals of actors in the political process' (Hausegger, Hennigar and Riddell 2009: 23). When we apply

5 An exception in New Zealand is Geddis (2009); (2007a); (2005) and the forthcoming Australian volume edited by Tham Costar and Orr (2011).

6 See also Geddis (2007a); Massicotte, Blais and Yoshinaka (2003); Norris (2004); Watt (2006); Forcese and Freeman (2005) and Orr, Mercurio and Williams (2003) for a similar approach.

this thinking to the legal regulation of political parties, an element of circularity appears in the relationship between law and democracy, in which parties are both the governors and the governed. Legal and electoral systems rely heavily on their 'democratic genesis' for legitimacy (that is, a system of lawmaking involving political parties; yet democracy only exists in an institutional and procedural form as it has been created by laws framed by political parties (see Geddis 2003: 53; Issacharoff, Karlan and Pildes 1998: 1–3).

Politics Shapes Lawmaking

The practice of politics inherently shapes the law, whether this occurs through the process of contestation and debate that occurs in the legislative chamber by elected representatives, or in the practice of interpretation and the application of laws and constitutions that is undertaken by the judiciary.

One interesting yet potentially problematic aspect of the legal regulation of parties is that the design of electoral systems and the legislation governing their conduct is initiated, debated and implemented by the parties themselves. Hence, there is opportunity for governing parties to reinforce pre-existing patterns of dominance, or to privilege their own positions in the design of particular legal regimes. In recent years, studies of party organization (and in particular the cartel party thesis, discussed below) have been concerned with this possibility, and it has also been noted by legal scholars (Feasby 2007; Geddis 2007a: 20; Carothers 2006: 194; Pildes 2004). As Carothers (2006: 194) argues, we need to be circumspect of both the underlying rationale and the potential consequences of electoral legislation: 'even when changes in party law are the cooperative project of all of the main political parties in a country, both those in government and the opposition, some part of the underlying motivation may not be democracy strengthening, no matter how the project is billed'. In other cases, legislation that is enacted may reflect or favour, more blatantly, the interests of the governing party, or privilege the interests of those parties currently represented in the legislature. Examples include party registration provisions, ballot access laws and the provision of public funding and subsidies to parties. Whether or not judicial review and constitutional oversight provides sufficient protection in this instance (assuming that courts are willing to flex their muscles in the wake of parliamentary sovereignty) is a topic that is open to debate, and one which I explore further in Chapters 4, 5 and 6.

However, despite the partisan and office-seeking motivations of the key actors involved in the process of formulating electoral law, viewing the legal regulation of elections and political parties from a 'rational choice, interest-group analysis misses an important aspect of what is involved' (Geddis 2007a: 20). Not least is the fact that electoral law is arbitrated and interpreted by the courts, who in their own right become important political actors. This has been readily acknowledged in the context of American legal scholarship, where the political nature of the courts (particularly the Supreme Court) is critically debated. Persily and Cain note that reading the case law on political parties that has emerged from the US courts reveals 'unforseeable results', which can more satisfactorily be explained by the 'worldview that judges and lawyers bring to these cases and particularly their differing philosophies as to the function political parties play in American democracy' rather than adherence to or reconciliation with existing precedent (2000: 777). Similarly, in cases involving democratic issues, Pildes (2004: 126) observes that the US Supreme Court has 'acted out of concern that judicial review is needed to ensure that democracy remains stable, orderly, and properly restrained'. These concerns reflect the:

> … implicit visions of democracy with which all judges must necessarily work: visions that reflect empirical assumptions, historical interpretations, and inherited understandings of democracy. Cultural sensibilities of this sort inevitably inform and influence how judges approach any specific case. (Ibid.)

Whereas the political nature of the appointments process and the democratic legitimacy of the judicial review of legislation has been key issues in US constitutional jurisprudence (see Graber 2008: 302–5 for an overview of some of the main debates), in democracies modelled on the British tradition of a strong separation of powers (Blackstone 2001), the political and social philosophies that judges might bring to their decisions remain largely obscured by a cloak of legalism.

Though the decisions of the courts in cases concerning political parties might reflect the normative views of the judiciary as to the place of parties in representative democracies, there is no reason as to why these views ought to be consistent between individual judges and courts over time. As the judgments discussed in this book will reveal, it is often difficult to reconcile a court's reasoning in a series of cases concerning parties. This may reflect the changing composition of the bench, a shift in political values, or as Garrett posits (2002: 96), a failure on the part of the legal community (in particular the judiciary) to 'develop sophisticated positive and normative views of political parties', which in part is caused by a lack of engagement with the discipline of political science. In this way, judges can affect legal and constitutional change, although as Schwartzberg argues (2007: 4), 'the distinction between deliberative and interpretive (i.e. "unintentional") change still has currency'. Persily and Cain (2000: 808–9) suggest that sometimes it is more illuminating to study constitutional decisions not in terms of constitutional provisions, but in examining the different political philosophies that are imbued within a judge's reasons (for example, pluralism and liberalism) that reflect where power should lie in a party system, and how many parties should compete in the electoral arena: 'judges then filter these philosophical predispositions through constitutional provisions in order to arrive at decisions in concrete cases'. Yet the dynamic nature of parties and politics necessitates some flexibility in judicial judgments, and as such it may not be possible to construct any sort of positive view of political parties. Furthermore, the full impact of judicial decisions and legal regulations on the roles and functions of political parties is not always apparent. As Kang (2005: 174–5) argues:

> Courts and commentators focus almost exclusively on the legal principles and articulated reform goals surrounding party regulation without adequately considering the political consequences of handing victory to one side in these party conflicts. Nonetheless, courts adjudicating party regulation cases are, in a sense, engaging in practical management of these political conflicts.

This begs the question as to whether courts are really an appropriate forum for the resolution of party disputes. That political parties are private organizations, incidentally, has been the prevailing view for much of the twentieth century. Thus we need to examine the balance between the desirability of courts refraining from entering the political arena (which I argue that inevitably they do) against the pressing concern that political parties operating within the logic of electoral competition might not be able to adequately regulate themselves.

Law Regulates Politics

Yet the law also plays a crucial role in legitimizing election processes and public decision making once a party assumes office. Election laws must reflect the normative or cultural expectations of democracy that are shared by members of a given society in such a way as to provide 'good reasons for all participants – losers and winners – to accept and abide by the outcome' (Geddis 2007a: 19). A diverse range of legislative instruments and judicial decisions regulates the activities of political parties not only in the conduct of elections but also has a significant impact – both directly and indirectly – on their internal organization and activities. The regime of party law in place affects the openness of the electoral market and the ease of entry of new competitors into the political system. The law impacts upon political parties at numerous stages in their life cycles: at the point of creation, where basic political freedoms are necessary (freedom of expression, communication, association, and so on), their registration and the manner in which they contest elections. However, this regulation will also have important 'flow on' effects for democracy at large. Given that political parties are a central institutional form through which mass participation in politics is organized, the legal and constitutional treatment of political parties has important implications for the activities of parties and therefore the conduct of elections and the practice of democratic governance (Pildes 2004: 101). Such effects might include the policy choices that voters are presented with at elections, and their opportunity to influence the election of party candidates and leaders.

In this sense, the law can assume a proactive function. Christodoulis and Tierney conceptualize the relationship between politics and the law as one both constraining and enabling political action. The 'logic of rule' operates, on the one hand, to maintain and underwrite 'patterns of power and weakness through political structures and processes' (2008: 1–2). On the other hand, public law may also be used to enable political action and redress patterns of inequality through the use of constitutional and legal authority. Applying this conceptual reasoning to the arena of electoral and party politics, the law has a dual function: to protect the interests of the governing and major political parties through the structure and processes surrounding the conduct of elections, but also to redress imbalances of power between parties in electoral contests and enable new players to enter what might ideally be conceived of as a 'level playing field'. Whether the public law achieves either of these aims is evaluated throughout the book. Hence, the law can be used as a mechanism to compel political parties to achieve their stated aims and fulfil their stated functions. Authors such as Gardner (2000: 671) consider the capacity of the public law, as the regulator of the institutional design of political parties, to enable them to fulfil a particular normative vision of democracy: that is, 'to serve simultaneously as conduits of virtue and bulwarks against unconstrained factionalism'. Alternatively, regulations can be used to serve partisan needs and entrench the interests of incumbents.

Who Makes the Law?

To understand the full impact of the law on political parties and representative democracy more generally it is necessary to acknowledge that there are numerous actors in both the political and legal arenas, and that analysing this legal framework involves looking at the interactions between these various political actors and institutions, whether they are political parties, interest groups, lobbyists, corporations, or judicial or legislative actors. Furthermore, often those who change the law or legislate for a particular outcome will be electoral participants themselves, and may even be the dominant power, as the US case *Tashjian v. Republican Party of Connecticut*[7] aptly demonstrates (discussed in Chapter 5). The state itself is not a neutral lawmaker, but comprises individual legislators who, for the most part, have some party allegiance.

Political parties constitute a particularly challenging case for regulators and legislators. Acting as both those entities that construct the rules and those who play by them, the conflict of interest created and the potential for partisan or incumbent interests to be privileged in any law making is a very real danger. For example, Kang (2005: 160) argues that:

> Party leaders and their allies have every incentive to foster a regulatory environment that benefits them. Party regulation, as a result, often represents politically motivated modification of the legal landscape to the calculated advantage of certain party actors and to the disadvantage of others.

7 479 U.S. 208 (1986).

This concern is shared by many other commentators (for example, Bennett 2009; Sayers and Young 2004: 7; Feasby 2007: 516). Yet nowhere is the concern greater than in the United States as partisan influence is possible at all stages of the electoral contest:

> When candidates seek access to the ballot, major party officials almost always review their eligibility. When a major party makes a legally questionable decision about how or when to spend its money, the Federal Election Commission, constituted by major party elected officials, assesses the decision's propriety. When electoral disputes lead to litigation, judges appointed and approved by major party officials – or, as in some states, elected on major party ballot lines – decide the cases. (Magarian 2003: 2047)

However, electoral engineering is not an exact science. Often legislative provisions will have unintended consequences and electoral actors may not respond in expected ways to regulation. For example, party organizational scholarship over the last half-century highlights the dynamism of parties as political actors and documents how parties successfully adapt to changed electoral, legal, technological and financial environments to ensure their long-term survival.[8] Hence, political parties are both institutions and actors, and this dual nature/structure makes legal and electoral regulation inherently difficult as such regulation needs to change the behaviour of dynamic and symbiotic actors, not simply institutions.

Nor are political parties unitary actors. They are fluid organizations that are constituted by their members and their supporters, working together in a set of relationships of various strengths, for a common purpose. It is very difficult to identify exactly where decisions are made within a political party, and, although the law may require the appointment of a party agent (or similar) to bestow some legal identity on the organization, these positions may have little relationship to the actual centres of power within the organization. Therefore, a party's legal personality may not necessarily reflect its political nucleus, complicating attempts to achieve transparency and effective accountability through legal means.

Furthermore, political parties differ remarkably between and within particular jurisdictions or states, and it is unreasonable to suggest that there is a common logic that drives all political parties. While parties may be defined by a common goal of electing members to public office, this is only one of many functions that political parties perform in representative democracies. Other functions include the communication of information, facilitating citizen participation and aggregating diverse citizen interests. This point is particularly important if we take a functional approach to regulation that acknowledges that different systems of regulation have varying impacts on these various functions, and that some parties may prioritize particular functions over others, which therefore may require a more nuanced regulatory approach.

8 See Chapter 2, 'The Emergence of Political Parties'.

The Public–Private Distinction

The idea of a public–private distinction in the regulation of political parties has been present in American jurisprudence for quite some time, particularly in First Amendment cases (see, for example, Magarian 2003: 1956–7). It has been used increasingly in cases concerning the internal operation of political parties in Australia, Canada, New Zealand and the United Kingdom. Whether a particular organization or an activity is classified as public or private will affect the legal framework that governs its conduct. In essence, the private realm is one of autonomy – the law has a legitimate place in facilitating decision making but its primary purpose is protecting individuals and groups from the encroachment of others (including the state). By contrast, the public realm is a 'world of government institutions, obliged to serve the public interest rather than private aims' (Freeman and Mensch 1987: 237).

The public–private dichotomy is particularly important in terms of state regulation as the distinction goes to the fundamental question of whether or not such regulation is desirable, the extent to which the state and the public law should intervene in the activities of political parties, and which of these activities it should regulate. If we categorize political parties as public organizations, regulating both their internal activities and the way in which they compete for political power may be normatively desirable, perhaps in order to implement particular democratic principles (for example, intra-party democracy) or outcomes (for example, gender or minority group quotas in candidate selection contests). If political parties are characterized as private bodies, state regulation (especially measures relating to candidate selection and the application of anti-discrimination law to such processes) may be seen as an undesirable intrusion upon the autonomy of these independent political entities and an unnecessary interference with the political expression of citizens.

The distinction between the private and the public realms in the political science scholarship concerning parties has gained a great deal of prominence in recent years. For almost all of the twentieth century, it was taken for granted that political parties had their base in civil society and in this respect were 'private organizations', or more accurately, organizations that did not form part of the state apparatus. However, since the mid-1990s, Katz and Mair's 'cartel party' thesis (2009, 1995) has provided one of the main catalysts for re-examining the relationship between political parties and the state. The main argument these authors make is that amidst a climate of growing public disengagement with conventional political institutions and weakening partisan attachments, in order to ensure their long-term survival, political parties (traditionally characterized as mass or popular associations with strong links to civil society) have transformed into what have been termed 'cartel parties'. In organizational terms, these changes have seen political parties become increasingly dependent on the state to provide material resources and legitimacy in lieu of those once provided by civil society. Driving this fundamental organizational shift is the 'ascendancy of the party in public office' over the other two faces of the party organization, the party on the ground and the party in central office (Katz and Mair 2002, 1993).[9] This dynamic in the relationship between the faces of the party stems from a combination of factors: the increasing financial resources associated with public office, the location of party staff and the centralization and professionalization of electoral campaigning. The cartel thesis sits alongside a more generalist political science scholarship that sees political parties becoming, more and more, organs of the state and less of civil society (see, for example, Epstein 1986: 157; van Biezen 2004: 705).

Of the previous studies that have been undertaken on the legal regulation of political parties, many authors choose to address the broader problem of the extent and character of legal regulation required from a private–public perspective (see, for example, Johns 1999; Persily and Cain 2000: 777). Put very simply, it is argued that political parties as such be subject to increasing legal regulation as they are becoming 'arms of the state', or that they perform public functions. Conversely, political parties as private organizations should be protected from judicial and state interference, free to conduct their activities according to their own rules and practices.

However, the public–private distinction is not necessarily synonymous with the proposition that political parties are, or are becoming, agents of the state (Johns 1999: 90). Johns argues that some political parties may choose to register, contest elections and become 'public' entities, but may never achieve office and/or receive state support. Conversely, political parties may achieve parliamentary representation and/or receive state support, yet remain private organizations in their internal affairs, closed to external scrutiny. They may also become public because of it (Ibid.). However, this perspective assumes that the public–private distinction is one based on the extent to which a political party is regulated by the public law or is labelled as one, not necessarily a reflection of the place and function of that particular organizational form in a modern representative democracy.

It is also difficult to categorize political parties as either public or private entities when these organizations are not, of themselves, unitary actors. Party scholars have outlined three different dimensions of political parties, which straddle the public–private divide. As outlined above, Katz and Mair's 'three faces of the party organization' and Key's distinction between the party in the electorate, office and the party organization recognize this much. The public–private distinction is further complicated by the fact that political parties combine elements of both the public and private spheres (Moss and Tham 2011; Geddis 2005: 108). This is evident in the functions that they perform: electing members to public office and governing a state is undoubtedly a public role. However, as voluntary membership organizations comprised of individuals pursuing a particular political agenda or a common cause, the role of political parties as private vehicles for the expression of

9 This threefold distinction is similar to that developed by Key (1964) in the context of American party scholarship, in which he refers to a party in the electorate, a party in office and a party organization. Applying Katz's and Mair's argument to this model, we might similarly expect to see the party in office dominate.

political thought in civil society comes to the fore. Consequently, the interpretation of whether or not a party is a public or private entity will shift with the function that is prioritized – between people and over time. It is therefore difficult to pigeonhole a political party into one category or the other, without dampening one or other of these important roles.

However, if party scholars such as Katz and Mair are right – that the balance between the three faces of the party organization is shifting towards the party in public office at the expense of the extra-parliamentary party organization and the membership, and in doing so fundamentally altering the functions parties perform – then perhaps it is reasonable to regard parties as increasingly 'public' entities. This raises an additional question: to what extent is regulation responding to the changing organizational nature of political parties and their place in democracy, or to what extent is this regulation shaping it? The fact that political parties and the public law are symbiotic is a key challenge for lawmakers, political scientists and legal scholars who want to understand the complex relationships between electoral actors and institutional design. A further difficulty is that any change in the nature of political parties (if it is occurring) is incremental and ongoing. Unlike other aspects of the electoral system, such as voting methods for example, political parties are not static. With this in mind, rather than regulating political parties on the basis that they are public or private entities, it is more fruitful to adopt a functional or purposive approach to regulation that seeks to regulate political parties based on the roles they perform (or ought to perform) in modern representative democracies.

The Countries for Analysis

Political Parties and Elections analyses the legal regulation of political parties in five common law democracies: Australia, Canada, New Zealand, the United Kingdom and the United States. Each of these states has been chosen on the basis of their shared common law foundations and their liberal democratic traditions and institutions, which have been built on the fundamental importance of voting as a mechanism of democratic expression by the people. Nevertheless, these states also vary in key aspects of the overall design of their representative democracies: electoral systems, legislatures and party systems. These variations provide fertile ground for analysing the effect and significance of party laws in different jurisdictions and political systems, and the historical and institutional contexts that have influenced their development. The comparative method is a useful technique for identifying idiosyncratic and autobiographical provisions in party, electoral and constitutional law that might otherwise be taken for granted or even missed when evaluated in isolation by country specialists, but which become apparent and highly significant in a comparative context.

A comparative approach is also sympathetic to the idea that the relationship between law and politics is symbiotic. Different party systems in different countries invoke different normative values of what the role of political parties should be. For example, a strong two-party system privileges ideas of coherent, effective governance and responsible government (as the majority party is also the government). In turn, these values shape lawmakers' attitudes towards the appropriate role of parties. However, the laws that regulate parties also serve to mould the contours and shape the character of the party system. In this section, I provide a brief introduction to the features of the representative democratic systems of each of the democracies in this study. A summary of the key institutional differences is presented in Table 1.1.

Australia

The Commonwealth of Australia was established in 1901 by the Constitution of the Commonwealth of Australia (an Act of the British Parliament). Australia is a federation of six States and two Territories, each of which has their own constitutions, parliaments and electoral legislation. However, for the purposes of this study and consistent with the approach taken to all the countries included I will predominantly analyse the federal parliament and national electoral system, although some limited illustrative examples will be drawn from the States and Territories. Constitutional principles regarding the structure of Australian government derive not only from the Constitution of the Commonwealth of Australia, but may also be found in ordinary legislation, judicial decisions and customs and traditions. The structure of representative democracy in Australia draws on elements from both the United Kingdom and United States constitutions. Often referred to as the 'Washminster' system, a parliamentary system of government has been adopted from the United Kingdom, coupled with a federal system with enumerated powers for both State and Territory governments that has been inherited from the US constitutional design.

The Australian federal parliament consists of two elected houses with roughly equal legislative powers.[10] Members of the lower house (the House of Representatives) are elected through an alternative vote (also called an 'optional preferential vote') in single-member districts. Members of the upper house (the Senate) are elected through a variant of proportional representation. Australia is characterized as having a strong two-party system comprising of two main political groupings: the Australian Labor Party (ALP) and the coalition of the Liberal and National parties. Third or minor parties (such as the Green Party) have gained representation in the Senate, but have never participated in any governing coalitions. The majority party in the lower house will typically form the government and controls the legislative agenda of the parliament, placing a great degree of power in practice in the cabinet and the executive arm of government.

10 The exception is bills with respect to supply, which must originate in the lower house.

Table 1.1 Key Features of the Representative System of Government

State	Legislature	Electoral system	Party system	Effective number of parties	Main parties	Unitary/Federal regulation	Key constitutional documents
Australia	Bicameral (equal powers)	Lower House: Alternative vote Upper House: proportional representation	Two-party	2.4	Australian Labor Party; Liberal/National Coalition	Combination of State and federal laws	*Commonwealth of Australia Constitution Act* 1901
Canada	Bicameral (lower house more powerful)	Plurality vote (first past the post)	Multi	3.0	Liberal Party; Conservatives; Bloc Québécois; New Democratic Party	Combination of Provincial and federal laws	*Constitution Act* 1867, *Canada Act* 1982 (including the Canadian Charter of Rights and Freedoms)
New Zealand	Unicameral	Mixed-member proportional	Multi	3.7	Labour; National; Greens; Maori Party; ACT	Unitary	Treaty of Waitangi 1840, *Constitution Act* 1986, *New Zealand Bill of Rights Act* 1990, *Electoral Act* 1993
United Kingdom	Bicameral (lower house more powerful)	Plurality (first past the post)	Two-party	2.4	Labour Party; Conservatives	Unitary	*Representation of the People Act* 1918, *Parliament Acts, Political Parties, Elections and Referendums Act* 2000
United States	Bicameral (equal powers)	Plurality (first past the post) (except Louisiana)	Two-party	2.0	Republican Party; Democrats	Combination of State and federal laws	*US Bill of Rights* and the *Constitution* 1787

Source: Gallagher and Mitchell (2005: 621).

Canada

Like Australia, Canada's system of representative democracy has been heavily influenced by the design of government in the United Kingdom and was originally established by the *Constitution Act* 1867. The Canadian Constitution has since been updated and consists of documents including the *Canada Act* 1982 and the *Canadian Charter of Rights and Freedoms*. Canada's federal parliament comprises two houses – the elected House of Commons and the appointed Senate. Although the powers of both houses are equal with respect to all bills (except supply), constitutional convention generally provides that the Senate should not obstruct the democratic will of the Commons. Members of the Commons are elected from single-member districts by a plurality voting system (first past the post). Federalism is a key feature of Canadian government; with a formal division of powers enumerated under Canada's various *Constitution Acts*. Up to five political parties are represented in the Canadian parliament, which currently include the majority parties the Liberal Party and the Conservatives, and two smaller parties, the Bloc Québécois and the New Democratic Party.

New Zealand

As with Australia and Canada, the British parliamentary system has had the greatest influence on the design of government in New Zealand. Key features inherited from the United Kingdom include parliamentary sovereignty, the cabinet system and constitutional ideals such as the rule of law, liberty, freedom and due process (Joseph 2007: 3). The constitutional documents of New Zealand include the Treaty of Waitangi (1840), the *Constitution Act* 1986, the *New Zealand Bill of Rights Act* 1990 and the *Electoral Act* 1993. New Zealand's parliament is unicameral, consisting only of the House of Representatives – New Zealand abolished its upper house, the Legislative Council, in 1947. For most of its history, New Zealand has been characterized by a strong two-party system, with the Nationals and the Labour Party dominating parliamentary representation under a first-past-the-post voting system. However, in the 1980s, New Zealand underwent a period of democratic and constitutional introspection, coupled with a debate on majoritarianism and representation, which led to widespread changes to the electoral system and significant reforms governing the legal status and operation of political parties. These reforms make New Zealand a particularly interesting case study, and I explore the history and context of these reforms in greater detail in Chapter 3.

A mixed-member proportional (MMP) electoral system was adopted by referendum in 1993 to elect members of the House of Representatives, introducing two votes: one for the party of a voter's choice and another for the local electorate member of the voters' choice. The overall composition of the parliament is designed to reflect the proportion of a party's share of the national vote. Up to six political parties now routinely gain representation in the parliament, and minority governments are not an uncommon occurrence.

The United Kingdom

The United Kingdom's political traditions are interesting because, on the one hand, they form the basis of the arrangements for government that have been adopted and adapted by all the other democracies in this study. On the other, the British system is constantly in a process of evolution, highlighted by recent calls for electoral reform and constitutional change (see, for example, Bogdanor 2009; Craig 1990: 10). In the absence of a formal written 'Constitution', Turpin and Tomkins (2007: 4) describe the British constitutional arrangements more broadly as a 'body of rules, conventions and practices which describe, regulate, or qualify the organization, powers and operation of government and the relations between persons and public authorities'. The British parliamentary tradition is based on the notion of one-party government, a situation that has been created by the first-past-the-post electoral system to elect representatives to the House of Commons (lower house). The parliament also consists of an appointed upper house (the House of Lords). Both constitutional conventions and legislation (the *Parliament Acts*) operate to severely restrict the ability of the House of Lords to reject or delay legislation that has been initiated in the Commons.

Like Australia, the United Kingdom has traditionally been regarded as having a strong two-party system: between 1945 and 1970, the Conservatives and the Labour Party shared 91 per cent of the vote between them. However, since the general election of 1974, this two-party dominance has started to break down. In the 2005 Parliament, 92 parliamentarians (approximately 15 per cent) came from political parties other than the major two: the Liberal Democrats and parties representing regional areas from within the UK, for example, the Democratic Unionist Party, the Scottish National Party, Sinn Fein and Plaid Cymru (see Bogdanor 2009: 36). The traditional assumption that the United Kingdom is a unitary and relatively homogenous state has come under increased scrutiny in an era of devolution, and with the emergence of these regionally based parties and the emergence of the extremist right-wing party, the British National Party (established in 1982). Low voter turnout at general elections (in 2001, turnout was 58 per cent and, in 2005, 62 per cent) and high levels of voter dissatisfaction with the current system of parliamentary government in the UK have invigorated an ongoing debate around electoral reforms such as proportional representation, the overhaul of existing political institutions such as parties and parliament (for example, reforming the House of Lords), and more decentralized forms of governance.

The United States

The constitutional design of the American system of government is characterized by two main elements. The first is a theoretical separation of powers between the legislature, the executive and the judiciary that is to some extent characteristic of all democracies in this study. The second is a federal system with a distinct division of powers between the federal government and the states (a feature shared with Australia and Canada). The US Bill of Rights and the Constitution (1787) have proved to be two of the most influential documents on comparative democratic design – advocating the ideals of liberalism, democratic representation and freedom from government that have been influential in the jurisprudence concerning political parties both in the United States and abroad.

The US differs from the other democracies included in this research with its presidential (rather than parliamentary) system of government with an executive branch of government that is distinctly separate and independent from the legislature. Nevertheless, the party system pervades both these arms of government and political party candidates contest both legislative and presidential offices in the United States. The American party system is a strong two-party system dominated by the Democratic and Republican political parties. Although many minor parties are in existence in the US, they very rarely gain representation in the legislatures (state or federal) or win more than a small percentage of the votes. Of the 7,300 state legislators in the United States, fewer than two dozen of these are Independents. Since 1901, both the Republicans and Democrats have together held more than 95 per cent of the seats in Congress. Another key point of difference is that parties as organizations beyond the legislature are fundamentally different in the United States to those in Australia, Canada, New Zealand and the UK. They have relatively little influence over individual legislators and are characterized by informal, candidate-centred networks that act as campaigning vehicles for candidates, in place of membership organizations. As Katz (2007: 88) comments, 'while partisan attachments and identifications structure much of American politics, parties as organisations … have almost no capacity to direct politics'.

The Body of Law Examined

Political science accounts of the legal regulation of political parties tend to focus predominantly on what is known as party law, and a limited body of ancillary law. Müller and Sieberer (2006: 435) suggest two definitions of party law: 'Party law can be understood as legislation specifically designed to regulate the life of party organizations. Alternatively, party law can be defined as the total body of law that affects political parties'. In this work, I adopt the wider definition, which draws on a more expansive range of sources spanning both public and private law and including constitutional law, electoral law, clubs and associations law, as well as contract, corporate and administrative law.

One of the key shortcomings of the literature on party regulation and party law to date (particularly within the political science discipline) is the tendency for scholars to look predominantly, if not exclusively, to legislation as the source of party law. For example, party law, according to Janda (2009: 14, 2005: 4) can be defined as 'any governmental regulations (whether in constitutions, statutes or administrative rulings) that govern the definition, composition, structure and activities of political parties'. This conception of the law as simply legislation ignores the body of case law that exists and which constitutes a fundamental component of the legal regulation of political parties as actors in the electoral contest. Regardless of the source of party law, it cannot be read in isolation from the judicial rulings that interpret it and which in many ways refine and develop the law.

The Status of Party and Electoral Law

A final point to note here is that in most of the democracies examined in this body of research, many of the laws governing the conduct of political parties and elections originate as ordinary acts of parliament – meaning that they can be created, repealed, or amended by any parliament without the need for a special majority or approval process. While this legislation (like all legislation) is subject to judicial review and express and implied constitutional limitations, the fluidity of these arrangements is notable in providing the legislature with the opportunity to amend electoral laws to reflect the prevailing and changing democratic, political and philosophical preferences of society. Whether or not this should be the case or whether these laws should be subject to a greater degree of entrenchment to avoid partisan manipulation is also a key element of the ongoing debate on the legal regulation of political parties. In this respect, the manner and form of the law matters just as much as its substance.

Outline of the Book

Chapter 2 examines the deliberate recognition (or non-recognition) of political parties in the constitutions of nation states, given the significance of these documents as the basic legal framework of how a political system should operate. Chapter 3 analyses the changing legal status of political parties in the laws of all states under consideration, and the trend towards an increasing acknowledgement of the role and significance of political parties – manifest in their greater recognition and consequent legislative regulation.

In Chapter 4, I analyse the various legislative regimes in place that regulate the structure and organization of a political party before it can contest an election, or in the instances of Australia and Canada, receive direct public funding for its election activities. Examples of the requirements and their variations that will be addressed include: the specific aim a party must have of contesting elections, that a party must have a membership of a certain number, and that a party must be established on the basis of a written constitution, which may prescribe a particular organizational structure.

Chapter 5 looks at the different provisions states have made for regulating the candidate selection contests (or primaries) of political parties. Given the importance of receiving party endorsement for the electoral success of a candidate, such contests have become increasingly significant and fiercely fought. Interestingly, there is a large variation in the inclusiveness of these contests and the extent to which they are controlled by the public law. For example, primaries in the US are open to registered party voters and are conducted under the provisions of electoral law, whereas in the UK, Australia and Canada candidate selection is entirely an internal matter for the party to determine.

Chapter 6 deals with the actual electoral contest and the regulation of the election campaign. The chief focus is on national elections. Given that the legal norm is to regulate the actions of individual candidates rather than party organizations, the chapter highlights specific instances of where the latter occurs (for example, the allocation of public broadcasting time, the regulation of parties' access to the media and election advertising) and explains how this reflects changing conceptions as to the nature of representative democracy and the reality of party government in modern democracies.

In Chapter 7, I outline the provisions for the public funding of election campaigns in the various states examined (notably Australia and Canada), and the implications of this for the financial organization of political parties and associated reporting requirements. I analyse the motivations for such funding, and the extent to which it privileges the activities of political parties over individual candidates and consolidates their relationship with the state apparatus. Finally, the chapter considers the relationship between public funding, increased regulation and the law's gradual intrusion into aspects of political party organization that were once considered matters solely for the internal management of the party.

In contrast to the provision of public funding to parties for their electoral expenses, Chapter 8 analyses the regulation of private sources of income for parties – in particular those which are directed towards fighting the electoral contest. The increasing cost of campaigns has been a salient and contentious topic of debate within modern democracies for the last several decades – particularly the impact of parties' aggregate spending on the perceived fairness of general elections. There is an extremely interesting contrast here between the United States, in which campaign spending is largely protected under the First Amendment as a form of political speech, and the regimes of many other states, such as Australia, Canada and the United Kingdom, where expenditure and contributions are regulated to encourage equality amongst parties in the electoral competition.

Shifting the emphasis away from the electoral contest to its outcomes, Chapter 9 examines the legal regulation of political parties (and individual parliamentarians as party members or representatives) in the legislature. In contrast to the increasing regulation that we are witnessing in the electoral arena, parliamentarians are overwhelmingly regarded by the law as independent representatives – free from interference from their party organization. I examine the extent to which legislators can be held legally accountable for party election promises and whether or not they are mandated to vote with their party group or are free to 'cross the floor'.

Chapter 10 concludes the book, providing a summary of the key findings of each chapter and reiterating the importance of alternate normative conceptions of representative democracy for explaining divergent patterns in the legal regulation of parties as electoral actors. The chapter also outlines many of the common challenges that face representative democracies in the future regulation of parties, for example, the role of the judiciary, and suggests some areas for potential reform.

Chapter 2
Political Parties and Constitutions

This chapter examines the recognition (or in some cases the deliberate non-recognition) of political parties in the constitutions of nation states, given the significance of these documents in presenting the basic legal framework through which a political system should operate. In many liberal democracies, the constitutional framers failed to mention political parties in the overall design of representative democracy – an omission that is treated with some curiosity today. In this chapter, I explain why this is the case, examining the organizational form of political parties at the time of drafting and the prevailing social attitudes towards the role and proper place of parties. However, the institutions and practices associated with representative democracy have evolved over the last two centuries, and this necessitates an analysis of the changing legal status of political parties in the laws of all the states under consideration in this research. In order to undertake this analysis, I describe how political parties have evolved as representative and participatory organizations over the course of the twentieth century, drawing on some of the theoretical frameworks established in the comparative political parties scholarship.

Constitutions, Parties and the Institutional Design of Democracy

A logical place to begin any examination of the legal status and management of political parties is with a state's constitution, the basic function of which is to establish, and regulate, how a political system should operate. Constitutions, according to Finer, Bogdanor and Rudden, not only define the democratic 'rules of the game', 'regulate the allocation of power, functions and duties among the various agencies or officers of government', 'define the relationships between these and the public', but also provide a 'textual source of the norms which aspire to govern the basic structure of power in a modern state' (1995: viii, 1). Constitutional design over the last century has provided a means for nation states to adopt particular systems of government (for example, parliamentary versus presidential), to provide for the inclusion of minorities in governmental processes, to codify political, social and economic rights, to determine appropriate electoral systems and to act as a catalyst for political mobilization (Lutz 2006: 9–15).

While they may provide for the 'bigger picture' of democratic design, constitutions as potential sources of law regulating the behaviour of political parties have often been overlooked by both political scientists and legal scholars (Janda 2005: 5–6). A common explanation provided for this oversight is that, with the exception of states such as Germany where political parties have been recognized as *verfassungsrechtliche Institutionen* ('institutions of constitutional law') (Müller and Sieberer 2006: 438–9), many constitutions simply fail to mention political parties in their texts and hence there is no express regulatory framework to analyse. Furthermore, constitutions are not necessarily contained in a single discrete document, which can create some difficulty in identifying and locating constitutional provisions in relevant pieces of electoral and other law. For example, although it is often labelled as unwritten, British constitutional provisions can be found in various Acts of Parliament including the *Representation of the People Act* 1918 and the *Parliament Acts* of 1911 and 1949.[1] Similarly, the New Zealand constitution consists of a collection of statutes (among them the *Constitution Act* 1986 and the *New Zealand Bill of Rights Act* 1990), the Treaty of Waitangi and letters patent.

Often what constitutions do *not* say about political parties is just as important as what they do. Constitutions do not provide for 'natural' forms of political organization but are a deliberately engineered 'human artifact' (Lutz 2006: 22). As such, the drafting and evolution of a constitution viewed within the broader context of the development of party law provides valuable insight into the historical place and changing role of political parties in modern democracies, and the normative values and democratic ideals that shape this conception.[2] Once we identify and understand how constitutions construct political parties within a particular interpretation of normative democratic theory, we obtain a better understanding not only of parties' place in the overall design of representative democracy, but how different regulatory regimes operate to facilitate, constrain and define their activities. For example, van Biezen and Kopecky (2007: 240) argue that the character of constitutional recognition of political parties today 'attests to a conception of democracy in which parties are seen as necessary institutions', one which 'signals that the state is assuming an increased role in the management of parties as an essential public good for democracy'. But what should these parties look like and how should they function? Different constitutional and legal provisions reveal distinct visions of parties' roles and form – not only between democracies, but also between members of the legislature and the judiciary.

The lack of attention to constitutions as a fluid source of party law also obscures the role that the judiciary plays in the interpretation and creation of constitutional provisions, albeit within institutional constraints (see, for example, Goldsworthy 2006). As discussed further in Chapters 3 and 4, constitutional courts have created a rich body of party law that derives from the interpretation of direct and also tangential, yet closely related, constitutional provisions. For example, while the US Constitution does not expressly mention political parties, many of the US Supreme Court's decisions affecting these organizations derive from the Court's reading and

1 See further Barendt (1998); Ewing (1987) and Rawlings (1988).

2 See, for example, Issacharoff (2000: 597).

interpretation of the First Amendment.[3] Similarly in Australia, cases concerning the requirements for registering a political party have been brought under sections 7 and 24 of the *Commonwealth of Australia Constitution Act* 1900, which simply state that parliamentarians are to be 'directly chosen by the people'.[4]

As this chapter will demonstrate, the prevailing historical trend in many established common law democracies such as the United Kingdom and the United States has been to exclude political parties from constitutional documents. This indicates a particular historical conception of parties' appropriate place in society as voluntary associations of individuals emanating from civil society and existing beyond the reach of the state. However, if we look beyond Britain and many of her former colonies that have been fashioned in a similar mould, it is evident that this lack of constitutionalization is by no means been a universal occurrence. In 1976, a survey conducted of national constitutions found that at least-two thirds mentioned political parties (Janda 2005: 6). For example, many constitutions in the new democracies of Eastern Europe acknowledge the role of political parties, as do Germany, Portugal and Spain (see also van Biezen 2004; van Biezen and Borz 2009).[5]

Scholars agree the basic pattern of constitutional codification is that political systems with long-established democratic traditions tend to omit parties from their constitutions, taking them almost for granted and acknowledging their existence only where need occurs, for example, in finance or electoral legislation (Müller and Sieberer 2006: 438). At this end of the spectrum, the constitutional traditions of Australia, Canada and New Zealand were drawn from the design of government of the United Kingdom and were heavily influenced by the constitutional structure of the United States. As such, political parties do not figure prominently in these documents. There is no mention of political parties in Canada's *Constitution Acts* 1867–1982 and New Zealand's *Constitution Act* 1986. Political parties were similarly absent from the *Commonwealth of Australia Constitution Act* 1900, existing as 'curiously private organisations',[6] until a minor reference to parties in the context of casual Senate vacancies was inserted by referendum in 1977. Why this might be the case has not yet been systematically explored in the academic literature.

---

3 The Constitution of the United States of America, Amendment I (1791) 'Religion, Speech, Press, Assembly, Petition' states that 'Congress shall make no law respecting an establishment of religion, or prohibiting the free exercise thereof; or abridging the freedom of speech, or of the press; or the right of the people peaceably to assemble, and to petition the Government for a redress of grievances'.

4 See for example *Mulholland v. Australian Electoral Commission* (2004) 220 CLR 181.

5 For an excellent online database that includes a comprehensive catalogue of the constitutional provisions regulating political parties in Europe, see The Legal Regulation of Political Parties in Post-War Europe, <http://www.partylaw.bham.ac.uk>, coordinated by Ingrid van Biezen (University of Leiden).

6 For commentary on political parties and the Australian constitutional tradition, see Gauja (2006b); Reid and Forrest (1989); Bennett (2002) and Somes (1996).

At the other end of the spectrum, the formal recognition of political parties in national constitutions tends to occur in democracies whose constitutions have been written after instances of conflict, periods of one-party dictatorship (Avnon 1995), or in the process of democratic transition. Although some liberal democracies in Europe followed the American and British mould in refraining from making reference to political parties and their role in the political system, many new democracies in Eastern Europe positively acknowledge the role played by political parties (van Biezen and Borz 2009: 1; Müller and Sieberer 2006: 438). An early exception to this was the Weimar Constitution (1919), which prohibited public officials from being members of political parties or receiving orders from them. In this instance, political parties were viewed as anti-democratic forces – to be restrained and regulated by the constitution rather than protected and liberated. As Mersel (2006a: 161) argues, in this period of history 'even when political parties were addressed legally, they were still perceived negatively, as a source of potential corruption'.

The trend towards the increasing recognition of political parties in national constitutions began in the aftermath of the Second World War, with the constitution of the Italian Republic (1947) and the Basic Law of the Federal Republic of Germany (1949). The German Basic Law is notable in a comparative context, as Article 21 of this document provides perhaps the most comprehensive constitutional regime for the regulation of political parties in post-war liberal democracies. This is, however, hardly surprising given that the Nazi Law of 1933 permitted only one party in the Third Reich. Article 21 of the Basic Law states:

1. The political parties shall participate in the forming of the political will of the people. They may be freely established. Their internal organization shall conform to democratic principles. They shall publicly account for the sources and use of their funds and for their assets.
2. Parties which, by reason of their aims or the behavior of their adherents, seek to impair or abolish the free democratic basic order or to endanger the existence of the Federal Republic of Germany shall be unconstitutional. The Federal Constitutional Court shall decide on the question of unconstitutionality.
3. Details shall be regulated by federal statutes.[7]

As a product of political history developed in response to Germany's experiences under the Nazi regime, the external enforcement of the democratic organization of political parties is viewed as a fundamental guard against the centralization of political power and as a means to ensure the popular control of government. This type of constitutional provision is common to other states with previous experiences of authoritarian and fascist regimes. For example, in Portugal, intra-party democracy is constitutionally protected: Article 51(5) of the Portuguese Constitution (1976) provides that a party 'must be governed by the principles of transparency, democratic organization and management and the participation of all of its members'. The internal organization

7 Translation provided by Finer, Bodgdanor and Rudden (1995: 137–8).

of Spanish political parties must also be democratic, as required by Article 6 of the Spanish Constitution (1978). This Article acknowledges the importance of, and key role played by, political parties in the Spanish system of democratic representative government:

> Political parties express democratic pluralism, assist in the formulation and manipulation of the popular will, and are a basic instrument for political participation. Their creation and the exercise of their activity are free within the observance of the Constitution and the laws.

We also observe similar constitutional provisions in many developing and transitional democracies, where the constitutional recognition and regulation of political parties is a key feature of democratization and institution building (for example, the democracies of Eastern Europe and others such as Nigeria and Nepal). Overall, we therefore see a great deal of variation between democracies as to whether or not political parties are acknowledged in constitutions, and the corresponding degree to which they are regulated by constitutional documents. However, departing from the liberal democratic tradition, over time the practice of constitutional recognition and revision has been followed in many other European polities to the point that 'most democratic constitutions in Europe today acknowledge the existence of political parties' (van Biezen and Borz 2009: 1). This trend also highlights the importance of the diffusion or transference of constitutional norms and principles in playing a key role in shaping the regulatory regimes of nation states. This transference is not a result of simply copying; but rather from the adoption of particular institutional designs that could potentially perform similar functions or effectively address problems common to a number of democracies.[8] As Lutz (2006: 10) argues, such diffusion and adaptation provides evidence that 'constitutional design makes a difference and that there are connections between institutional design and general political outcomes'. Given that political parties are a common occurrence in most democracies and generally perform similar functions (see page 38), we might expect that the existence of laws concerning these organizations proliferate across the globe. Hence, diffusion is based just as much on pragmatism and practicality as it is on ideological arguments or persuasions.

Explaining Constitutional Non-recognition

Despite evidence of the increasing constitutionalization of political parties in recent decades, the prevailing historical trend up until the Second World War in many common law liberal democracies was the exclusion of political parties from constitutional documents. As previously noted, the constitutional traditions

8 For a more general account of constitutional and institutional 'borrowing', see, for example, Hall and Taylor (1996); Peters (1999); Sajo (1993) and Osiatynski (2003).

of Australia, Canada and New Zealand were in large part drawn from the design of government of the United Kingdom and were also heavily influenced by the constitutional structure of the United States. The US Constitution of 1787 did not designate any role for political parties. Similarly, the constitutional arrangements in the United Kingdom did not provide for a 'general statute of parties' (Finer et al. 1995: 96) until electoral legislation passed only quite recently.[9] This influence spread to other states of the Commonwealth: there is no reference to political parties in Canada's *Constitution Acts* 1867–1982 and New Zealand's *Constitution Act* 1986. Parties were also absent from the original constitution of the Commonwealth of Australia that was drafted at federation.

This omission is often treated as somewhat of a curiosity, given the prominent role that parties play in these representative democracies. As Barendt (1998: 149) notes, given the importance of political parties to the functioning of modern party government:

> One might, therefore, expect constitutions to lay down some framework rules for political parties, at least to prevent them from adopting totalitarian policies and to safeguard the rights of individual members. But constitutions rarely say much about parties, while some have totally ignored their existence.

I argue that rather than treating the relationship between the practical significance of political parties and their constitutional recognition as a curious paradox or an 'ambiguous relationship' (van Biezen 2003: 174), it is necessary to analyse more closely why political parties were omitted from the constitutions of the countries under consideration in this study.

I offer four possible explanations for this omission. The first is that political parties were not significant organizational entities at the time that the constitutional documents were drafted, or that their subsequent political influence and institutionalization was not anticipated. Secondly, prevailing social and elite attitudes at that time indicated that parties were viewed negatively and not as appropriate or desirable constitutional actors worthy of codification. Third, the minimalist designs of many constitutional texts precluded the inclusion of parties, primarily as a mechanism for preserving flexibility in the design and regulation of future forms of representative democracy. Finally, the dominant ideals of parliamentary independence, the influence of Burkean notions of representative democracy stood, and continue to stand, in tension with the concept of party government. Each of these factors is discussed in comparative context, below.

The Infancy of Political Parties as Organizations

The work of American political scientists and historians suggests that political parties, as the organizations we know today, did not develop until well into the

9 *Political Parties Elections and Referendums Act* 2000 (UK).

nineteenth century.[10] At the time the US Constitution was drafted, political parties were in their infancy – existing as divisions and factions in colonial assemblies, groups which, according to Hoadley (1986: 30–31) did not constitute a party 'in the modern sense of the word'. Political parties were not created as formalized organizations until the 1790s and evolved to accommodate the conflicting interests associated with the nature and operation of the constitutional Republic, notably the extent to which government in the new Republic should be centralized, and they crystallized into two main political groupings: the Federalists and anti-Federalists (Crotty 2006: 27).

Political parties in Australia, Canada, New Zealand and the United Kingdom did not evolve until even later. The tendencies of the Canadian Liberal Conservatives (who advocated a programme of nation building and territorial protection from the US) and the opposition Clear Grits of Canada East and the *rouges* of Canada West (who advocated free trade with the Americans) only coalesced into cohesive organizations in the 1880s. Similarly, structured political parties did not emerge in the UK and New Zealand until the late 1800s, with the Tories, Liberals and early manifestations of the Labour Party in the UK, and the Liberals in New Zealand (Barendt 1998: 150; Miller 2005: 27; Atkinson 2003: 98).

Australia presents an interesting and in many respects typical case study of the dynamics of colonial and pre-party politics.[11] Political parties also did not feature prominently in Australian colonial politics until the end of the nineteenth century (Loveday, Parker and Martin 1977: 6–15). While organizational groupings had formed to serve the interests of individual parliamentarians, these factions were transient, prone to destabilization and based on pragmatism rather than policy or ideology. This was despite all Australian colonies except Western Australia having become self-governing, and displaying characteristics of responsible government familiar to the Westminster system. Lower houses were elected, and the executive of each colony was appointed by the Governor on advice from a member of Parliament who commanded majority support in the lower house. To emphasize the similarities between colonial and British politics, parliamentarians were given the general labels of either 'liberal' or 'conservative'. However, these partisan tendencies were usually transient, and meant little more than support for a particular body of reforms or a section of the community.

To retain their seats, parliamentarians in the colonial polities had to engage with their electorate to a far higher degree than that which is usual in Westminster democracies today – it was 'necessary to pay close attention to the affairs of their constituencies and be able to show something for their parliamentary work, particularly something material like a bridge or a road' (Ibid.: 8). However, in Parliament, leaders could not survive by standing for general causes or constituency

10 See, for example, Chambers (1963); Hofstadter (1969: 212–70); McLaughlin (1912); Risjord and DenBoer (1974: 984).

11 See, for example, McKenzie (1963: 1–8), Namier (1952) and Jennings (1961) on the British experience of pre-party politics.

interests alone, but also had to monitor the particular interests of other members in order to form transient and expedient coalitions and to win majorities (Ibid.: 13).

Despite the pragmatic necessity of 'networking', members were keen to retain their status as 'independents' in the interests of maintaining electoral support. Parliamentarians were reluctant to admit any connections to each other publicly, for fear of damaging their reputation as being able to put 'the general above the particular interest and measures above men' (Ibid.: 14). Although factions (as a precursor to political parties) were a feature of colonial politics and the government and Opposition included a recognized leader and group of followers, these groupings were never large enough to govern outright and were prone to disintegration and destabilization when a leader lost support. Furthermore, factions were not necessarily polarized along conservative or liberal lines – votes were not dictated by principle or ideology alone, but rather a more pragmatic concern for constituency outcomes. An important distinguishing characteristic of these factions was the absence of any structured or coordinated extra-parliamentary party organization.

Given that parties had not yet formed as coherent organizational entities in all colonies by the time of the Constitutional Conventions at which the framework and content of the Australian constitution was discussed (1891 and 1897–98), it is not surprising that they did not feature prominently in the federation debates. An analysis of these debates reveals that although there was no sustained discourse amongst the participants as to the role or place of parties in society, the inevitability of their formation and even their embryonic existence was acknowledged by the framers. For example, John Macrossan and Alfred Deakin raised the general query that political parties may in fact form the basis of representation in the Australian upper house (the Senate), and may 'coalesce and throw in their lot with each other … irrespective of state boundaries altogether'. Macrossan predicted that 'the influence of party' would be such that 'instead of members of the Senate voting, as has been suggested, as States, they will vote as members of parties to which they belong' (see Gauja 2006b: 285). However insightful these observations may have been in hindsight, the convention participants did not pursue the issue further.

What is significant about the development of political parties and party systems in the democracies surveyed is that parties evolved (rather than being planned) and were 'created out of need, instituted as a practical and effective mechanism (whatever their faults) for mobilizing and representing the mass of people' (Crotty 2006: 26). They developed as a response to the inevitable coordination problem created by universal suffrage, an expanding electorate, the increasing size and complexity of representative legislatures and the development of political and social issues that extended beyond local concerns. Parties have evolved in a pragmatic and extra-legal fashion, in some cases constitutions simply pre-dated them; in other instances their significance as institutional mechanisms of representation was overlooked.

Social Attitudes Towards Political Parties

The prevailing social attitudes towards political parties and the development of party politics at the time at which responsible government was established at a national level was far from positive. For example, in each Australian colony prior to Federation, the 'ruling ideal of "independence" was taken to mean that men should not attach themselves regularly to parties, leaders or causes but should instead exercise independent judgment on all matters which came before Parliament' (Loveday et al. 1977: 42; cited in Gauja 2006b: 285). Not only did political parties threaten to corrupt the free judgement of parliamentarians, they also threatened the independence of, and cooperation between the States of the newly established Commonwealth.

This perception of parliamentary independence and the corrupting influence of parties is entirely consistent with the Burkean conception of representative democracy reflected in the constitutional documents of the United Kingdom (see Barendt 1998; Ewing 1987; Rawlings 1988) and the liberal democratic thinking that influenced the drafting of the United States Constitution (Hoadley 1986: 30–31). Epperson documents a similar animosity towards political parties held by America's founding fathers and leading politicians at the time of Confederation. Although political parties were present in American politics prior to the ratification of the US Constitution and the first government quickly divided into partisan groups that formed the basis of the nation's first party system (Epperson 1986: 3), political discussion during the eighteenth century was 'pervaded by a kind of anti-party cant' (Hofstadter 1969). Parties were criticized as unnecessarily divisive, the cause of needless social conflict, appealing to and acting as the instruments of narrow and special interests (the tyranny of the minority) (Epperson 1986: 4). In writing *The Federalist Papers*, both Alexander Hamilton and James Madison contemplated the role of parties, regarding them as a pestilence contaminating the body politic (Rossiter 1961: 171, 231). Maddison was concerned with the potential of political parties to dominate state legislatures, advocating the views of a small minority or particular interest at the expense of the general welfare (*The Federalist Papers*, No. 10). Thomas Jefferson regarded party affiliation as 'the last degradation of a free and moral agent', whereas George Washington warned against 'the baneful effects of the spirit of party' (cited in Gardner 2000: 667–8). In his farewell address in 1796, Washington made a plea to the nation to reject political parties:

> This spirit [of party], unfortunately, is inseparable from our nature, having its root in the strongest passions of the human mind. It exists under different shapes in all governments, more or less stifled, controlled, or repressed; but, in those of the popular form, it is seen in its greatest rankness, and is truly their worst enemy. The alternate domination of one faction over another, sharpened by the spirit of revenge, natural to party dissension, which in different ages and countries has perpetrated the most horrid enormities, is itself a frightful despotism … the

> common and continual mischiefs of the spirit of party are sufficient to make it the interest and duty of a wise people to discourage and restrain it. [12]

Given this animosity, 'it is not at all surprising that the Constitution made no mention at all of political parties and, in fact, the Electoral College was constructed on the assumption that parties would not exist' (Hoadley 1986: 30–31). The complex division and separation of powers and authority inherent in the federal US Constitution was designed to mitigate against the influence of 'factions', conceived as both 'dangerous majorities or interested minorities' (Banning 1989: 1; see also Bennett 2009: 6–7; Barendt 1998: 150; Schattschneider 1942: 6–10). The historical consensus is thus overwhelmingly in favour of the proposition that the non-inclusion of political parties in the US Constitution was entirely deliberate, and was meant to control or counteract political parties. In the nineteenth century, when political parties consolidated their position as the dominant electoral actors, this occurred entirely against the expectation and wishes of the Founding Fathers (Schlesinger 1973: xxxiv; Hofstader 1969: viii). As Hofstader aptly describes it, the design of the US Constitution represents a 'Constitution against parties' (1969: 40).

However, as Gardner (2000: 668) has observed, 'the Framers never clearly explained why the presence of political parties should be capable of so thoroughly thwarting the achievement of [democratic] goals that nothing could be done except to condemn parties and hope fervently that they did not survive'. And yet, somewhat ironically, those men who were so opposed to the formation of parties were instrumental in the creation of the American party system. Epperson (1986: 6) notes that Hamilton, Adams, Jefferson and Madison were heavily involved in the organization and activities of the early manifestations of the Federalist and Republican parties. To these men, the establishment of parties was but a temporary phase in American politics, which would eventually collapse as one side of politics persuaded and absorbed 'the more acceptable and innocent members of the other' (Hofstadter 1969: 8). However, one cannot help wondering whether the dichotomy between the interests and actions of these men might parallel the criticisms made of political parties and their parliamentarians today in developing regulatory regimes when it suits them, and refraining from doing so when it does not. The difficulties described that arise in electoral regulation when political parties and parliamentarians are both legislators and political actors are considerations that appear to have arisen at the very genesis of the US party system.

The Constitutional Design of Representative Democracy

Another reason for the omission of political parties from constitutional documents concerns the design of representative democracy and the frameworks for governance established in the various constitutions under consideration. A significant element

12 Washington's Farewell Address, 1796, available at the Avalon Project <http://avalon.law.yale.edu/18th_century/washing.asp>.

in examining the legal status of political parties is to acknowledge that it can also be viewed as a normative debate over the boundaries of representative democracy and the level at which participation should be secured. In this sense, we may reasonably look to a constitution to provide some indication of how representative democracy ought to function.

Australia's Constitution is notable for its brevity. The provisions of the Australian Constitution require a system of voting by electors for members of both houses of Parliament, but the exact nature of the electoral system, who should be given the right to vote and the place of political parties within this scheme are matters left to the Commonwealth Parliament to determine. The High Court has noted on numerous occasions that although the Constitution provides for representative government, the power to legislate for the structure and form of electoral democracy is vested in the Parliament, subject only to a small number of express and implied limitations (see Gauja 2006b: 285–6). This minimalist constitutional design is also common to the United States, where power to legislate for electoral matters is the prerogative of the state legislatures and Congress.[13]

A key question of institutional design then arises. Why should the framers of the Australian and US constitutions have sought to codify political parties when they declined to include other (arguably crucial) details, such as rules governing the election of the legislature, beyond the basic requirement (as in the Australian case) that they be 'directly chosen by the people'?[14] Rather than providing detailed rules for governance, the framers' design sought to prioritize the flexibility of the constitutional arrangements, and the necessity that they respond to developments in public opinion and shifting democratic standards.[15] Political parties may simply have been regarded as another element of the political landscape that could be more appropriately legislated for by elected representatives. Consequently, the omission of political parties in the Australian and US constitutions should not necessarily be interpreted as conferring an 'inferior' or extra-legal status upon political parties; it could alternatively be seen as simply shifting the venue for their regulation to the federal and/or state/regional legislatures.

A similar flexibility is evident in the Canadian constitutional arrangements. In assessing the constitutionality of the registration requirements for political parties in *Figueroa v. Canada (Attorney General)* [2003] 1 S.C.R. 912, members of the Supreme Court noted that:

> The right of each individual to meaningful participation sets the limit on what is permissible, but up to that limit, many options might reflect quite different, but equally acceptable, versions of democratic representation. Within constitutional limits, the choice among these options should be viewed as a matter of political and philosophical preference in which it is not in this Court's role to intervene.

13 The *Constitution of the United States of America*, Section 4.

14 *Commonwealth of Australia Constitution Act* 1900 ss 7, 24.

15 *Mulholland v. Australian Electoral Commission* [2004] HCA 41.

> The Constitution of Canada does not require a particular kind of democratic electoral system, whether it is one that emphasizes proportionality and the individual aspects of participation or one that places more emphasis on centrism or aggregation, to be frozen in place. It does require courts to be vigilant in ensuring that the system does not unduly compromise any of the values comprised with the concept of effective representation – especially the primary value of individual participation in fair elections on a basis of relative equality.[16]

Democracy is a multi-dimensional and open-ended concept, and one that is constantly evolving. Unless a constitution expressly institutionalizes particular features (such as representative democracy or parliamentary supremacy), constitutions are open to modern reinterpretations. Or, as Brooks argues, the representative and democratic nature of Canadian political institutions was 'simply assumed'.[17] The centrality of the democratic principle was taken as a baseline 'against which government would operate' and hence there was no need for the framers of the written Canadian Constitution 'to state what all assumed to be obvious' (Brooks 2009: 133).

The New Zealand *Constitution Act* 1986 does not make any mention of political parties, despite being drafted in an era when the prominence of political parties in the electoral arena, and in the everyday operation of government, was clear. This can in part be explained by the fact that, although described as New Zealand's 'premier constitutional statute' (Joseph 2007: 126), the *Constitution Act* originated from a constitutional crisis that followed the 1984 general election and concerned the transfer of power to an incoming government. Rather than being drafted as a document laying the foundations for a new political order at a time of democratic transition (as the written constitutions of the United States, Canada and Australia sought to do), the *Constitution Act* 1986 (NZ) was rather more modest in its aims: merely consolidating 'in a structured and systematic way, the most important constitutional provisions that were scattered throughout the statute book' (Ibid.: 126).

Therefore in New Zealand and the United Kingdom, which both do not have a single written constitutional document, constitutional principles are sourced from a combination of statutes, the common law and conventions. For example, the New Zealand Constitution comprises not only of the *Constitution Act* 1986, but also the *Electoral Act* 1986, the *New Zealand Bill of Rights Act* 1990, the Treaty of Waitangi, the *Standing Orders of the House of Representatives*, and various conventions. In similarity to the Australian Constitution (and since the achievement of universal suffrage with the enactment of the *Representation of the People Acts* 1918 and 1928), constitutional law experts argue that the British Constitution embodies the principle of representative democracy (in relation to the House of Commons), but that the exact form and means by which to achieve it are matters

16 *Figueroa v. Canada* [2003] I S.C.R. 912 at para. 161 per LeBel J.

17 See also Supreme Court of Canada, *Reference re Secession of Quebec*, Aug. 1998 at page 21 of online decisions.

for the legislature to determine (Turpin and Tomkins 2007: 35). The comparative fluidity of this constitutional arrangement means that political parties have been recently recognized and progressively incorporated into the constitutional design of representative democracy in these nations, particularly through parliamentary conventions and legislative instruments such as the *Electoral Act* 1986 (NZ) and the *Registration of Political Parties Act* 1998 (UK) (Turpin 1999: 511; Gay 2001). More attention to the significance of these instruments is given in the next chapter. However, at this point it is important to note that the structure and content of the British and New Zealand constitutions effectively transfer the ongoing design of the constitutional democracy to the Parliament, maintaining a degree of fluidity that is comparable to that achieved in the minimalist designs of the Australian, Canadian and US constitutions. Again, this highlights the importance of political parties not only as political actors that are regulated *by* the law, but actors that potentially also shape the design of political institutions and processes:

> Any analysis of so peculiar an animal as the uncodified British constitution is likely to prove historically contingent, that constitutional *forms* depend upon political *forces*, and that the future shape of our constitution is likely to depend upon the evolution of our party system. (Bogdanor 2004: 733)

The Independence of Parliament and Burkean Notions of Representation

> The first duty of a member of Parliament is to do what he thinks in his faithful and disinterested judgement is right and necessary for the honour and safety of Great Britain. His second duty is to his constituents, of whom he is the representative but not the delegate … It is only in the third place that his duty to party organization or programme takes rank. All these three loyalties should be observed, but there is no doubt of the order in which they stand under any healthy manifestation of democracy.
>
> Sir Winston Churchill[18]

The failure to legislate for political parties' existence is also linked to attitudes as to the nature of parliamentary representation and the fundamental (and ongoing) tension between the pragmatic reality of party government and the Burkean tradition of independent representation that has traditionally characterized Westminster parliamentary politics (see further, Chapter 9). In this mould, legislatures are constituted by independent representatives who pursue the national interest, unconstrained by party interests. This much is evident in the elite and social attitudes towards political parties that were described previously, but it is a view that has persisted in modern times. For example, in recognition of this independence, in 1947, the House of Commons (UK) resolved the following:

18 On 'The duties of a Member of Parliament' (King-Hall 1954: 302).

> It is inconsistent with the dignity of the House, with the duty of a Member to his constituents, and with the maintenance of the privilege of freedom of speech, for any Member of this House to enter into any contractual agreement with an outside body, controlling or limiting the Member's complete independence and freedom of action in Parliament or stipulating that he shall act in any way as the representative of such outside body in regard to any matters to be transacted in Parliament; the duty of a Member being to his constituents and to the country as a whole, rather than to any particular section thereof.[19]

As Turpin and Tomkins (2007: 527) note, the 1947 resolution was reinforced again in a more recent statement of 6 November 1995 with respect to lobbying for reward or consideration. Canadian members of Parliament share a similar ideal of independence, and there is a distinct notion amongst these individuals that 'a greater loyalty was owed to Parliament than to any political party. Clearly the party was only seen as an instrument of election' (Courtney 1978: 34). Although the relatively strong party discipline and uniform voting behaviour evident in all the democracies surveyed in this book (bar the United States) would seem to indicate otherwise (see, for example, Kam 2009), in terms of role perceptions parliamentarians in the United Kingdom, Australia and New Zealand today still prefer to think of themselves as representatives independent of party interests (see Gauja 2010). The idea of maintaining independence from partisan interests is not as prominent in the US Congress, where 'representation occurs mostly independent of party' and 'to a substantial extent, congressional partisanship is an elite (and perhaps interest group related) phenomenon' (Page et al. 1984: 751; see also Katz 2007: 143–5).

Hence, Burkean notions of parliamentary independence have also worked to some extent to inhibit the formal legal recognition of political parties as electoral and constitutional actors.[20] That legislators in Australia, Canada, New Zealand and the UK choose to ignore one of the fundamentals of party and parliamentary politics 'by continuing to subscribe to the view that parties were not to be acknowledged formally', has served to 'widen the gap between theory and practice' (Courtney 1978: 35–6). However, as I argue in Chapter 9, in modern times the independence of the member of Parliament must be analysed in the context of party government. The overwhelming majority of parliamentarians are elected not as individuals, but on the basis of party endorsement or a party label – a fact that has since been acknowledged by electoral registration arrangements that allow candidates to place their party affiliations on the ballot paper.[21] Nevertheless, the prevailing attitude that

---

19 House of Commons Debates, vol. 440, col. 365, 15 July 1947.

20 However, the adoption of parliamentary standing orders that recognized political parties as parliamentary actors has contributed to parties' acceptance – albeit in an extra-legal fashion (see next chapter).

21 *Representation of the People Act* 1969 (UK); updated in the *Representation of the People Act* 1983 (UK); *Commonwealth Electoral Act* 1918 (Aust.) s. 214; *Electoral Act* 1993 (NZ) s. 150, Form 11, Schedule 2; *Canada Elections Act* 2000 s. 117.

parliamentarians are (and should be) independent of party influences has presented a key barrier to the constitutionalization of political parties in democracies, particularly those characterized by single-member districts. New Zealand after the adoption MMP is an interesting counterpoint to this trend, and this is discussed further in Chapter 9.

The Emergence of Political Parties

Notwithstanding the thinking of political theorists and the previously expressed attitudes towards political parties, actual political practice changed rapidly in the late nineteenth and early twentieth centuries when an expanding franchise and the onset of mass electoral politics led to the inevitable formation of political parties as organizations to contest elections. The expanded franchise increased the legitimacy of the Parliament as representing the political will of the people, but the need to appeal to an enlarged electorate was a key catalyst in the gradual strengthening of party organizations as an efficient means by which to supply the labour resources necessary to gather votes and mobilize supporters. Unlike in previous decades, 'buying' votes or securing them on the basis of patronage was no longer practicable (Craig 1990: 39).

By the early years of the twentieth century, a basic pattern of party competition had developed that continues to characterize democracies today. In contrast to the anti-party sentiment that had characterized the eighteenth and nineteenth centuries, during the course of the twentieth century political parties came to be viewed as indispensable elements of democracy. For example, in 1976 the UK Report of the Committee on Financial Aid to Political Parties made the following statement:[22]

> Effective political parties are the crux of democratic government. Without them democracy withers and decays. Their role is all pervasive. They provide the men and women, and the policies for all levels of government – from the parish council to the European Parliament. The parties in opposition have the responsibility of scrutinizing and checking all the actions of the Executive. Parties are the people's watchdog, the guardian of our liberties. At election times it is they who run the campaigns and whose job it is to give the voters a clear-cut choice between different men and different measures. At all times they are the vital link between the government and the governed. Their function is to maximize the participation of the people in decision-making at all levels of government. In short they are the main-spring of all the processes of democracy. If parties fail, whether from lack of resources or vision, democracy itself will fail.

In 1950, the American Political Science Association's Committee on Political Parties issued a report in defence of the role of political parties in modern American democracy, and argued the need for a stronger, responsible two-party system:

22 Cmnd 6601/1976 at para. 9.1 Quoted in Turpin and Tomkins (2007: 539).

> Popular government in a nation of more than 150 million people requires political parties which provide the electorate with a proper range of choice between alternatives of action. The party system thus serves as the main device for bringing into continuing relationship those ideas about liberty, majority rule and leadership which Americans are largely taking for granted. (APSA 1950: 22)

The APSA Report reveals a very clear normative role for parties that centres upon effective majority representation that, as we shall see, is in some ways quite specific to the American context. However, more broadly, political scientists believe that parties perform several crucial functions in modern systems of representative governance, by creating a chain of linkage between citizens and the state (see, for example, Lawson 1988; Key 1961; Schattschneider 1942). As part of this chain, political parties serve to reconcile and aggregate diverse and often conflicting interests in society; to provide an arena for citizen participation in politics; serve as vehicles for political communication; to recruit political elites through processes of candidate selection and once elected to the legislature, perform a governance function, to represent diverse and partisan interests in society, and through the mechanism of regular general elections, act as a conduit through which the government can be held accountable.

The Evolution of Political Parties and Party Models

During the course of the twentieth century, political parties became firmly entrenched in the electoral and parliamentary politics of the United States, the United Kingdom, Canada, Australia and New Zealand. As politics began to be defined in terms of partisan struggles, consequently the academic writings and social commentaries on political parties shifted from whether they were desirable at all, to a more descriptive discussion of party types and features (Scarrow 1996: 17). In this section, I introduce readers to the main theoretical models that political scientists have used to analyse and understand the evolution of political parties throughout the twentieth century, and their implications for the legal regulation of these organizations.

Political parties have moved through a number of stages or organizational transformations in the last century. The earliest type of party, generally referred to as the elite or cadre party, evolved from the support networks that organized to assist in the electoral and campaigning efforts to elect prominent politicians to the legislature. Rather than attracting a wide social base and encouraging popular participation in politics, elite parties were interested only in mobilizing an active political elite reflecting the limited franchise of the time. As voting rights expanded in the early 1900s, the elite party was superseded by the 'mass' party, the organizational form that characterized electoral politics until the middle of the twentieth century. Mass parties sought the election of the candidates for public office through the development of a large organizational base, consisting of an expansive membership that contributed labour and resources to the party, which was expected to represent a distinct social strata in the Parliament (for example, the social democratic parties that represented the working classes).

The lessening of class cleavages in the post-war period, a growing middle class and changes in campaign technology are generally attributed to have encouraged the development of what are termed 'catch-all' and 'electoral professional' parties (Panebianco 1988). The political practice of these parties differed significantly from the mass parties that preceded them; rather than representing a segment of society or a set of interests, these parties turned their efforts to capturing the support of the 'median voter', producing policies to appeal to the electorate at large, often at the expense of ideological purity. This approach was facilitated by unprecedented improvements in campaigning technology that emerged with the mass media. Rather than working through traditional channels and using party members as a resource for door-knocking, conducting public meetings and mobilizing support, party leaders were able to reach a significant percentage of the population through television, radio and printed publications.

This shift in practice has, in turn, affected the theoretical role of parties in modern democracies. As electoral pragmatism replaced an ideologically driven agenda, the function of representation has shifted from aggregating (and responding to) the views of a party's members and its supporters to formulating policies perceived to be popular with the entire electorate. This, in Kirchheimer's (1966: 199) words, has created a party characterized as 'non-utopian, non-oppressive and ever so flexible'. The role of parties as avenues for democratic participation has also been downgraded, as members' roles in policy making, fund raising and campaigning are reduced and replaced by paid professionals. Consequently, the locus of power within the party organization has shifted from the membership and the extra-parliamentary organization, which emphasized participation and ideology, to the 'more electorally ambitious and pragmatic parliamentary elite' (Miller 2005: 71).

Nowhere is this change in the nature of parties as organizations more evident than in the decline of party membership. Half a century ago in the United Kingdom, one of every 11 eligible voters belonged to a political party. Now only one in 88 does. In this time, the Labour Party's membership has dropped from one million individual members to 150,000, and the Conservatives from 2.8 million to 250,000 (Bogdanor 2009: 292). In the last 40 years, Australian party memberships have dropped from over 4 per cent of the electorate to just 1 per cent (McAllister 2002: 389–91; Sawer, Abjorensen and Larkin 2009: 134–5). Party membership in New Zealand declined from a peak of 12.5 per cent of the electorate in 1981, to 4.8 per cent in 1999 (Vowles 2002: 416). Canadian parties experienced a drop in members from 4.45 per cent in 1988 to under 2 per cent in 1994 (Carty 2002: 355).[23]

23 Political parties in the United States do not have formal 'memberships' akin to the other democracies analysed, thus reliable comparative figures for this state are unobtainable.

More recently, the introduction of public funding for parties' election expenses has prompted theorists to re-evaluate the relationship between parties and the state. The 'cartel party' represents the latest model in the evolution of party types; one in which governing parties (or those established in the legislature) are able to utilize the resources of public office to the exclusion of new parties and other competitors (Katz and Mair 2009, 1995; Blyth and Katz 2005). This includes obtaining and manipulating direct election funding, parliamentary expenses to subsidize party activity and the allocation of publicly funded broadcasting time. Like a catch-all party, the locus of power in a cartel party resides in the parliamentary party (especially the leadership) who receive and control the distribution of state resources, and the influence of the extra-parliamentary wing of the party organization is minimized.

One key feature of a cartel party is that it can *prima facie* appear to be internally democratic – individual members are offered greater participatory opportunities to influence policy and select candidates, typically through direct ballots. However, internal democracy is largely illusory, as the focus on largely inactive and moderate individual members privileges the parliamentary party by circumventing party activists and other centres of power within the party such as national conferences, regional and local branches (Blyth and Katz 2005). The decision-making power and influence within the party becomes ever more centralized in the party in public office and the leadership. As Katz (2001: 293) aptly describes, it is a strategy of 'empowering while decapitating the membership'.

In terms of representation, theorists predict a distinct policy convergence between the political parties in any given political system as established parties continue to pursue policy positions that are electorally agreeable, reducing the options available to voters and the diversity across the policy spectrum. Furthermore, within the cartel party model, policy is increasingly influenced by the 'perspectives and priorities of the state bureaucracy' (Miller 2005: 73), shifting the impetus for policy formulation away from parties to the executive. Policy commitments are increasingly becoming 'externalized' and delegated to experts, particularly in the area of economic policy. For example, in 1997, the UK Labour government granted the Bank of England the effective power to set interest rates, subject only to the advice of a government-appointed Monetary Policy Committee. This delegation of responsibility and power was not mentioned in the party's election manifesto, and would have been deemed unthinkable by previous governments, regardless of party type (Blyth and Katz 2005: 47). The full implications of these trends is explored in greater detail throughout the book, but at this point it is sufficient to note that how political parties are regulated by the law has important implications for the functions that they perform; but that such regulation should also take into account the dynamic nature of political parties as adaptive organizations, and in particular, the increasing importance of the party in public office.

Conclusion: The Implications for Electoral Regulation

As the first part of this chapter demonstrated, in large part the constitutions of the nation states examined in this research do not explicitly acknowledge, or regulate political parties in modern democratic society. I advanced four main reasons for this occurrence: the infancy of political parties as organizations when constitutions were drafted; negative social attitudes towards parties; the need to preserve flexibility in constitutional arrangements, and the dominance of Burkean (or independent) attitudes towards parliamentary representation. Given this constitutional absence, responsibility for party regulation is left to the legislatures and the courts. However, without an overarching constitutional statement as to the place of political parties in society, much of this regulation has the tendency to be *ad hoc* – occurring only when the need occurs by legislators and the judiciary. While this lack of entrenchment does allow party laws and regulations to remain contemporary in character; it also comes with the possibility that legislators may exploit their position as both party members and law makers to create regulatory regimes that serve an incumbent or partisan interest. This possibility is discussed in greater detail in the chapters that follow.

The second half of the chapter discussed the emergence of political parties and the changes that they have undergone in the last century. However, the dynamic and adaptive nature of political parties serves to complicate electoral regulation. Although political scientists generally agree that political parties have over the last century performed a number of important functions in democracies (aggregating interests, providing a forum for citizen participation, communicating with the public, recruiting leaders, governing and representing partisan interests), as both societies and political parties change, the balance between these various functions also shifts. The changes in party organization (from cadre, to mass, to catch-all and cartel) over the last century consequently alter the nature of what it is that the laws are seeking to regulate. For example, we know that political parties are no longer the mass associations that they once were, attracting hundreds and thousands of members into their fold. Therefore, are laws that continue to judge the legitimacy of political parties on the basis of their financial membership still relevant today? Furthermore, if political parties are becoming increasingly reliant on the resources of the state, and are forging greater links to entrench themselves in office, do we need new laws that might ensure the accountability of parties if general elections are becoming less effective? Given the possibility that political parties are converging in their policy positions, is there a case for legislation to ensure a greater level of policy competition between parties in the interests of diverse representation? How might we balance this with other normatively desirable ends such as the need to achieve cooperation, stability and non-violence? As Bogdanor (2009: 298–9) suggests:

> The demise of the mass party raises fundamental problems for democratic government. In the past, political parties were the prime institutions linking the

> aspirations of voters with the machinery of government. But, if they are not longer the primary vehicles of political engagement, then, inevitably there will be radical changes in the relationship between people and the government.

Besides responding to the changing nature of political parties, the law can also be used as a mechanism to achieve change within parties. Regulations on campaign finance that seek to control sources of party funding are a good example of laws that have an indirect effect on the internal organization of political parties (discussed further in Chapter 8). Hence we need to ask ourselves what it is we want political parties to do, or to look like, and structure our laws accordingly. If we judge that citizen participation in politics through political parties is an important function, we might look to establish laws that encourage intra-party democracy (see Chapter 3). Similarly, if we value the primacy of centrism, interest aggregation and 'strong' government, then laws which privilege the major party actors would be desirable, whereas diverse representation in the legislature might be better achieved through a system of party regulation that encourages minor party competitors. Although I have argued that the law can potentially be used as a mechanism with which to structure party competition and influence the organization of political parties, questions remain over the effectiveness of legal measures – particularly when viewed amongst other forces that shape party behaviour (for example, socioeconomic changes in society).

These are all questions that are open to debate; yet first and foremost they need to be actually asked. As the next two chapters will demonstrate, although the law is potentially an important force in shaping the actions of political parties, it has developed in an unreflective manner – keeping up with the development and increasing prominence of political parties rather than systematically addressing what roles they should play in modern democracies.

Chapter 3
The Gradual Legal Recognition of Political Parties

Given the political acceptance of parties as a commonplace feature of representative democracy and their organizational evolution over the last century, this chapter examines the extent to which they have been recognized by the law. Paralleling their importance in everyday political practice, I catalogue a clear trend towards an increasing acknowledgement of the role and significance of political parties as electoral actors – manifest in their greater legislative and judicial recognition and consequent legal regulation. Nevertheless, there is a clear difference in the extent to which the law regulates the activities of parties in electoral campaigns and their internal organization. These patterns of regulation have arisen due to a number of factors, which although are common to most of the democracies surveyed, vary in their salience throughout: the emergence of party (rather than candidate) competition; a need to stem perceived corruption; to allocate and regulate financial resources (both from the state and private sources) and provide for transparency and accountabilities in how these funds are spent or allocated.

The Legal Recognition of Parties in Australia

In the first few decades following federation, political parties were barely recognized, let alone regulated by Commonwealth legislation. A telling example of the status of parties is the fact that 'for many years official Australian election results gave voting figures as if all candidates were independents, treating the parties as electorally non-existent' (Bennett 2002: 2). The primary legislative recognition of political parties in Australia occurred with the passing of amendments to the *Commonwealth Electoral Act* 1918 in 1983,[1] which allowed for the formal registration of political parties to contest federal elections. This regulation was necessitated by the introduction of public funding for election campaigns. In the late 1960s and early 1970s, political campaigning began significantly changing in Australia. Campaign techniques such as opinion polling and widespread political advertising were first used in the 1967–68 re-election campaign of South Australian Premier Don Dunstan, and then at the federal level by the Whitlam opposition in the 1972 'It's Time' Campaign (Young 2004). The increasing sophistication and expense of election campaigns occurred

1 *Commonwealth Electoral Legislation Amendment Act* 1983 (Cth).

simultaneously with the rise of the 'electoral-professional' party organization, which prioritized the role of hired campaign professionals to appeal to the median voters at the expense of the party membership and ideological orientation (Panebianco 1988: 264).

Both major parties had difficulty in meeting the rising cost of campaigning, having spent AUD$12 million which could not be met due to a shortfall in donations. The major parties advocated public funding on the basis that it would lessen reliance on corporate donors. Communicating policies to the electorate so that voters could make an informed choice at the ballot box was regarded by the parties as a civic duty, one worthy of financial subsidy from the public purse (Young 2004: 116). Subsequently, public funding for the conduct of federal electoral campaigns was introduced by the Hawke government in 1984, although it had previously been in place for New South Wales State elections from 1981 (see further Chapter 7). It was this provision of public funding that created the catalyst for greater legal regulation. As Bennett (2002: 6) notes, 'Where parties once benefited from the freedom which came from their legislative non-existence, the introduction of public funding produced legislative changes which began to see parliamentary "interference" in their operations'. Such interference was deemed necessary in order to satisfy demands for transparency and accountability in the provision of taxpayers' funds.

Prior to the enactment of the *Commonwealth Electoral Legislation Amendment Act* 1983, which provided for the public funding of parties, political parties were inserted into the text of the Australian Constitution in 1977, in an amendment approved by popular referendum in the aftermath of the sacking of the Whitlam government and the 1975 'constitutional crisis'. The crisis arose following the actions of several State Parliaments in appointing senators to fill casual Senate vacancies who were not members of the political party that originally held the seat. The practical effect of these appointments was to reduce the government's already tenuous control of this house of Parliament to a minority position, which left it unable to pass supply bills and prevented it from governing.

In May 1977, a constitutional amendment was presented to the electors of Australia, which was designed to prevent a similar crisis from reoccurring. Section 15 of the Commonwealth Constitution, pertaining to casual Senate vacancies, was amended to 'ensure so far as practicable that a casual vacancy in the Senate is filled by a person of the same political party as the Senator chosen by the people and for the balance of his term'.[2] The referendum received bipartisan political support and passed successfully both nationally and within all six States,[3] carrying significant

2 Australian Electoral Office, 'AEO Referendums to be held on Saturday May 21, 1977 – Arguments for and Against', 28 March 1977.

3 Under s. 128 of the Australian Constitution, in order to succeed a referendum must be passed by both a majority of electors nationwide, and by a majority of electors in each of the six Australian States. Nationally, 72.02 per cent of electors supported the amendment whereas 26.2 per cent voted against it. See Blackshield and Williams (2002: 1307). The

implications for the legal recognition of parties as legitimate and 'official' actors in the political process.

The debate surrounding the desirability of the constitutional change is an important case study of the Australian public's attitudes towards party government. An analysis of the 'yes' debate reveals that parties were regarded as an indispensable element of representative democracy, and their constitutional recognition was 'fundamental to [the] rights [of] a voter that representation in the Senate should always reflect the wishes of the electorate' (AEO 1977: 4). Those opposed to the amendment acknowledged the importance of parties as political actors, but maintained that they should remain the subject of unwritten conventions, rather than 'rigid constitutional requirements' (Ibid.: 14). It was feared that the codification of parties would transfer power to political parties at the expense of State Parliaments and 'complete the process of making the States' House entirely a party political house'.[4] In this regard, it is plausible to interpret the success of the referendum as reflecting popular support for the 'official' and legitimate role of parties as actors in political and electoral processes, and their consequent codification in Australia's constitutional document (Gauja 2006b: 290).

Judicial attitudes as to the appropriate legal status of political parties in Australia have largely responded to these legislative developments, though arguably have been slower in acknowledging the development of political parties as institutions fundamental to representative democracy. For most of the twentieth century, political parties were characterized at common law as 'voluntary associations'. The case of *Cameron v. Hogan* (1934) 51 CLR 358 (hereinafter *Cameron*), heard a quarter of a century after the consolidation of the party system in Australia, placed the internal affairs of political parties largely beyond the reach of the law. According to the majority judgment of the High Court (at 370–71), such voluntary associations were:

> Likely to be formed without property and without giving to their members any civil right of a proprietary nature. They are for the most part bodies of persons who have combined to further some common end or interest, which is social, sporting, political, scientific, religious, artistic or humanitarian in character, or otherwise stands apart from private gain and material advantage. Such associations are established upon a consensual basis, but, unless there was some clear positive indication that the members contemplated the creation of legal relations inter se, the rules adopted for their governance would not be treated as amounting to an enforceable contract.

As I will argue in the following chapter, this characterization of parties as voluntary associations has had a significant impact upon the rights of party members.

success of the referendum should also be appreciated in its historical context: while there have been 44 referenda held in Australian since 1901, only eight have carried.

4 AEO (1977: 14).

However, this situation changed in the latter half of the twentieth century when the courts began contemplating the public role and importance of parties. The historical progression highlights the symbiotic relationship between judicial and legislative developments in the regulation of political parties. Both are closely related – with the former using the legislative and constitutional recognition of parties as a justification for judicial intervention in what was once considered the 'domestic concern' of the parties.[5]

The first decision to express concern with the High Court's categorization of political parties in *Cameron* was *McKinnon v. Grogan* [1974] 1 NSWLR 295 (*McKinnon*). Although this case concerned the rules of association of a football club, Justice Wooten took the opportunity to question the continuing pervasiveness of the High Court's decision in *Cameron*, which dealt with 'an area of human affairs which has changed and continues to change greatly in social significance' (at 297). Justice Wooten suggested in *obiter* that perhaps the time had come to reconsider the nature of political parties in Australian society and hence their legal classification:

> *Cameron v. Hogan* was 40 years ago, and I suspect that in that period it has been more frequently distinguished or ignored than it has been applied, simply because its application in full rigour has been increasingly out of tune with the felt needs of the time. The High Court has not had occasion to reconsider it squarely, and I venture to suggest that when such an occasion does arise there will at least be some qualification of what was there said. With the greatest respect to the eminent and forward-looking judges who gave the decision, it has tended to justify judicial abdication from areas the orderly regulation of which has become of ever-increasing importance. The resultant categorization in legal analysis of a great political party … with a group of friends agreeing to meet for tennis, is simply inadequate. (at 297)

This conclusion, albeit arrived through a slightly different line of reasoning, was also reached by the Supreme Court of Queensland in *Baldwin v. Everingham* [1993] 1 Qd R 10 (*Baldwin*). *Baldwin* concerned a dispute between a member of the Queensland Liberal Party and the party's executive over alleged irregularities in the party's candidate selection process. As in *Cameron* and *McKinnon*, the central question was whether the party's rules and procedures were justiciable – or whether, as a voluntary association, they stood beyond the reach of the law. In *Baldwin*, Justice Dowsett applied the earlier approach of Justice Isaacs in *Edgar v. Meade* (1916) 23 CLR 29. This earlier case concerned an internal dispute within a trade union, and the matter was found to be justiciable on the ground that the union was a entity that had received statutory recognition,[6] which took it beyond the status of a voluntary association (at

5 Cameron at 376 per Starke J.

6 Section 55 of the *Conciliation and Arbitration Act* 1904 (Cth) provided for the registration of trade unions.

43–4). Similarly, in *Baldwin*, Justice Dowsett considered the effect of the provisions of *Commonwealth Electoral Act* 1918 upon the legal status of political parties. He observed (at 15) that 'For a very long time, the parliamentary system functioned upon the assumption that parties had no official status in the electoral process. The Act indicates that such is no longer the case' (Gauja 2006b: 293).

By analogy with the reasoning of Justice Isaacs in *Edgar v. Meade*, Justice Dowsett concluded that the internal disputes of political parties were justiciable owing to the legislative recognition of such organizations in the *Electoral Act*. However, Dowsett's conclusion differed from that in *Cameron v. Hogan*, '*not because changing policy considerations dictate a different result, but rather because the Commonwealth Parliament, in conferring legislative recognition upon political parties has taken them out of the ambit of mere voluntary associations*' (at 20) [emphasis added]. This decision was followed several years later by the South Australian Supreme Court in a case that dealt with the controversial political practice of branch-stacking:[7] *Clarke v. Australian Labor Party (SA Branch)* (1999) 74 SASR 109. In determining whether this matter was justiciable, Justice Mulligan examined the provisions of the *Electoral Act* 1985 (SA) and concluded that it was due to this 'statutory recognition by the South Australian Parliament of political parties' (at 65) that political parties' internal matters came under the ambit of judicial adjudication. There has been substantial academic criticism of the approach that the judicial regulation of political parties (particularly with respect to their internal affairs) should be premised solely on legislative recognition rather than taking account of broader policy considerations (see, for example, Forbes 1995).

The Recognition of Parties in Canada

Although the origins of the Canadian party system date back to as early as 1880, political parties in Canada did not receive official legislative recognition until almost a century later with the passing of the *Canada Elections Act* (1970). As the Canadian Supreme Court noted in *Figueroa v. Canada (Attorney General)* [2003] 1 S.C.R. 912 (hereinafter *Figueroa*):

> Parties are such important actors in our political system that, although they are private and voluntary organizations, they also possess some of the characteristics of a public institution. It is therefore to be expected that the identification and regulation of parties should have become one of the functions of Canadian elections law; indeed, it is rather surprising that the existence of political parties was not recognized at all in federal electoral legislation until 1970.[8]

7 Branch-stacking is the act of paying for the memberships of individuals in a particular political party solely for the purpose of supporting a particular candidate in a nomination contest. It is discussed in further detail in Chapter 5.

8 *Figueroa* at para. 143.

At that time, Canadian political parties were viewed as private and voluntary associations, and consequently beyond the reach of the law. For example, in *Young and Rubicam Ltd. v. Progressive Conservative Party of Canada* (22 March 1971), C.S. 803–933, the Quebec Superior Court dismissed a case brought by an advertising agency against the Progressive Conservatives seeking damages for the party's failure to pay its accounts as such a case could not be brought against the party. Although 'well founded in facts and law', the Court found that 'no claim of this kind can be drawn up against a political party' as it has no 'legal existence' (Courtney 1978: 36; see also 1993: 401).

In similarity to the Australian experience, the impetus for the legal recognition and hence regulation of political parties had its origin in campaign finance. The formal legislative recognition of parties in Canada came in response to the recommendations of the Committee on Election Expenses (the 'Barbeau Committee') in its report issued in 1966 (*Report of the Committee on Election Expenses*). The report noted that before the amendments to the *Canada Elections Act* only the fund raising and spending of individual candidates were regulated, and as political parties played a fundamental role in Canadian electoral politics this meant that effectively electoral financing remained virtually unregulated. This created opportunities for corruption and the possibility that both parties and legislators would be less accountable to voters and less likely to act in conformity with the public interest.

The Barbeau Committee's report recommended that a formal registry of political parties be established and public subsidies provided for basic campaign expenses to reduce the distorting effect of large private contributions, coupled with donation and expenditure disclosures. The Committee also proposed the use of tax incentives to encourage a broad individual base of donations to parties, and the printing of candidates' party affiliations on the ballot paper. Parties were required to comply with registration requirements before accessing these benefits (Committee on Election Expenses 1966: 37–48). Many of these recommendations were adopted in major amendments to the *Canada Elections Act* in 1970 and 1974 (see further Chapters 7 and 8).

The Act was also amended to allow candidates' party affiliations to be printed on the ballot paper. This move followed the pragmatically motivated recognition of political parties in the Canadian Parliament. As Courtney (1978: 37) writes, after the 1963 general election, the victorious Liberal Party 'wasted no time in seeking to consolidate [its] position as the new governing party in a house of minorities'. In passing an amendment to grant financial support of $4,000 per annum to a parliamentary political party with 'a recognised membership of 12 or more in the House of Commons', the government was able to extend benefits to the newly formed *Ralliement des créditistes* (with 17 MPs), whilst marginalizing the existing Social Credit Party (with 11 MPs).[9]

Today, an extra-parliamentary political party is defined by the *Canada Elections Act* 2000 as 'an organization, one of whose fundamental purposes is to

9 *Senate and House of Commons Act*, R.S.C. 1970 c. S-8, s. 41(2).

participate in public affairs by endorsing one or more of its members as candidates and supporting their election'.[10] The Act also imposes several registration requirements upon political parties seeking to contest elections and receive public funding, including meeting certain membership requirements. Like the somewhat arbitrary numerical threshold for the recognition of a parliamentary party adopted after the 1963 election, such 'gatekeeper' or threshold provisions may serve to entrench the interests of the existing parties and/or dominant players (see further Chapter 4, 'Gatekeeper Provisions').

Despite registration requirements and the regulation of parties' financial activities in return for public subsidies, the Canadian courts have generally regarded political parties as private entities, which according to Forcese and Freeman (2005: 95) is also the prevailing view in political circles, and hence there is a corresponding perception that they should therefore be free to regulate themselves. As noted above in the extract from *Figueroa*, the Supreme Court has expressed its opinion as to the importance of parties as electoral institutions and this has paved the way for the courts to regulate parties in the context of the electoral contest; however, the courts have largely remained reluctant to regulate the internal affairs of parties, which continue to exist as 'private and voluntary organizations' (*Figueroa*).

This position has caused some controversy in the conduct of Canadian parties' candidate and leadership selection contests. The status of political parties as 'clearly non-statutory bodies' was reaffirmed in *Cureatz v. Progressive Conservative Party of Canada* [1997] O.J. No. 2309 (at para. 17 per LaForme J), which dealt with a dispute over the party's candidate nomination process. However, the court suggested that it could review the decisions of such bodies in very limited circumstances, 'in the nature of certiorari', and only where there is an error of law (including a denial of procedural fairness or natural justice), not a dispute over the construction of party rules (at paras 17 and 21). This view of political parties was reiterated in a more recent case, *Knox v. Conservative Party of Canada* [2007] 286 DLR (4th) 129, where the Alberta Court of Appeal declined to review a party's candidate selection method, owing to the fact that:

> Neither constituency associations nor political parties are given any public power under the *Canada Elections Act* S.C. 2000, c. 9. They are essentially private organizations. It is true that their financial affairs are regulated: they may only give tax receipts in certain circumstances, and they may only spend the money they raise in certain ways. However, merely because an organization is subject to public regulation does not make it a public body subject to judicial review … It is argued that the democratic process, elections, and the activities of political parties are of great public importance. That is undoubtedly true, but public importance is not the test for whether a tribunal is subject to judicial review. (per Berger, Watson and Slatter JJ at paras. 26–27)

10 *Canada Elections Act* 2000 s. 2.

Therefore, while legislative developments have allowed the legal recognition and regulation of political parties in matters concerning party finances and the conduct of the electoral contest, unlike their Australian counterparts, Canadian courts appear more reluctant to examine and arbitrate in matters that are internal to the party.

The Recognition of Political Parties in New Zealand

New Zealand's political parties did not emerge as coherent, unified entities until the last decade of the nineteenth century. The 1893 election marked a turning-point, when the 'loose' combination of members of Parliament pledging their support to the previous ministry became a reasonably disciplined caucus under the label of the Liberal Party and united behind a coherent economic and social programme (Atkinson 2003: 98). However, despite their emergence a century earlier, political parties in New Zealand did not receive noteworthy legislative recognition until 1993, with the passing of the *Electoral Act*. Prior to this, political parties were only referred to in passing in statutes, concerning matters such as representations regarding electorate boundaries, the display of campaign material on election day and the ability (from 1975) of candidates to place their party affiliation on the ballot paper if they so wished (Geddis 2005).

However, unlike Australia, Canada and the United Kingdom, where the statutory recognition of political parties has been incremental, the *Electoral Act* 1993 (NZ) pushed political parties to the centre of the stage in completely overhauling New Zealand's electoral machinery from a first-past-the-post to a proportional representation system and acknowledging the crucial role parties play in this system of representative government.

It is this sudden transformation that warrants New Zealand as an interesting case study of the legal regulation of political parties, and necessitates a closer examination of how these widespread changes came about. Electoral reform in New Zealand originated from, on the one hand, a strong dissatisfaction with existing first-past-the-post electoral institutions, and on the other, the complex interplay between key political actors both inside and outside Parliament, and 'ultimately, a series of political miscalculations or accidents' (Atkinson 2003: 201; see also Jackson and McRobie 1998). It is also an excellent, and unusual, example of an electoral reform agenda driven from outside the legislature (through a combination of referendums, public pressure and the central importance of an independent, extra-parliamentary committee), which together were in large part able to circumvent the actions and preferences of the dominant parties that opposed reform.

Discontent with first-past-the-post and the strong system of two-party competition that it created was a sentiment that had its origins as early as the 1960s, but gathered pace in the 1970s and 1980s in a climate of economic insecurity, the implementation of a neo-liberal programme of economic reform without public support, and negative attitudes towards elected representatives who were seen as unaccountable and representing a narrow set of partisan interests. During this time, New Zealand earned the label and reputation of being 'an executive paradise', where a majoritarian first-past-the-post electoral system combined with strong party discipline and the Westminster style of parliamentary democracy to effectively fuse together the legislative and executive arms of government. Very few institutional checks and balances existed to hold governments to account and the ruling party occupying executive office could essentially push through any legislation it chose, 'subject only to the normal vicissitudes of political calculation' (Geddis 2007a: 29).

The early push for reform was driven by the NZ Labour Party, which although it had won a greater share of votes in both the 1978 and 1981 elections than its main opponent, the Nationals, failed to gain a majority of seats and hence remained in opposition. During both these election campaigns, Labour pledged to initiate an inquiry into various aspects and outcomes of the electoral process. When the Labour Party finally won government in the 1984 election, it established a Royal Commission on the Electoral System (1985). The Commission sat for 18 months, received over 800 written submissions, undertook consultations in major New Zealand cities and visited Australia, Canada, Ireland, the United Kingdom and West Germany, at a total cost of NZ$1.3 million (Atkinson 2003: 204).

The Commission's recommendation that New Zealand adopt a German-style mixed member proportional (MMP) representation system was seen by those in power as too radical, and received little support from both the Labour Party (which had commissioned the Inquiry) and the National Party. In its report *Towards a Better Democracy*, the Commission concluded that MMP was 'the best voting system for New Zealand's present and future needs' as it would overcome 'the disproportionality between parties that is inherent in plurality [first past the post] voting' (Wallace 1986: 11–12). The new system was seen to be more equitable towards smaller political parties and would encourage a broader spectrum of representation in the Parliament.

Anticipating that its findings may not be entirely welcomed by the political parties that enjoyed dominance in the legislature, the Commission devised a method of implementation for the reforms by way of a popular referendum. A referendum would only require the support of a simple majority of electors, in contrast to the special majority of 75 per cent of parliamentarians that was an alternate means to changing the electoral arrangements under the *Electoral Act* 1956 (NZ) and effectively 'take the ultimate decision out of politicians' hands' (Atkinson 2003: 205). Although both political parties played down the report and tried to suppress the issue in light of these recommendations, the debate took an unexpected and fortuitous turn during a televised leaders debate in the lead up to the 1987 general election. In this debate, the National Party's leader Jim Bolger attempted to embarrass the government over its neglect of the Commission's Report, to which Prime Minister David Lange promised to hold a referendum on the issue by 1990 – a commitment that he later admitted was a 'colossal' mistake owing to a misreading of his briefing notes (Geddis 2007a: 31; Atkinson 2003: 206).

After Labour's election, the issue was referred to a parliamentary select committee (the Electoral Law Committee) composed of four Labour and three National parliamentarians, who recommended that the first-past-the-post system be retained in the interests of simple and effective government. In April 1989, the government announced that there would be no electoral referendum. However, the issue was kept alive by a handful of MPs, grassroots groups such as the Electoral Reform Coalition, the Women's Electoral Lobby, academics, trade unions and newly established small parties such as the Greens who would benefit in the transition to such a system. Furthermore, the National Party continued to embarrass the Labour government for reneging on its electoral reform promises, and carried to the 1990 election a pledge to hold a binding electoral referendum prior to the end of 1992. The Labour Party responded during the campaign with a counter-promise for an indicative referendum to be held by October 1991 (Atkinson 2003: 209). Consequently, and as a result of pure political expediency, there was bipartisan consensus for holding an electoral referendum in the 1990 campaign, despite both parties' reluctance to pursue reforms they perceived to be against their own interests.

Two referendums were subsequently held prior to the introduction of MMP. An indicative referendum was held in September 1992 that attracted a turnout of 55.2 per cent, of whom 84.7 per cent favoured changing the electoral system. Seventy per cent supported the transition to MMP. The second, binding referendum was held concurrently with the 1993 general election and attracted a much higher turnout of 85.2 per cent of electors. MMP was endorsed by a majority of voters (54 per cent to the 46 per cent who remained in favour of first-past-the-post), and achieved majority support in both the North and South Islands and in the Maori seats.

The electoral legislation that was designed to implement and support MMP explicitly recognized the existence of political parties by tying the overall composition and representation in the House of Representatives to the vote obtained by each political party at a general election (through the mechanism of party list seats). Margaret Wilson, past president of the NZ Labour Party and head of the Prime Minister's Office under Geoffrey Palmer, saw the reforms as the means by which:

> Political parties have achieved formal recognition, if not legitimation, of their role within out constitutional arrangements. Although political parties have played a dominant role for a long time in New Zealand, their role has been masked, through a combination of a cloak of secrecy that has traditionally surrounded their internal activities, and the notion that governments are non-political. (Wilson 1998: 169)

However, arguably this system only really formalized the place of parties in the New Zealand electoral system rather than fundamentally transforming it. In 1998, the New Zealand High Court commented:

> In one sense, it may be seen as the law more closely reflecting voters' wishes, since for over 100 years nationwide political parties have in fact been central to the electoral process, the formulation of policies, the selection of candidates and, as a result, the decisions that individual voters make about how to cast their votes. (*Lange v. Atkinson* [1998] 3 NZLR 242, per Blanchard J at 463)

Nevertheless, the *Electoral Act* 1993 (NZ) imposed several key regulatory requirements upon political parties such as registration, financial and reporting obligations, and the requirement of internally democratic candidate selection procedures (discussed further in Chapters 4 and 5). Furthermore, the fundamental role and importance of political parties in the legislature was also acknowledged in the parliamentary standing orders of the New Zealand House of Representatives. Standing Orders 34–35 facilitate the formal recognition of parliamentary parties as a group of six or more MPs. Interestingly, the House of Representatives also introduced the additional requirement that a new political party must first register with the Electoral Commission before it is able to receive parliamentary recognition (S.O. 34(2)(b); see Joseph 2007: 352). The number of members a parliamentary party has determines the allocation and order of speaking opportunities in parliamentary debates (S.O. 102), and the proportion of party representation in select committees (S.O. 186).

Yet despite their formal importance in the institutional design of MMP, the legal status of political parties and the character and extent to which they should be regulated remains an unsettled matter in New Zealand (Geddis 2005). Prior to the introduction of MMP, in a similar approach to that taken by the courts to the status of political parties in Australia and the United Kingdom, parties were essentially regarded as private unincorporated associations and any internal disputes were to be resolved by way of the application of the principles of contract law (*Peters v. Collinge* [1993] 2 NZLR 554). *Peters* concerned an action brought by Winston Peters, a disgruntled former cabinet minister in the National Party, to review the party's process of candidate endorsement and its decision to fail to re-nominate him for election. The New Zealand High Court found that in this case:

> The National Party is an unincorporated society. Fundamentally, the jurisdiction to review steps taken by such a society is to be found in contract. In some special situations a private body may be subject to non-contractual judicial review, for example where it exercises quasi-public functions … or contemplates an action of significant direct impact upon the public … Time constraints permit me to say only that in my view this is not one of those exceptional cases which fall outside the scope of contract. It must be kept in mind that we are dealing here with the manner in which the controlling executive of a political party may exercise its power to decline to approve a Member of Parliament as its candidate in the forthcoming general election, not an expulsion, disciplinary, or restraint of trade case. (per Fisher J at 39–40)

However, this statement did leave the door ajar for the possibility of review where a political party might exercise a quasi-public function, or more specifically, intra-party processes dealing with expulsion or disciplinary action. Justice Fisher went on to comment that in this instance, the decision as to the selection of an appropriate candidate was a party matter:

> Politics is a notoriously volatile, not to say fickle, business. Just as ideas and policies change, so must there be room for change in allegiances and loyalties … Whether a political party is so out of sympathy with its Member of Parliament that it no longer wants him as a candidate is something which one would expect the party to be free to decide from time to time with relatively little constraint. It is essentially a political question in which one would expect a robust level of discussion, lobbying and preconception. (at 47)
>
> … For legal purposes, political parties are private bodies. They have no statutory or public duties. If they wish, parties can assist individuals onto the stage of public life and offer support and suggestions from the wings while they are there. But it is to the elected individuals themselves that we then turn when we look for performance of public and statutory duties. It is not the parties who helped to get them there. The fact that a party has supported a successful candidate does not impose any fresh legal status or responsibilities upon that party. The party remains in the wings as a private entity. (at 68)

The conception of the limited function of a political party changed significantly after the transition to MMP, and in particular, with the legislative requirement that political parties adopt democratic procedures for candidate selection (*Electoral Act* 1993, s. 71). Although the exact requirements of this provision are discussed in greater length in Chapter 5, the way in which a political party conducted its candidate selection processes and the nature of this function as public duty became issues for determination in *Payne v. New Zealand National Party* [2008] 3 NZLR 233, in which the court stated that political parties are 'free to regulate how they will go about the selection of constituency candidates at general elections. The freedom to structure their own arrangements for candidate selection, however, was made subject to the requirement of s. 71 in the 1993 Act' (per Panckhurst J at para. 58). However, the rather minimalist way in which the court interpreted these requirements indicates a continued perception that political parties are essentially private actors when it comes to determining their internal affairs, even within an MMP regime.

The Recognition of Parties in the United Kingdom

Writing as late as 1963, political scientist Jean Blondel observed that political parties in the United Kingdom were 'private associations to which the law does not give more rights and duties than to other private organizations' (1963:

87). Indeed, until the end of the twentieth century, political parties were only acknowledged in statute and parliamentary practice in a very piecemeal and *ad hoc* way. In some ways like Canada, the initial legal recognition of parties in the United Kingdom had its origins in the realm of parliamentary politics. In 1937, the *Ministers of the Crown Act* recognized and provided a salary for the office of the Leader of the Opposition, the Opposition Chief Whip and the office of Prime Minister and the Cabinet. As Bogdanor (2004: 724) argues, this Act also gave statutory recognition for the first time to the fact that the House of Commons was composed of political parties (a government party and an Opposition) rather than being composed of individual members of Parliament. As the Liberal MP Dingle Foot commented in a Commons debate at the time, 'this is the first time in any statute that we have recognised the existence of a party caucus' (29 April 1937, cited in Bogdanor 2004: 724).

In 1969, the *Representation of the People Act* provided a further step toward recognition by allowing candidates to state their party affiliation on the ballot paper. However, this Act did not provide for the full statutory recognition of political parties, as a proposal to establish a corresponding 'Registrar of Political Descriptions' was opposed by the Conservatives on the basis that it did not fit with the party's structure and would make registration of all the party's constituent organizations impractical. It was also defeated in Parliament on the grounds that 'by making the ownership of a party label a justiciable matter, the law is, quite unnecessarily, brought into politics' (see Ibid.: 726). Somewhat deficiently, as Bogdanor argues, and as a bizarre consequence of legislative compromise struck, there was therefore no requirement that a party description be accurate, nor was there any remedy available to voters if the description or label was misleading (Ibid.: 726).

A number of parliamentary committees in the 1970s also recognized the importance of political parties: the Committee on Financial Aid to Political Parties (1976) and the Kilbrandon Report, Cmnd 4460-I (1973). The authors of the Memorandum of Dissent to this report argued that any contemplation for constitutional reform in the United Kingdom must be concerned with political parties, which were described as 'the chief motivating force of our main governmental institutions'. In 1975, the Parliament took further steps to institutionalize the role of political parties in the legislature, providing what is called 'short money' to assist all opposition parties (not just the official Opposition) in carrying out their parliamentary duties. In order to be eligible for assistance, a political party had to meet a minimum threshold of the election of two parliamentarians or one parliamentarian and 150,000 votes nationwide. However, despite the fact that all political parties (at least in their parliamentary capacity) were now being supported by public funds, the issue of statutory recognition was again avoided as the proposal to provide short money was carried by parliamentary resolution and not statute (Ibid.: 728). Hence we observe a situation where political parties were able to provide their own publicly resourced benefits, but were also able to escape the obligations of statutory recognition.

Indeed, political parties did not receive constitutional recognition or statutory regulation until very late in the twentieth century, with the passage of the *Registration of Political Parties Act* 1998 (UK) and the *Political Parties, Elections and Referendums Act* 2000 (UK) (PPERA). This latter act provides for a system of party registration that requires political parties to nominate office holders, provide a copy of their constitution and financial arrangements to the electoral commissioner, and places controls and obligations upon parties' fund raising and spending. Prior to this, although parties had been mentioned in various Acts and secondary legislation, the only Act that dealt with parties in any substance was the *Sex Discrimination Act* 1975, which excluded political parties from its operation – 'the purpose being to allow the women's sections on Labour's National Executive Committee to continue' (Ibid.: 718; Ewing 1987). Like Australia and Canada, the motivation for the statutory recognition of political parties in the United Kingdom has also largely been driven as a by-product of the debate on political finance and how best to regulate it, and to enable party lists in the European elections, rather than as a measure to rectify their arguably anomalous status as voluntary associations (Bogdanor 2004: 717).

Like the statutory recognition of political parties, the judiciary's attempt at adjudicating matters concerning political parties has evolved in an *ad hoc*, yet quite creative way. The current common law status of political parties in the United Kingdom gradually evolved from decisions pertaining to trade unions, which could be regarded as broadly analogous to political parties in their organization and operation. The British courts have held that political parties remain as 'unincorporated associations' at law, but are subject to some common law regulation in that their internal affairs are justiciable. Faced with several cases in the 1970s and 1980s concerning the enforcement and interpretation of party rules in intra-party disputes, the English courts realized that 'voluntary associations' were often incapable of protecting the rights of their members, and a way to overcome this lack of enforcement and redress had to be found. That mechanism came by way of the 'legal fiction'[11] that the rules of associations were of such social importance that they must have been intended by their members to be contractually binding.[12] This principle originally pertained only to trade unions, but was applied to the Labour Party in a latter case in which the contractual nature of the party rules and constitutions was assumed to be binding upon the organization and its members.

Lewis v. Heffer [1978] 1 WLR 1061 concerned a factional dispute within a constituency branch of the UK Labour Party, which culminated in an inquiry into the branch's conduct and the suspension of two factional leaders by the party's central executive body, the National Executive Council (NEC). One of these leaders, Julian Lewis, sought a declaration that the actions of the NEC were *ultra vires* and an injunction restraining the NEC from making the suspensions.

11 *Enderby Town Football Club Ltd v. Football Association Ltd* [1971] Ch 591 at 606 per Denning LJ.

12 *Lee v. Showmen's Guild of Great Britain* [1952] 2 QB 329.

In making its ruling that the actions of the NEC were within its power under the party's rules and constitution, the court considered the legal status of the Labour Party and its constituency parties. Denning MR had no doubt that the dispute was justiciable on the basis that the rules of the association formed a binding contract upon all members of the party, despite the party's status as an unincorporated association:

> There is no doubt that the solution of this case must depend on the rules of the parties. We have to discover what is the true relationship between the national party and the local constituency party, and to do this we have to look at the rules. Each of these parties, the national party and the local constituency party, is in law an unincorporated association ... But they are inextricably tied together ... When a person joins a local constituency party, he becomes automatically a member of the national party. In the eye of the law he enters into two contracts – one with the other members of the local constituency party – the other with the other members of the national party. He is taken to have agreed to both: and be bound by the rules of both. (per Denning MR at 1071)

Lord Justice Ormrod similarly held that 'rules of associations of this kind ultimately derive their legal effect from the acceptance, by the members, of the terms and conditions of the association when they join the group' (at 1076).

The Court in *Lewis v. Heffer* made several interesting observations about the nature of political parties as organizations and the distribution of power within them. In examining the relationship between the national party and its constituency organizations, Lord Justice Ormrod accepted the party's argument that it was 'essentially a central organization working through satellites in the constituencies, with control firmly at the centre and all power and initiative flowing outwards to the periphery and not inwards to the centre' (at 1076). Lord Denning described political parties as akin to 'a regiment or an army or a ship of a fleet. Each individual is a member of his unit but he is also a member of the whole. His unit is subject to the directions of the High Command: and so is he' (at 1071). Both these comments suggest that parties can, and necessarily need to be organized so as to maintain a degree of centralized control and power. This characterization of the party organization is somewhat out of character with comments expressed by Lord Denning in *obiter* that if the NEC had the ulterior purpose of 'promoting sectional differences of one faction against the other – I should have thought that would have invalidated the suspensions' (at 1073–4). If a political party is subject to commands from the leadership, should they not be able to choose the political direction of the party and favour one faction over another if a dispute arises? Nevertheless, despite its scope and motivation, the exercise of this power is subject to the rules and procedures of the party, and the principles of natural justice (although the rules of natural justice did not apply in this particular case).

However, in *Conservative and Unionist Central Office v. Burrell (Inspector of Taxes)* [1982] 1 All WLR 522, the Conservative Party, for the purposes of taxation law, was found not even to be an unincorporated association. Rather, it existed 'as a political movement' and lacked 'the characteristics of an unincorporated association for the purposes of the taxing statute. There are no mutual understandings between all the members, no mutual rights and obligations and no rules governing control where it clearly lies, which is in the leader' (at 527 per Lawton LJ). In some ways, it is difficult to reconcile this judgment with the Court of Appeal's conclusions in *Lewis v. Heffer*; however, the relatively more fluid organizational structure of the Conservative Party may have been as distinguishing feature. Furthermore, unlike *Lewis v. Heffer*, which concerned the adjudication of an intra-party dispute, *Burrell* was concerned with the more specific question of the characterization of a political party for the purposes of the applicability of taxation provisions. Of the two cases, *Lewis v. Heffer* should be regarded as the more expansive and broader reading of a party's significance and status at law.

In contrast to the approach of the Australian courts, the contractual enforceability of the rules of political parties is the legal means by which judges claim to have the jurisdiction to settle intra-party disputes in the United Kingdom.[13] It is interesting to note that although some cases concerning disputed candidate selection processes were characterized as falling under the scope of employment law from 1996 to 2008, the House of Lords has now returned to contract law as the basis for settling such disputes (discussed further in Chapter 5).

The Recognition of Political Parties in the United States

As noted in the previous chapter, anti-party sentiment has been historically strong within the United States, reflected in the fact that parties were deliberately omitted as constitutional actors. However, and somewhat ironically, this scepticism of the place of political parties in public life also meant that unlike the *laissez-faire* approach evident in the United Kingdom, Canada, Australia and New Zealand, political parties became the interest and subject of state regulation comparatively early on. This is so much the case that, as Justice Scalia has noted, 'Americans have made the regulation of political parties one of the principal tasks of political legislation' (quoted in Pomper 1992: 116), and in effect, have made them public property (Johns 1999: 91). Nevertheless, the extent to which political parties should be regulated, how, and by what means (self-regulation, judicial or legislative) are substantial and yet unresolved streams of political discourse in the United States.[14]

A number of state legislatures began to regulate (and by default recognize) party activities during the Civil War, a process that gained momentum in what was known as the 'Progressive Era' (Ibid.). The motivation behind such regulation was to remove

13 The principle was more recently upheld in *Weir v. Hermon* [2001] NICh 8. See also *Mortimer and Ors v. Labour Party*; Ch D (Parker J) 14 January 2000 (unreported).

14 See for example, Epstein (1989); Lowenstein (1993) and Fay (1982).

power from the hands of corrupt party officials and return it to the people, and the main mechanism by which this was achieved was the party primary (for more detail on the development of primaries in the US, see Chapter 5).[15] Like the other states surveyed in this research, regulating 'money politics' was also a key catalyst for legislative regulation. In 1974, Congress passed the *Federal Election Campaign Act* (followed by the *Bipartisan Campaign Reform Act* 2002),[16] but by this time political parties had been substantially brought within the realm of statutory recognition through legislative measures to regulate primaries at the state level.

The first reference to political parties in the decisions of the US Supreme Court dates back to *Neal v. Delaware* 103 U.S. 370, 391 (1880), which dealt with the exclusion of African Americans from serving in juries in Delaware, almost a hundred years after the ratification of the US Constitution. However, *Neal v. Delaware* and several other jury decisions in this period[17] only make mention of the existence of political parties, without making any comment on their function or how they should operate in the system of government and representative democracy. Parties' role, however, was hinted at in the dissenting opinion of Justice White in the income tax case of 1895, *Pollock v. Farmers' Loan and Trust Co.* (*Pollock I*)[18] and the majority opinion, written by Chief Justice Fuller, in *Pollock v. Farmers' Loan and Trust Co.* (*Pollock II*) (Nelson 2005: 93).[19] In *Pollock I*, Justice White described the role of the Supreme Court as an arbiter, 'removed from the contentions of political parties and the animosities of factions',[20] and in *Pollock II*, Chief Justice Fuller noted that contentious questions such as the desirability of income tax regimes were best resolved within the political realm, that is, belonging 'to the controversies of political parties, and cannot be settled by judicial decision'.[21] Such statements reflect an attitude that the law and the courts sat above the base world of party politics, and that these two arenas – the judicial and the political – should remain separate. Consequently, non-recognition and regulation of parties can be viewed as a consequence of this early and somewhat arguably arbitrary distinction.

The first Supreme Court decision to directly address the role of political parties in the American system of government was *Ex Parte Curtis*,[22] which examined the constitutionality of federal legislation that prohibited employees of the federal government asking for or accepting campaign contributions from other governmental employees. Justice Waite, writing for the majority, upheld the constitutionality of

15 For a detailed account of this process, see Petterson (1995: 112–13); Ranney (1975).

16 See further Chapter 8.

17 *Pointer v. United States* 151 U.S. 396, 407 (1894); *United States v. King* 147 U.S. 676 (1893); *Agnew v. United States* 165 U.S. 36 (1897).

18 157 U.S. 429 (1895).

19 158 U.S. 601 (1895).

20 *Pollock I*, 157 U.S. 429 (1895) at 650–52.

21 *Pollock II*, 158 U.S. 601 (1895) at 634.

22 *Ex Parte Curtis*, 106 U.S. 371 (1882). See Nelson (2005: 96–8).

the law as a means to prevent corruption and protect public service employment, but acknowledged the role of parties in American democracy:

> Political parties must almost necessarily exist under a republican form of government; and when public employment depends to any considerable extent on party success, those in office will naturally be desirous of keeping the party to which they belong in power. The statute we are now considering does not interfere with this. The apparent end of Congress will be accomplished if it prevents those in power from requiring help for such purposes as a condition to continued employment.[23]

Although political parties were again briefly alluded to in several Supreme Court judgments relating to the electoral process in the late nineteenth century,[24] decisions in the early years of the Court do not amount to any sort of constitutional tradition of political parties in the American system of government, nor do they 'recognize any special place or privilege for these political organizations' (Nelson 2005: 103). Nelson further argues that:

> The paucity of cases brought before the Court during these early years can be viewed as a reflection of the endogenous nature of political parties – creatures developed within the politics of the political actors of the day and not within constitutional jurisprudence. If on the other hand, political parties are, indeed, viewed as part of a constitutional tradition, then the scanty involvement of the Supreme Court – as the interpreter of the Constitution – in issues related to the political parties appears to be problematic. (Ibid.: 104)

Despite the absence of a constitutional tradition of political parties in the jurisprudence of the early Supreme Court, recent pronouncements from the Court appear to suggest that political parties now have a special or privileged role within the institutions of American government.[25] Political parties have been described by the Court as a 'constitutional tradition', with Justice Kennedy proclaiming in *California Democratic Party v. Jones* 530 U.S. 567 (2000) that:

> Our constitutional tradition is one in which political parties and their candidates make common cause in the exercise of political speech, which is subject to First

23 *Ex Parte Curtis*, 106 U.S. 371 (1882) at 376.

24 See, for example, *Ex Parte Yarbrough* 110 U.S. 651 (1884); *Connors v. United States* 158 U.S. 408 (1895); Nelson (2005: 100–103).

25 See, for example, *McConnell v. Federal Election Commission*, 540 U.S. 93, 320 (2003); *Colorado Republican Federal Campaign Committee v. Federal Election Commission*, 518 U.S. 604, 630 (1996) at 630.

> Amendment protection. There is a practical identity of interests between parties and their candidates during an election.[26]

In light of this history of legislative and judicial regulation, Epstein (1986: 157) defined political parties in the American context as agencies 'performing a service in which the public has a special interest sufficient to justify governmental regulatory control, along with the extension of legal privileges, but not governmental ownership or management of all the agency's activities'. Although the American debates on the legal status of political parties tend to focus on the need for reduced regulation, rather than whether it should be expanded, the fundamental question in all democracies remains the same. How, if at all, should political parties be regulated by the law? What is an appropriate level of regulation? What form should it take? Is regulation appropriate or necessary for political parties in performing certain democratic functions within society?

Conclusion: Patterns of Legislative and Judicial Recognition

When analysing the legal status of political parties across democracies, it is helpful to disaggregate the nature of this regulation into two distinct subcategories. First, from what source does the regulation of parties originate, or who undertakes the regulatory task (for example, is it self-regulation, judicial regulation, or legislative regulation). Secondly, what is the character of this regulation? Does it seek to control the actions of political parties as they interact with other political parties and voters, or does it extend to the party's internal activities and processes, such as candidate selection, policy formulation and patterns of participation? Finally, what have been the key drivers behind this recognition and regulation?

Table 3.1 presents a comparative summary of the key instruments and rationales for legal recognition and regulation. The regulation of political parties is overwhelmingly achieved through statutory measures, although in some states certain statutes may have constitutional status (for example, the *Political Parties Elections and Referendums Act* in the United Kingdom). With the exception of the United States, statutes that regulate political parties have only been enacted in the last few decades. In Australia, Canada and the United Kingdom, these instruments have emerged as a regulatory response to the problem of party finance, and thus seek predominantly to regulate parties' actions in the electoral contest. Both New Zealand and US statutes purport to control aspects of parties' internal decisions (such as candidate selection), however, the origin of these laws derives from different sets of motivations. In the United States, it was an early response to negative public perceptions of political parties and an attempt to avoid corruption through the centralization of political power in party

26 *California Democratic Party v. Jones*, 530 U.S. 567 (2000) at 589. Cited in Nelson (2005: 85–6).

leaderships. In New Zealand, such regulation stems from an attempt to secure diverse representation in the Parliament and to ensure an appropriate nexus between citizen participation in politics through parties, and the overall party composition of the legislature. The reality of party government (that is, parties' presence in Parliament) has also provided an important catalyst for recognition in Canada and the United Kingdom.

Judicial regulation of political parties has been more restrained, but in turn responds to legislative developments. For the greater part of the twentieth century, political parties were regarded as private entities – voluntary associations – beyond the reach of the law. This continues to be the dominant paradigm in Canada and the United Kingdom, although the courts in Australia and New Zealand appear to be more willing to acknowledge political parties as organizations with a legitimate public function – as has been the approach in the United States for almost a century. An interesting question also arises as to the interplay between recognition and regulation. Did the former facilitate the latter? With respect to judicial regulation this appears to be the case. For example, in Australia, legislative recognition has been used to justify review by the courts of intra-party processes. However, it has not mandated such review. In contrast, legislative recognition and legislative regulation are symbiotic – most legislative instruments that recognize the existence of political parties also seek to impose some conditions upon their behaviour bestow a benefit upon them. Given that political parties are not recognized in constitutions, their status at law is neither protected nor prescribed.[27] Hence we observe a situation where governments, courts and political parties are in a constant struggle to determine the limits of freedom of these organizations, a battle complicated by the fact that parties are also legislative actors.

As illustrated in Table 3.1, and arguably as a by-product of this contest, there continues to be an imbalance between the regulation of parties' external actions (for example, how they spend their money during election campaigns) and their internal decision-making processes (for example, policy making and candidate selection) in favour of the former. Whether or not this is normatively desirable is a question for debate. Provided they conform to the provisions of the general law, it is arguably against liberal principles to regulate the internal activities of political parties. However, as we shall see in the next few chapters, this relative balance has created a situation whereby entry to elections is tightly controlled and political parties (particularly the entrenched electoral actors and incumbents) are receiving increasing levels of public subsidies, yet they operate under very few constraints as to how they spend this money or select their candidates who will in turn contest elections and form government.

27 However, see discussion in the next chapter 'The Freedom to Associate and the Requirement to Register'.

Table 3.1 The Legislative Recognition and Regulation of Political Parties: Key inStruments and Catalysts for Change

State	Constitutional changes	Legislative instruments	Parliamentary resolutions	Target of regulation	Catalysts
Australia	Casual Senate vacancies (1977)	*Commonwealth Electoral Act* (1983 amendments)		Financial affairs	Public funding; Financial transparency and accountability
Canada		*Canada Elections Act* (1970)		Financial affairs	Public funding; Allocation of parliamentary resources
New Zealand		*Electoral Act* (1993)	House of Representatives Standing Orders	Financial affairs; Candidate selection	Electoral reform; Financial transparency and accountability
United Kingdom		*Representation of the People Act* (1969) *Registration of Political Parties Act* (1998); *Political Parties, Elections and Referendums Act* (2000)	*Ministers of the Crown Act* (1937); Short money (1975)	Financial affairs	Allocation of parliamentary resources; Party competition; Financial transparency and accountability
United States		Various state laws mandating primaries (from late 1800s); *Federal Election Campaign Act* (1974); *Bipartisan Campaign Reform Act* (2002)		Candidate selection; Financial affairs	Minimizing corruption; Regulating electoral competition; Financial transparency and accountability

Chapter 4
Requirements for Party Registration and Internal Organization

In this chapter, I examine the rules that political parties must abide by and the conditions that they must fulfil in order to be recognized as 'official' participants in the electoral process. Although political parties are generally free to form and associate as they wish (subject to some constitutional limitations), achieving the status of a 'registered' and thus state-sanctioned political party confers several important benefits upon a political organization, such as financial subsidies. I argue that it is therefore effectively impossible to be a significant political force in a general election without fulfilling the requirements of registration. The bulk of this chapter examines party registration requirements in a comparative context, and analyses how they operate to definite the character of party competition within a given political system, and how they privilege some political parties at the expense of others. The chapter concludes with an evaluation of how (if at all) the law shapes the internal activities of political parties, and discusses whether a certain proscribed standard of internally democratic decision making should be required of political parties operating in modern representative democracies.

The Freedom to Associate and the Requirement to Register

The ability of political parties to form, or to associate, is one of the fundamental freedoms enshrined in the constitutions of the United States and Australia,[1] the Canadian *Charter of Rights and Freedoms*, the *New Zealand Bill of Rights Act* and the European Convention on Human Rights. It is crucial to the practice of representative democracy that citizens have the ability to come together collectively (subject to certain constitutional limitations described below) to express their political views and preferences.

Freedom of association cases with political parties as litigants have been most common in the United States, where political parties have invoked the First Amendment to challenge the legislative regulation or prescription of their existence and activities (both electoral and internal). The majority of the cases have concerned procedures for selecting congressional candidates, and as discussed further in Chapter 5, the US Supreme Court has used the implied freedom of association

1 However, note that in Australia this is an implied rather than express freedom – see below.

contained within the First Amendment to uphold parties' preferences as to the exact form of primary elections. However, this freedom is not absolute, and much depends upon where the boundary between elections (as public activities) and the private affairs of political parties is drawn. The US Supreme Court has upheld the general act of holding state-mandated primaries and has ruled that a state might seek to maintain the overall integrity of the electoral process, to provide for the secrecy of the ballot, to increase voter participation in primary elections and to prevent the harassment of voters, and these interests go to the conduct of the primary and do not justify a substantial intrusion into the associational freedoms protected by the Constitution's First and Fourteenth Amendments.[2]

The right to form political parties in the United Kingdom is protected by Article 11 of the European Convention on Human Rights (1950), which provides:

1. Everyone has the right to freedom of peaceful assembly and to freedom of association with others, including the right to form and to join trade unions for the protection of his interests.
2. No restrictions shall be placed on the exercise of these rights other than such as are prescribed by law and are necessary in a democratic society in the interests of national security or public safety, for the prevention of disorder or crime, for the protection of health or morals or for the protection of the rights and freedoms of others. This article shall not prevent the imposition of lawful restrictions on the exercise of these rights by members of the armed forces, of the police or of the administration of the State.

However, this freedom is not absolute. Groups that repudiate democratic principles or advocate violent means to achieve their goals are not protected by the Convention.

In New Zealand, the freedom to associate is codified in Article 17 of the *New Zealand Bill of Rights Act* 1990, but is subject to 'such reasonable limits prescribed by law as can be justified in a free and democratic society' (Article 5). The *Canadian Charter of Rights and Freedoms* also provides for freedom of association in Article 2, subject to 'such reasonable limits prescribed by law as can be demonstrably justified in a free and democratic society' (Article 1). In both cases, we have seen courts assume the jurisdiction under their respective national charters to adjudicate disputes concerning party and electoral law dealing with association, and it is expected that they will continue to do so. As Courtney (1993: 405) notes:

> Legal challenges … to electoral statutes and to regulatory and administrative decisions affecting the operation of elections will almost certainly continue to be a feature of future elections. The subject-matters … will depend on little more

2 *Eu v. San Francisco County Democratic Cent. Committee*, 489 U.S. 214 (1989); *Democratic Party of U.S. v. Wisconsin ex rel. La Follette*, 450 U.S. 107 (1981).

> than a modicum of human ingenuity and an interest in testing the limits to which the *Charter* might be pushed.

While there is no express right to freedom of association in the Australian constitution, the High Court has found this freedom to be implied within the document to the extent that it is required for the operation of free political discussion and representative government. In *Australian Capital Television* (1992) 177 CLR 106, it was suggested that 'the notion of a free society governed in accordance with the principles of representative parliamentary democracy may entail freedom of association, and, perhaps, freedom of speech generally'.[3] In what has been described as one of Australia's greatest constitutional triumphs (Winterton 2003: 108), the High Court struck down legislation that attempted to ban the Communist Party of Australia. Passed by a conservative Liberal-National coalition government, the *Communist Party Dissolution Act* 1950 (Cth) was designed to ban the Communist Party and its affiliated bodies under the ambit of the Commonwealth's defence power.[4] The Act stated that:

> … it is necessary, for the security and defence of Australia and for the execution and maintenance of the Constitution and of the laws of the Commonwealth, that the Australian Communist Party, and bodies of persons affiliated with that Party, should be dissolved and their property forfeited to the Commonwealth …[5]

The High Court held in *Australian Communist Party v. Commonwealth* (1951) 83 CLR 1 (the *Communist Party* case) that while the government had the power to prohibit subversion, the legislation was invalid on the grounds that it simply declared the Party and its individuals as being subversive without allowing the courts to judge that factual connection.[6] The *Communist Party* case is not precedent for the suggestion that *all* political parties are protected from dissolution, but that any law purporting to ban political parties would be subject to scrutiny. As Winterton (2003: 134) argues, the Court may well uphold legislation dissolving, not a specific political party, but one with specified undesirable characteristics that

3 Per Gaudron J at 212; see also Justice Murphy's judgments in *McGraw-Hinds (Aust) Pty Ltd v. Smith* (1979) 144 CLR 633 and in *Miller v. TCN Channel Nine* (1986) 161 CLR 556; *Lange v. Australian Broadcasting Corporation* (1997) 189 CLR 520 at 567–8.

4 Section 51(vi) of the Australian constitution provides that 'the Parliament shall, subject to this constitution, have power to make laws for the peace, order and good government of the Commonwealth with respect to … the naval and military defence of the Commonwealth'.

5 *Communist Party Dissolution Act* 1950 (Cth), Preamble. Section 4 of this Act declared the Party to be an unlawful association, and section 7(1) provided that any person continuing to operate as an officer of the Party or carrying or displaying anything indicating that he/she was associated with the Party would be liable for up to five years' imprisonment.

6 This reasoning was adopted by five of the 6:1 majority (Justices Dixon, McTiernan, Williams, Fullagar and Kitto). Chief Justice Latham dissented and Justice Webb's reasoning was quite divergent from that of the majority.

the legislature was justified in suppressing (for example, incitement to violence) and if this suppression were proportionate to concerns for public safety. This approach is consistent with the express limitations to the right to association that are provided for in the human rights charters discussed above.

The approach in these liberal democracies is substantially different from other societies that have experienced non-democratic regimes or are far more heterogeneous, with multiple cleavages that facilitate the emergence of extremist political parties. As noted in the previous chapter, the German Basic Law declares political parties that 'seek to impair or abolish the free democratic basic order or to endanger the existence of the Federal Republic of Germany' unconstitutional. This provision was used to declare some extremist right-wing groups such as the *Republikaner* unconstitutional in the 1990s (Ignazi 2003: 73–4) and to outlaw the German Communist Party (KPD) and the neo-Nazi party (*Sozialistische Reichspartei*) in the early years of the Republic. Similar provisions are also included in the constitutions of Spain, Portugal and Poland (see Müller and Sieberer 2006: 439–40). In contrast to these democracies, the design of the electoral systems in Australia, Canada, the UK and the US favours single-member plurality districts, making it more difficult for extremist and anti-democratic parties to gain representation (Mersel 2006a: 168–70). However, these societies are not entirely immune from the emergence of extremist political parties, as the recent experience of Pauline Hanson's anti-immigration 'One Nation' party in Australia, and the British National Party in the UK demonstrate.

Therefore, subject to some 'justifiable' limitations necessary for the maintenance of free democratic societies, anyone is free to form a political party to contest elections at various levels of government: national, regional and local. As I will explain in this chapter, many democracies have also established regimes for the registration of political parties that wish to contest elections, which bring a number of benefits such as public subsidies, party affiliation printed on ballot papers, access to the electoral roll, and so on. However, registration is not compulsory.

While there is a crucial theoretical distinction between the freedom of citizens to associate and form a political party, and the requirement to register it; the harsh reality of electoral competition in the current climate is that party registration is almost essential to contesting public elections. If the ultimate aim of a political party is to contest public office (a definition agreed upon by both legislators and political scientists alike); then registration is necessarily tied up with the effective ability to associate to pursue an organization's aims and ideological principles. Therefore, despite the constitutional freedom of citizens to associate, there remains a fundamental normative question regarding the ability and ease with which new competitors and political parties should be able to enter the electoral arena. As Müller and Sieberer (2006: 437) argue, there are two issues that must be considered in this debate: the need for effective and open electoral competition (achieved by placing relatively few restrictions on the freedom of the electoral market-place), traded off against the potential problem of the fragmentation of the party system and its consequent inability to coherently structure issues and interests.

Placing registration requirements on political parties in order to contest elections is one legal mechanism by which the state can attempt to control the effective number of parties that participate in elections. A higher registration threshold, which for example could be achieved by placing a minimum membership requirement upon parties or the lodgement of a deposit, might be expected to reduce the number of competitors, whereas a lower threshold would potentially see more political parties enter into the electoral contest. Another means by which the number of competing political parties can be controlled is through the nature of the voting system that is adopted in any given election, and there is a vast political science literature that analyses this.[7]

Why should the state seek to impose requirements for registration that may reduce electoral competition? Intuitively, unrestricted competition between political parties may seem desirable for democracy. However, an atomized party system (with a large number of smaller parties) would likely result in government instability and 'insufficient political problem-solving capacity' (Müller and Sieberer 2006: 437) as there is no incentive for individuals and smaller parties to seek collective solutions, aggregate multiple opinions and organize on a larger scale. Müller and Sieberer also argue that given the infrequency of elections and the fact that citizens will only have limited opportunities to vote during their lifetime, 'eliminating "loony" parties or candidates and forcing the others to demonstrate some level of support before they are allowed to contest elections is legitimate and beneficial to voters' (Ibid.: 437). For these authors, the law cannot guarantee an 'optimal' or correct number of parties, but it can be used as a tool with which to cut back excessive supply.

Often registration requirements are tied to the allocation of public resources to political parties, such as election funding. In this sense, the requirements imposed upon parties could also potentially perform an accountability and transparency function in necessitating political parties to have adequately transparent financial structures and accounting systems in order to account for the ways in which taxpayers' money is spent. This argument could even be taken further to suggest that in return for public funding, registration requirements also provide some means by which the public (or their elected or appointed representatives) control, or have some say, over the way in which public funds are expended by political parties and how they are internally organized.

The Requirements of Registration

Regardless of whether or not regulating the effective number of political parties contesting elections is viewed as normatively desirable, all the democracies surveyed in this research impose some registration requirements upon political

7 For an overview of the main debates in a comparative context, see Gallagher and Mitchell (2005); Norris (2004); Blais and Massicotte (2002).

parties, although there is considerable variation between them. However, as a general point of comparison, the requirements that a party must meet in order to be registered are an important determinant of the ease of entry into the political system, and the structure of party competition within a democracy.

In Australia, parties registered for the receipt of public funding under the *Commonwealth Electoral Act* 1918 (Cth) must be established on the basis of a written constitution, have a minimum of 500 financial members or one Member of Parliament, and are required to submit an annual disclosure of the sources of party funding. The benefits of registration include the use of the party name beside individual candidates on ballot papers, public funding provided that the party's endorsed candidates poll at least 4 per cent of the primary vote, and a copy of the electoral roll containing the postal contact details of all enrolled electors, which parties can make use of for campaigning purposes.[8] Although registered political parties require a formal written constitution under the provisions of the *Commonwealth Electoral Act*, the structure and content of the party constitution are essentially regarded as internal matters for individual political parties to determine. The *Electoral Act* requires only that the aims of the party (one of which must be the endorsement of candidates to contest federal elections) be enumerated, in addition to the terms and conditions of party membership (for example, the procedures for accepting or terminating membership). It is important to note that like the aims of the party, the Act requires only that the terms and conditions of party membership be formally codified in the party's constitution, and does not impose any requirements as to their actual content. Although recommended by the Australian Electoral Commission,[9] the current regulatory regime does not require political parties to formulate rules for the appointment of office bearers within the party organization, or to detail procedures for amending the party's constitution. Nor does the Act require the party to submit any details of its structure (AEC 2005: 10–11).

The situation is similar in the United Kingdom. Under the *Political Parties, Elections and Referendums Act* 2000 (UK) (hereinafter PPERA), party registration is not compulsory, but is open to any party that declares its intention of contesting one or more elections (see Bradley and Ewing 2003: 155–8). Under the current regime, only candidates representing a registered party may be nominated for election; other candidates must be nominated as independents or without description.[10] Although a party must provide details of its financial structure and a copy of its constitution upon registration, again, there are no formal requirements as

8 *Commonwealth Electoral Legislation Amendment Act* 1983 (Cth).

9 The Australian Electoral Commission (AEC) is the statutory body responsible for conducing federal elections and referenda, maintaining the Commonwealth electoral roll, administering election funding, financial disclosure and party registration requirements.

10 *Political Parties, Elections and Referendums Act* 2000 (UK) ss 22, 28. This provision was inserted to overcome the problem of candidates adopting similar names to the parties to confuse electors. For example, in one instance a candidate stood as a Liberal Democrat (*Sanders v. Chichester* (1994) SJ 225).

to what it should contain. The UK Electoral Commission (2006: 13) suggests that a party's constitution contain provisions as to the structure of the party (branches, headquarters, affiliated organizations, and so on), how it is run (frequency of meetings, decision-making procedures, appointment of officers, and so on) and its aims and objectives. However, again these are merely recommendations. In what is a unique provision amongst comparable common law liberal democracies, registered political parties in the UK are eligible for policy development grants from the Electoral Commission, with a total pool of £2 million each year to be divided among eligible registered parties.[11] In order to be eligible for this financial support, political parties must have gained parliamentary representation.

Party registration in the United Kingdom is split into two types: registration for political parties and registration for minor parties.[12] The distinguishing feature is the level at which the party may contest government – minor parties are eligible to be listed on the Great Britain register, but can only contest council elections in England and Wales. Minor parties are not required to submit as much information to the Electoral Commission upon registration as are political parties (for example, there is no requirement that a party draft a constitution), nor are they subject to as vigorous financial controls as political parties. Nevertheless, those wishing to register either a political or minor party in the United Kingdom must pay a lodgement fee of £150.

In an application for registration under the *Canada Elections Act* 2000, a political party must provide the details of its leader, party officers, agent and auditor. It must also provide the names, addresses and signatures of 250 electors and their declarations in the prescribed form that they are members of the party and support the party's application for registration.[13] Finally, the party must also submit a declaration from its leader that one of its fundamental purposes is to participate in public affairs by endorsing one or more of its members as candidates and supporting their election.

Under Part 4 of the *Electoral Act* 1993 (NZ), a political party must register with the New Zealand Electoral Commission before it can contest the party vote at general elections under the MMP system.[14] New Zealand is the only democracy of those surveyed that requires a party to formulate and provide a copy of the party membership rules upon registration that show what is required for current financial membership and that detail candidate selection rules that provide for the democratic involvement of members in the process.[15] The party rules and candidate selection procedures then become a public document available for inspection and displayed on the Elections New Zealand website, thereby encouraging transparency in internal

11 *Political Parties, Elections and Referendums Act* 2000 (UK) s. 12. This provision is discussed further in Chapter 8, 'The Public Funding of Election Campaigns'.

12 *Political Parties, Elections and Referendums Act* 2000 (UK) s. 23(3).

13 *Canada Elections Act* 2000 ss 366, 380.

14 *Electoral Act* 1993 (NZ) ss 62–71B.

15 Ibid., s. 71.

Table 4.1 Requirements for Party Registration in Australia, Canada, New Zealand and the United Kingdom

State	Rules/ Constitution	Minimum membership	Registration fee	MPs	Minimum candidates	Financial/ Accounting
Australia	Yes (no detail)	500	$500	Yes	No	Yes
Canada	No	250	No	No	Yes	Yes
New Zealand	Yes (detail)	500	No	No	No	Yes
United Kingdom	Yes (no detail)	No	£150	No	No	Yes

management. In addition, the *Electoral Act* also imposes a minimum membership threshold of 500. However, despite the broad requirement of democratic selection procedures (discussed in further detail in Chapter 5 'Regulating Party Candidate Selection Contests'), there is no further legislative guidance given as to how the party should be structured, or what 'democratic involvement' actually involves.

Table 4.1 summarizes the requirements for party registration in the four Westminster-style democracies in this research (Australia, Canada, New Zealand and the United Kingdom). All democracies require their registered parties to provide detail of or implement certain financial/accounting arrangements (for example, audits) and all but Canada require a political party to be established on the basis of written rules or a constitution. However, the detail of the governance arrangements is left for the party to determine. Only the United Kingdom does not require a minimum number of members of its registered parties – all other democracies require some measure of popular support, whether this be a membership threshold, minimum number of candidates (Canada) or, in lieu of a membership, a current parliamentarian (Australia).

Unlike the other democracies analysed in this research, the United States has no truly 'national' system of elections, with congressional elections better thought of as state events that are run simultaneously (Katz 2007: 59). Consequently, within constitutional limitations, each state is free to choose its own electoral system, party registration regime and ballot access laws. The registration and official recognition 'or qualification' of political parties is inherently connected to the act of participating in elections and the popular support gained at the polls. As the Supreme Court held in *Timmons v. Twin Cities Area New Party*, 520 U.S. 351, 373 (1997), a political party is separated from other political associations by the right to be on the election ballot (Stevens J dissenting), not simply access to public funding or other privileges that may come with registration.

There is considerable variation in the registration requirements in each of the States. For example, in California, a political party must have polled at least 2 per cent to retain their place on the ballot paper, or in the lead-up to an election, 1 per cent of registered voters must have declared their affiliation with that particular political party. A new party can also qualify for ballot access by petition, in which case the signatures of 10 per cent of registered voters are required.[16] Prior to seeking ballot access and qualification as a party, a political body must hold a caucus or convention where temporary officers are elected, the name of the party determined (which cannot conflict with any existing parties), and notice given to the Secretary of State that the body has organized, elected temporary officers and intends to qualify as a party pursuant to section 5100 of the Elections Code.[17] In other states, political parties must gather a minimum number of signatures of support, which can range from 1,000 (Colorado) to 50,000 (New York). Many states also declare or confirm the status of political party *retrospectively* based on previous election performance.

Political party committees must register with the Federal Election Commission once they have received contributions or made expenditures of over $1,000 associated with federal campaigns in a calendar year, raised more than $5,000 in a year for use in future campaigns, or spent $5,000 or more on ‘exempt activities’. The Commission then determines (by advisory opinion) whether an organization will qualify for state or national political party committee status. For state status, the FEC has looked to see if the organization has engaged in day-to-day activities commensurate with a political party at the state level, and whether or not the committee has gained ballot access for its federal candidates. In order to determine national status, the FEC employs several criteria: whether the party nominated qualified candidates for presidential and congressional office in a number of states; whether it engaged in mobilizing activities such as voter registration drives; publicizing the party’s issues; holding a national convention, and setting up a national office. Once a party committee achieves this status, the party is eligible for federal public funding if it agrees to abide by expenditure limits.

Registration imposes annual reporting obligations upon a political party, but also brings benefits. For registered parties in all the democracies surveyed, the name of the party can appear alongside the candidate’s name on the ballot paper,[18] and registered parties are usually given access to electoral rolls for campaigning purposes.[19] More importantly are the financial benefits that accrue to registered parties. Canada and Australia introduced public subsidies to underwrite election costs and limitations on expenditure relatively early: Canada in 1974 and Australia in 1984. In Canada, a registered party is entitled to free broadcast time, the right to purchase reserved broadcast time, the right to the partial reimbursement of election expenses subject to receiving a certain percentage of the vote, the right of a candidate to transfer unspent election funds to the party (rather than returning them to the government),[20] and finally, the right to issue tax receipts for donations

16 *California Elections Code*, Division 5, s. 5100.

17 Ibid.

18 See, for example, *Canada Elections Act* s. 100; *Commonwealth Electoral Act* 1918, s. 214(1),(2).

19 *Commonwealth Electoral Act* 1918 s. 90B.

20 *Elections Act* s. 232.

received outside the election period.[21] New Zealand and the United Kingdom do not provide for the direct public funding of parties' election expenses,[22] although a system of party registration and financial regulation was introduced in New Zealand in 1993 and in the United Kingdom in 1998. Hence the incentives for political parties to register with their respective electoral authority are significant, and arguably begin to blur the line between association, formation of a political entity and its registration.

Refusal to Register, Deregistration

In addition to the failure to meet the criteria for registration discussed above, electoral authorities can typically refuse to register a political party on several other grounds. For example, the Australian Electoral Commission must refuse to register a party if its name or abbreviation comprises more than six words, is obscene,[23] closely and confusingly resembles the name or abbreviation of an unrelated 'recognised'[24] party, comprises the words 'Independent Party', or contains the word 'Independent' together with the name of an unrelated registered party. Similarly, the Electoral Commission of New Zealand is obliged to register a political party unless the name of the party is indecent or offensive, excessively long, likely to cause confusion or mislead electors, or contains reference to a title or honour.[25] Similar restrictions apply in Canada under the *Elections Act* (s 368) and the United Kingdom under the PPERA (s 28(4)). This latter Act also prohibits party names in anything other than the Roman script or that include any word or expression prohibited by order made by the Secretary of State after consulting the Commission. Granting ballot access to political parties is a matter for individual states in the US, which will have varying legislative requirements.[26]

None of the Electoral Commissions has the ability to refuse registration on the grounds of objection to a party's policies or ideology. This was demonstrated in

21 Provided for in s. 127(3) of the *Income Tax Act*, R.S.C. 1985, c. 1 (5th Supp).

22 None the less, the state provides other important benefits that amount to significant subsidies such as free postage to candidates, tax credits and broadcasting time.

23 *Commonwealth Electoral Act* 1918 s. 129.

24 'Recognised' refers to a parliamentary party; another federally registered party; or a party registered or recognized in a state or territory that has endorsed candidates in the last five years. See *Commonwealth Electoral Act* 1918 s. 129(2).

25 *Electoral Act* 1993 (NZ) s. 65.

26 For example, s. 5102 of the *California Elections Code* states: 'no party shall be recognized or qualified to participate in any primary election that either directly or indirectly carries on, advocates, teaches, justifies, aids, or abets the overthrow by any unlawful means of, or that directly or indirectly carries on, advocates, teaches, justifies, aids, or abets a program of sabotage, force and violence, sedition or treason against, the government of the United States or of this state'.

2006 when the New Zealand Electoral Commission registered the National Front party despite public objection and when the Australian Electoral Commission registered the Sex Party in 2009, despite complaints from the public. In registering the National Front, the New Zealand Electoral Commission took the step of issuing a media release explaining its decision:

> The commission found the application to be in order and the proposed logo to meet the legal requirements of not being confusing, misleading, indecent, offensive, or in breach of someone else's intellectual property rights. In reaching its decision commissioners carefully considered 28 objections received in response to public notices advertising the application, 11 of which were the same petition with a total of 127 signatures. Objectors were generally concerned with the cross-like element of the logo, its perceived associations with Christian, Nazi or military imagery, and an alleged offensiveness that resulted. Responses from the applicant and counter-responses were also considered. Cross-like imagery is widespread and used in many contexts, so we could not accept the objectors' arguments. *Many of the objections were explicitly related to opinions of the applicant party's policies or beliefs, however these matters are outside the scope of what the law requires the commission to both consider and confine itself to.* (Elections New Zealand 2006, emphasis added)

The Australian Electoral Commission took a similarly cautious approach in issuing a five-page advice of the relevant case and statute law relating to the name of a party being 'obscene' for the purposes of s. 129(1)(b) of the *Commonwealth Electoral Act* 1918, after four objections were made to the registration application lodged by the Australian Sex Party (AEC 2009a). Nevertheless, the Commission concluded that:

> when the Party name and abbreviation are assessed in light of the guidance afforded by existing case law and statute on the word 'obscene', the name 'Australian Sex Party' and the abbreviation 'Sex Party' are not prohibited under s129(1)(b). (AEC 2009b)

The various Electoral Commissions of the states analysed may deregister a political party at the request of the party, if it no longer exists, has failed to endorse candidates for election in a prescribed period, has not updated or provided information to the Electoral Commission as required, the party has fewer than the minimum required number of members or, in Australia, has no parliamentary representation, or the original registration was obtained by fraud or misrepresentation.[27] Again, these

27 *Commonwealth Electoral Act* 1918 s. 137(1), *Elections Act* 1993 (NZ) s. 70, *Political Parties, Elections and Referendums Act* 2000 (UK) s. 33, *Canada Elections Act* 2000 ss 385–8.

are predominantly technical criteria that reflect the fact that there is currently no electoral legislation in place in the democracies examined in this research that purports to ban anti-democratic parties.

Parliamentary Parties as the Basis for Registration

The basic principle behind registration is that a political party needs to demonstrate sufficient levels of popular support to be recognized as a qualified or 'official' electoral actor. This can be demonstrated in several ways, such as previous electoral performance, a minimum number of members or candidates, minimum fund-raising efforts or a threshold level of voters pledging support or petitioning for the registration of a particular political party. Australia has a unique provision amongst the democracies analysed in this research, which enables a political party to be registered if it has one parliamentarian present in either house of the federal Parliament. Section 123 of the *Commonwealth Electoral Act* 1918 provides that a political party eligible for registration can be either a political party with at least 500 members and established on the basis of a written constitution, or a parliamentary party with at least one member in the Commonwealth Parliament. Prior to the *Commonwealth Electoral Amendment Act (No 1)* 2000, political parties could also be registered federally on the basis of representation in one Australian State or Territory.

At first glance, it is plausible that a political party that has had one of its members elected to Parliament would by virtue of that fact, have demonstrated significant levels of public support. However, the provisions of the Act do not exclude parliamentarians resigning from the political party under which they were first elected to Parliament to begin another. For example, this occurred in the Australian State of New South Wales when upper house MP Franca Arena left the Labor Party and after sitting as an Independent, created the Franca Arena Child Safety Alliance. The Alliance polled just 0.4 per cent of the popular vote at the 1999 election. Secondly, by virtue of the electoral system that is used to elect Senators to the Australian Senate (the upper house of the Australian parliament) – a variant of proportional representation – it is possible for Senators to be elected with a very small percentage of the popular vote. The reforms to the *Commonwealth Electoral Act* enacted in 2000 that removed the ability of members of a State or Territory Parliament to register a political party federally were, in part, motivated by the desire to stop former One Nation Party leaders from registering 'sloganistic' parties with the Commonwealth Electoral Commission. Concerns were expressed that these political parties, registered without popular support, could have been used to channel voters' preferences to other parties, or to earn a profit for their leaders through the public funding scheme if more than 4 per cent of the vote was achieved (Orr 2000: 43).[28]

28 As discussed further in Chapter 7, Australian political parties are reimbursed at a set rate per vote if they achieve more than 4 per cent of the total vote for either house of Parliament – it is not necessary to provide proof of actual electoral expenditure.

Therefore, the definition of a 'parliamentary party' for the purposes of party registration under the *Commonwealth Electoral Act* 1918 is very expansive and arguably allows the registration of parties (or more accurately individuals) that have not necessarily demonstrated significant levels of public support. Indeed, the opposite situation exists in New Zealand, where the House of Representatives introduced the requirement that a new party must first register with the Electoral Commission before it is able to receive parliamentary recognition as a parliamentary party (Standing Order 34(2)(b); see Joseph 2007: 352). Recently, the Australian Government's Green Paper on Electoral Reform, in light of a submission made by the Democratic Audit of Australia, has suggested that the *Electoral Act* be amended to disallow parliamentarians who have resigned from the party under which they were elected to use this opportunity to create and register a new party (Australian Government 2009: 120).

Gatekeeper Provisions

Given the importance of the financial and other benefits given to political parties through registration, it is important to appreciate the practical consequences of the eligibility requirements for registration. The registration requirements of a minimum number of members and a declaration to contest elections impose 'gatekeeper provisions' upon the electoral process in that only groups meeting threshold requirements may participate fully in elections. Typically, only groups that can demonstrate the 'seriousness' of their purpose can meet this threshold. Whereas the UK has no minimum membership requirement for registration, Australia and New Zealand impose a threshold of 500 members, whereas Canada requires a minimum of 250. The method of verifying the party's membership may also differ across jurisdictions. Within Australia, for example, the State of New South Wales requires individual declarations from the members upon which the party is going to rely on for registration. By contrast, the State of Victoria requires only a statutory declaration of the party secretary that the party has the required number of members (Ibid.: 114). This is similar to New Zealand, where a party must submit an annual statutory declaration that it still has 500 current financial members and intends to continue running candidates in elections (*Electoral Act* 1993 s. 71A).[29]

Until 2003, the *Canada Elections Act* also required a registered political party to run candidates in at least 50 electoral districts, thereby imposing an additional threshold requirement not seen in any other common law liberal democracies. This provision was struck down by the Canadian Supreme Court in *Figueroa v. Canada (Attorney General)* [2003] 1 S.C.R. 912[30] (hereinafter

29 However, as Geddis (2007a: 78) argues, New Zealand political parties incur no penalty in failing to abide by this requirement, nor does it allow for the cancellation of a party's registration.

30 See MacIvor (2004) for further commentary on this case.

Figueroa) as violating section 3 of the *Canadian Charter of Rights and Freedoms*, which provides for 'the right to vote in an election of members of the House of Commons or of a legislative assembly and to be qualified for membership therein'. The action seeking a declaration of unconstitutionality was brought against the Attorney General by Miguel Figueroa, who was at that time the leader of the Communist Party of Canada. The Communist Party was founded in 1921 and had been registered as a political party under the *Canada Elections Act* since party registration began in 1974. In the 1993 federal general election, the party lost its registered status and the associated benefits when it failed to field 50 candidates. Consequently, the party was forced to liquidate its assets, pay its debts and remit the outstanding balance to the Chief Electoral Officer.

The Court held that the requirement that parties field 50 candidates in a general election to be eligible for the benefits of registration was too restrictive and not reasonably and demonstrably justifiable in a free and democratic society (Forcese and Freeman 2005: 90).[31] In defending the legislation, the Attorney General of Canada submitted that the objective of the threshold was to 'enhance the effectiveness of Canadian elections, in both their process and outcome', and to advance three separate goals. First, to improve the effectiveness of the electoral process through the public financing of political parties. Secondly, to protect the integrity of the electoral financing regime. Third, to ensure that the process is able to deliver a viable outcome for the Canadian form of responsible government.

In holding the 50-candidate threshold set by the *Elections Act* unconstitutional, the Court emphasized the importance of political parties in the Canadian system of democracy:

> Political parties enhance the meaningfulness of individual participation in the electoral process for reasons that transcend their capacity (or lack thereof) to participate in the governance of the country subsequent to an election. Irrespective of their capacity to influence the outcome of an election, political parties act as both a vehicle and an outlet for the meaningful participation of individual citizens in the electoral process.[32]

In making its judgment, the Supreme Court constructed a particular vision of political parties, how they fit into the Canadian form of democratic politics, and how they provide for 'effective representation' as guaranteed by section 3

31 In order to justify the infringement of a *Charter* right under s. 1, the government must demonstrate that (1) the object of the legislation is sufficiently substantial and pressing to warrant violation of a right; and (2) the infringement is proportionate. See *R. v. Oakes* [1986] 1 S.C.R. 103; *Vriend v. Alberta* [1998] 1 S.C.R. 493; *Thomson Newspapers Co. v. Canada (Attorney General)* [1998] 1 S.C.R. 877; *M. v. H.* [1999] 2 S.C.R. 3.

32 *Figueroa v. Canada* [2003] I S.C.R. 912 at para. 39.

of the *Charter*.[33] The Court rejected the view that parties that provide 'effective representation' are only those that possess the capacity to aggregate interests on a national level and can participate in the governance of a country subsequent to an election. Rather, parties (large or small) that allow citizens to 'play a meaningful role in the electoral process' through participation in party activities and the dissemination of a broad range of ideas and opinions should not be precluded from the benefits of registration under the *Electoral Act*.[34] The Court noted that:

> All political parties, whether large or small, are capable of acting as a vehicle for the participation of individual citizens in the public discourse that animates the determination of social policy. For example, marginal or regional parties tend to dissent from mainstream thinking and to bring to the attention of the general public issues and concerns that have not been adopted by national parties. They might exert less influence than the national parties, but still can be a most effective vehicle for the participation of citizens whose preferences have not been incorporated into the political platforms of national parties. It is better that an individual citizen have his or her ideas and concerns introduced into the open debate of the electoral process by a political party with a limited geographical base of support than not to have his or her ideas and concerns introduced into that debate by any political party at all.[35]

Therefore, in the Supreme Court's view, the function of political parties as the means by which policy preferences are expressed is of just a great value and importance as their ability to win seats in general elections. Irrespective of the outcome of an election, a vote for a political party or candidate is not merely about the selection of parliamentary representatives, but is also an expression of support for a particular policy approach or platform. The Court also noted the importance of regional political parties and the fundamental role they played in representing the opinions of citizens along geographic lines in a federated nation, and found that the 50-candidate rule conflicted with the principle of regional representation because of its disparate impact on different provinces and the regions of the country.[36]

The Supreme Court suspended its judgment for 12 months, enabling Parliament to re-examine and legislate again on the issue. However, it failed to do so until just before the June 2004 election, rushing through legislation that merely required parties to run one or more candidate(s) in a single electoral district,

---

33 *Figueroa* at para. 21; *Reference re Provincial Electoral Boundaries (Sask.)* [1991] 2 S.C.R. 158 ('Saskatchewan Reference'); *Haig v. Canada* [1993] 2 S.C.R. 995; *Harvey v. New Brunswick (Attorney General)* [1996] 2 S.C.R. 876; *Thompson Newspapers Co. v. Canada (Attorney General)* [1998] 1 S.C.R. 877.

34 *Figueroa* at paras 28, 40, 41.

35 *Figueroa* at paras 41–42.

36 *Figueroa* at paras 162–169, 174.

and maintaining the requirement that political parties have a minimum number of members, although this was increased from 100 to 250.[37] Although there was some concern and reservations were expressed by members of both the House of Commons and the Senate as to the possible effect and desirability of the new registration threshold, both the government and opposition parties supported the bill in principle, and it was passed by both Houses on 13 May 2004 – only three months after it had been introduced into Parliament. The thresholds for registration (one candidate and 250 members) set by *An Act to Amend the Canada Elections Act and the Income Tax Act* S.C. 2004, c.24 remain in force today and have not yet been revisited in parliamentary debate or challenged in the courts.

It is unclear from the Supreme Court's judgment in *Figueroa* whether the candidate threshold needs to be as low as one. The majority decision appears to indicate that a court would be suspicious of any attempt to increase the threshold (Forcese and Freeman 2005: 91): it 'may well be that the government will be able to advance other objectives that justify a 12 candidate threshold. But suffice it to say, the objectives advanced do not justify a threshold requirement of any sort, let alone a 50-candidate threshold'.[38]

However, Justices Gonthier, LeBel and Deschamps were more sympathetic in their concurring judgment towards the idea of a threshold set above a single candidate, arguing that 'a requirement of nominating at least one candidate, and perhaps more, in order to qualify for registration as a party would not raise any serious constitutional concerns'.[39] In making this argument, they acknowledged the possibility that groups or individuals could potentially abuse the party registration regime. Even though:

> Many of the registration benefits are virtually meaningless outside the context of electoral competition ... some, such as tax credits to contributors, could be attractive to groups that do not seriously intend to compete in elections. Making them available to such groups as well as genuine parties could undermine the purposes of the registration scheme ... Nominating candidates and competing in the electoral process is fundamental to the nature of parties as opposed to other kinds of political associations, such as interest groups.[40]

Commentators (for example, Forcese and Freeman 2005: 91–2) have expressed concern that the low registration threshold could make it easier for interest groups to form into political parties to gain the financial benefits offered under the *Elections Act*, and in order to circumvent the caps currently in place to restrict third-party advertising expenditures. By forming a 'flag of convenience' political party for

---

37 *Elections Act* ss 366, 370 and 385. The requirement that parties have a minimum of 250 members was amended by cl. 3(3) of Bill C-3*: An Act to Amend the Canada Elections Act and the Income Tax Act* (2004).

38 *Figueroa* at para. 92.

39 *Figueroa* at para. 149.

40 *Figueroa* at para. 148.

the purposes of registration and running one or two candidates, the combined candidate and party spending cap under the *Elections Act* would well exceed the limit imposed on third-party spending that interest groups would otherwise face. As it currently stands, the *Elections Act* cannot guard against these sorts of abuses, and this is a pertinent example of the difficulty inherent in defining or codifying a political party and its activities, and where these limits should be drawn.

In their concurring judgment, Justices Gonthier, LeBel and Deschamps highlighted another important consideration in the formulation of electoral gatekeeper provisions: the need to balance the right of each citizen to play a meaningful role in the electoral process against other democratic values, for example, the aggregation of political preferences and the promotion of cohesiveness over factionalism.[41] Essentially, this becomes an exercise in balancing individual and collective interests. In suggesting this balancing exercise, LeBel J looked to the form of the current electoral system (first-past-the-post elections that tend to favour the mainstream parties) as reflecting the prevailing majoritarian political values in society; 'because our FPTP electoral system is one of Canada's core political institutions, it is reasonable to conclude that this virtue remains consistent with certain values of our democratic culture'.[42] Consequently, Justice LeBel concluded that political aggregation as a core democratic value should be taken into account when determining the meaning of 'effective representation' under s. 3 of the *Charter* and the constitutional limits that this provision sets upon electoral choices open to the government.[43]

Looking back to the context within which the 50-candidate threshold was adopted, the Lortie Commission regarded a breadth of appeal and a high level of commitment to electoral competition as two of the main indicators of a party suitable for registration:

> A political party that nominates candidates in 50 constituencies would demonstrate serious intent to engage in the rigors of electoral competition at a level that indicates relatively broad appeal for its program and ideas. Moreover, experience since 1974 shows that this level is neither unduly onerous nor too lenient for registration. We believe that this threshold should continue to serve as a benchmark in determining which parties may be registered under the *Canada Elections Act*.[44]

Nevertheless, this deference to mainstream and majoritarian values as expressed by the structure and operation of the current electoral process was rejected by Justice Iacobucci (writing the majority judgment):

41 *Figueroa* per LeBel J at para. 151. However, see the contrary view of the majority judgment, paras 36 and 37.

42 *Figueroa* at para. 157.

43 *Figueroa* at para. 159.

44 Canada. Royal Commission on Electoral Reform and Party Financing. *Reforming Electoral Democracy: Final Report*, Vol 1. Ottawa: The Commission, 1991. Vol. 1, 249.

> … the fact that our current electoral system reflects certain political values does not mean that those values are embedded in the *Charter*, or that it is appropriate to balance those values against the right of each citizen to play a meaningful role in the electoral process. After all, the *Charter* is entirely neutral as to the type of electoral system in which the right to vote or to run for office is to be exercised. This suggests that the purpose of s. 3 is not to protect the values or objectives that might be embedded in our current electoral system, but, rather, to protect the right of each citizen to play a meaningful role in the electoral process, whatever that process might be.[45]

Gatekeeper provisions also have a significant effect in other Commonwealth nations. In New Zealand, parties who fail to register are excluded from contesting the party vote,[46] which in an MMP environment, effectively negates their chances of successfully electing members to Parliament. As Geddis (2005: 120) notes, in New Zealand 'the registration requirement for political parties has the practical effect of restricting potential membership of parliament to those candidates who are backed by a group of supporters that is both able and prepared to meet' such provisions. However, they have not yet been challenged in the courts by political parties blocked from registering under the regime.

The Australian requirement that a political party have at least 500 financial members for the purposes of registration was challenged by the Democratic Labor Party (DLP) in the High Court in *Mulholland v. Australian Electoral Commission* [2004] HCA 41 (hereinafter *Mulholland*). The DLP faced deregistration on the grounds that it could not prove that it had 500 current financial members to the Australian Electoral Commission. Originally, the regulatory scheme was adopted following a report of the Joint Select Committee on Electoral Reform, delivered in September 1983. The report recommended that a system of public funding for election campaigns necessitated the registration of political parties, the adoption of a list system for Senate elections, and the printing of the political affiliation of candidates on ballot papers,[47] which was designed to 'assist voters in casting their vote in accordance with their intentions'.[48] The membership threshold of 500 was agreed upon after lengthy discussions, although the Committee's exact reasons for selecting this figure are not known.[49]

---

45 *Figueroa* at para. 37.

46 Section 127 of the *Electoral Act* 1993 (NZ) states: 'At any general election any secretary of a political party *that is registered under Part 4* may forward to the Chief Electoral Officer a list of candidates for election to the seats reserved for those members of Parliament elected from lists submitted under this section' [emphasis added].

47 Parliament of the Commonwealth of Australia, Joint Select Committee on Electoral Reform, *First Report*, September 1983 at para. [3.43].

48 Parliament of the Commonwealth of Australia, Joint Select Committee on Electoral Reform, *First Report*, September 1983 at para. [12.1].

49 *Mulholland v. Australian Electoral Commission* [2004] HCA 41 per Gleeson CJ at [2]. Similar thresholds exist in most Australian States: Victoria 500 persons (*Electoral*

Unlike the Canadian Supreme Court's approach in *Figueroa* with respect to fielding a minimum number of candidates in an election, the High Court of Australia held that the '500 rule' did not infringe the Australian constitutional requirement of direct choice in elections. A common theme emphasized by the majority of the Court in *Mulholland* was the flexibility of these constitutional arrangements, and the necessity that they respond to developments in public opinion and changing democratic standards.[50] This was a theme also expressed by the Canadian Supreme Court in *Figueroa*, but it is interesting that it was only emphasized in Justice LeBel's concurring judgment.[51] Consistent with its previous position in several cases concerning the constitutionality of electoral laws,[52] the High Court reiterated the right of Parliament to legislate for its own affairs and determine the structure of the electoral system. As Justice Kirby optimistically noted:

> The Constitution does not impose rigid limitations on the power of the Federal Parliament, in enacted electoral law, to respond to changing attitudes concerning the conduct of elections. The future will doubtless be no less adaptive in this respect than the past. Successive Parliaments will continue to search for new and improved ways to reflect the representative character of the Parliament and of the senators and members of the House of Representatives who are elected.[53]

Despite affirming Parliament's broad power to legislate to regulate the conduct of elections, the Court also noted that it is subject to certain express and implied constitutional limitations;[54] most importantly the express requirement in sections 7 and 24 that members of both the House of Representatives and Senators be 'directly chosen by the people'. However, the Court held that in this instance, the requirement was not breached. Several different 'balancing exercises' were employed by members of the Court to achieve this conclusion. Evaluating the objective of the laws, Justices Gummow and Hayne required a 'consistency' or conformity with the objectives of a system of representative government. For Justices Callinan and Heydon, there was no indication that the discrimination was

---

Act 2002 (Vic) s. 45(2)(e)); Queensland 500 persons (*Electoral Act* 1992 (Qld) s. 70(4)(e); South Australia 150 persons (*Electoral Act* 1985 (SA) s. 36); Western Australia 500 persons (*Electoral Act* 1907 (WA) s. 62E(4)(d)); Tasmania 100 persons (*Electoral Act* 1985 (Tas) ss 3(1), 55(1)(b)); New South Wales 750 persons (*Parliamentary Electorates and Elections Act* 1912 (NSW) ss 66A(1), 66D).

50 McHugh J at [63]–[65]; Gummow and Hayne JJ at [154]–[155]; Kirby J at [212]–[213]; Heydon J at [344]; Gleeson CJ at [9], [14].

51 *Figueroa v. Canada* [2003] I S.C.R. 912 at para. 161.

52 *Langer v. Commonwealth* (1996) 186 CLR 302; *McGinty v. State of Western Australia* (1996) 186 CLR 140; *Muldowney v. State of South Australia* (1996) 186 CLR 352; *McKenzie v. Commonwealth* (1984) 57 ALR 747.

53 *Mulholland*, per Kirby J at [213].

54 *Mulholland*, per McHugh J at [61]; Kirby J at [214]; Gleeson CJ at [61].

irrational or *unreasonable*.[55] Therefore, the High Court's judgment in *Mulholland* indicates that although they are subject to some constitutional limitations, gatekeeper provisions that affect access to the electoral system are within the power of the Parliament to determine, and that the judiciary should generally be reluctant to interfere in this process.

Similar gatekeeper provisions exist in the United States. For example, individual States restrict ballot access by requiring both minor party and independent candidates to demonstrate a significant measure of community support before they can be included on the ballot paper, as well as automatic ballot access for the major parties.[56] Furthermore, such provisions, coupled with the requirement of party registration as a precondition for voting in primary elections have the effect of reinforcing major party dominance and 'encouraging voters to think of themselves as Republicans or Democrats' (Rosenblum 2000: 832). The regulations are defended on the grounds of preserving the integrity of the process, avoiding voter confusion, and maintaining the stability of the party system.[57] In *American Party of Texas v. White* 415 U.S. 767 (1974), the Supreme Court upheld Texas laws requiring Independents to demonstrate minimum levels of support on the basis of such 'vital' state interests and supported the proposition that 'political parties appearing on the general ballot demonstrate a significant, measurable quantum of community support'.[58] Similarly, in *Jenness v. Forston* 403 U.S. 431 (1971), the Supreme Court held (at 442):

> There is surely an important state interest in requiring some preliminary showing of a significant modicum of support before printing the name of a political organization's candidate on the ballot – the interest, if no other, in avoiding confusion, deception and even frustration of the democratic process at the general election.

However, the key phrase here is 'significant modicum of support', and when contrasted with the gatekeeper provisions in the other liberal democracies covered in this volume, ballot access requirements in US states such as California (where almost 89,000 voter registration affidavits were required for the 2010 Primary Election) appear to set a very high threshold for new political parties to achieve. Like all gatekeeper provisions, the exact provisions and thresholds are essentially a balancing exercise between the right of parties and individuals to contest elections and concerns over the integrity of the ballot, voter confusion and factionalism. The United States' courts' approach to ballot access has therefore been described as enabling states to 'condition access to the ballot upon the demonstration of a

---

55 *Mulholland*, per Callinan J at [332]; Heydon J at [351].

56 See *Tashjian v. Republican Party of Conn.*, 479 U.S. 208, 225 (1986).

57 See *American Party of Texas v. White*, 415 U.S. 767, 782 (1974); Barendt (1988: 159).

58 *American Party of Texas v. White*, 415 U.S. 767, 782 (1974) per White J (for the majority).

significant measurable quantum of community support, but cannot require so large or so early a demonstration of support that minority parties or independent candidates have no real chance of attaining ballot positions' (Tribe 1988: 1110–11). This is a position that reflects a reasonably consistent view of representative democracy that privileges a strong two-party system, echoing the recommendations and conclusions of the 1950 American Political Science Association report (see p. 37–8).

Finally, registration may also impose certain financial burdens upon a political party. In Australia, a fee of $500 is payable upon application for registration,[59] or for a change of party name or abbreviation.[60] Application fees within Australia range from $2,000 (New South Wales) to nothing in Queensland, Western Australia, South Australia, Tasmania and the Australian Capital Territory. There is no application fee in New Zealand or Canada. Registered party applicants in the United Kingdom are required to pay a fee of £150.

Candidate Deposits

Although they effectively function as another gatekeeper mechanism, an example that illustrates the fact that the conduct of elections remains to a large extent regulated at the individual level is the requirement that a deposit be paid by individual candidates, rather than political parties. For example, in the United Kingdom, candidates are required to lodge a deposit of £500 in order to stand for election in a particular seat and this is refundable if the candidate secures 5 per cent or more of the registered vote.[61] In New Zealand, the amount of this deposit is set at $300, which is forfeited to the Crown unless the candidate receives 5 per cent or more of the constituency vote in his or her electorate.[62] In Canada, the deposit is $1,000, refundable if the candidate complies with election reporting requirements.[63] Candidates for the House of Representatives in Australia must lodge a deposit of $500 with the Australian Electoral Commission, and $1,000 if the candidate is standing for a Senate seat. These deposits are refundable if the candidate achieves 4 per cent of the first preference votes in their electorate.[64]

In practice however, it is usual for a political party to pay a candidate's deposit upon securing a party nomination. To facilitate easier electoral administration, section 146 of the *Electoral Act* 1993 (NZ) provides a process whereby political parties can also submit bulk nominations of candidates to the Electoral Commission, as an alternative to the nomination of individual candidates in each electoral district. However, a deposit of NZ$300 per candidate is still payable (s. 146F). Although

59 *Commonwealth Electoral Act* 1918 s. 126(2)(g).

60 *Commonwealth Electoral Act* 1918 s. 134(2)(d).

61 *Representation of the People Act* 1983 (UK), Schedule 1, rules 9(1), 53(4).

62 *Electoral Act* 1993 (NZ) s. 144(1).

63 *Canada Elections Act* ss 72, 468.

64 *Commonwealth Electoral Act* 1918 ss 170, 173.

expressed in terms of individual candidates, the requirement of a deposit is similar in its effect to the gatekeeper provisions previously discussed with respect to the initial registration of parties, in that depending on the amount requested, it may discourage some 'serious independent candidates' and create difficulties for less affluent political parties who are deprived of a significant sum (if candidates are endorsed in multiple electorates) during the period of the campaign (Turpin and Tomkins 2007: 508). In essence, these individual-level regulations none the less have consequential effects for political party and campaigning organizations, and reflect a particular pattern of party competition that has its roots in the two-party system and privileges the existing, entrenched major party players.

The Significance and Comparative Consequences of Gatekeeper Provisions

Gatekeeper provisions present an excellent case study of an example of institutional design that significantly alters the conduct of electoral politics, and reflects particular normative visions of democracy, the character of the electoral contest and the place of parties within it. It is through establishing registration requirements and ballot access provisions that the state is able to effectively define what constitutes a political party. However, it is important to note that registration requirements and gatekeeper provisions not only define what is a political party, but more specifically, what is an *official* political party – one authorized through its compliance with these conditions to nominate candidates on the official ballot (Gardner 2000: 686–7).

Gardner (2000: 687) identifies two models of electoral politics – popular and pluralist – which are supported by different gatekeeper provisions and different thresholds. Populist electoral design should reflect the views of the majority of citizens, therefore it would be justifiable to restrict ballot access to those candidates commanding popular support and thus best able to articulate policies that appeal to a broad set of electors. Conversely, under a pluralist model of politics, gatekeeper provisions should be directed at producing candidates who advocate the views of a section of the population, that those views might be expressed in the legislature. Laws that produce high thresholds (for example, ballot access laws in most US states) facilitate the former, whereas lower thresholds (for example, access to registration and the ballot in the UK) favour the latter. Nevertheless, the fact that both these states have reasonably different gatekeeper provisions yet strong two-party systems indicates that there are also several intervening factors at play, for example, the design of the electoral system (in these cases, first-past-the-post) and the cost and financing of electoral politics.

The Internal Organization of Political Parties

One of the main elements that characterizes electoral laws in common law democracies is that registration requirements, by and large, set very fluid limits upon or do not seek to prescribe the internal arrangements and conduct of political parties. The analysis of the legal history of political parties and their evolving status presented thus far indicates that while political parties have become subject to increased regulation, these measures predominantly address the public face of parties: how they interact with one another and the electoral system. There is relatively less regulation or legislative interference in the internal workings of political parties, for example, how parties select their candidates for public and party office, formulate their policies, decision-making procedures and the administration of the party on a day-to-day basis. With a few exceptions, any directives in this arena tend to be the product of the common law, and essentially constitute 'judicial opinion as to how parties ought to conduct their internal affairs' (Gauja 2006b: 284).

Given this lack of regulation, the organizational development of political parties has been a response more to pragmatic political concerns (for example, the maximizing votes) rather than to legal requirements.[65] Indeed, political parties, as organizations or associations, have generally been reluctant to expose their internal operation to the scrutiny of the law. The constitutions of two Australian political parties serve as an illustration of this sentiment. The current constitution of the Australian Labor Party states in a resolution preserved from the 1955 Annual Conference:

> This conference resolves that as a general principle it cannot concede the right of any member of the Party to initiate legal proceedings for the purpose of establishing the constitutional behaviour of the Labor Movement. We emphasise that, with a few isolated exceptions, the history of our Party discloses we have functioned on the basis of a complete determination in accordance with our own rules and our own interpretation of them. We insist we must continue to create our own procedures, taking care of our own business without the introduction of lawyers and law courts.[66]

Similarly, the constitution of the Christian Democratic Party states:

> It is intended that this document and everything related or implied within it, or any agreement or transaction entered into on the basis of this document shall not give rise to any legal relationship or any consequence which will be legally enforceable or be the subject of litigation. All arrangements, agreements and transactions are binding on the basis of trust only.[67]

---

65 See further the discussion of the evolution of party organizations in Chapter 2.

66 Australian Labor Party, *National Platform and Constitution 2004* (as amended at the 43rd ALP National Conference 2004) Part E, Section 1.

67 Christian Democratic Party (Australia) *NSW State Branch Constitution and Rules*, Article 1.

As Bennett (2002: 3) argues, this view is also shared within other Australian political parties and is consistent with the attitudes of parties in other liberal democracies. However, there is some difficulty in verifying this position, given that these 'exclusionary clauses' tend to be an Australian phenomenon arising from particular historical circumstances. Indeed, courts in the United Kingdom (and implicitly in Australia) have held that nothing within a party's constitution or rules can oust the courts' jurisdiction in internal party disputes (see *Weir v. Hermon* [2001] NICh 8 per Girvan J). However, Bennett's argument develops to suggest that this attitude can be extrapolated from other sources, such as the Canadian Royal Commission on Electoral Reform and Party Financing, which found that Canadian 'parties enjoyed the status of private organizations, and suggested that they remain so "for very good reasons"' (Bennett 2002: 3–4).

This argument reflects a strong belief that is shared by both political practitioners and many political scientists, namely, that intra-party democracy, or simply dictating the internal affairs of a political party is 'incompatible with democratic government' (McKenzie 1982: 195; see also Sartori 1965: 124). This side of the debate is developed in further detail below, but for now it is sufficient to note that this view (as the dominant strand of thinking with respect to party organization and freedom of association) has helped to maintain a clear line of demarcation between legislation that regulates a party's activities as they relate to the competitive electoral system and its internal activities. For example, while states typically regulate the way in which political parties spend money during elections and how they advertise their policies, states have *not* legislated to regulate how parties administer their organizations on a day-to-day basis, make political and/or policy decisions, or resolve disputes within the political party itself. Candidate selection is regulated in some democracies but not in others (see Chapter 5).

The extent to which the internal operations of political parties are subject to the scrutiny of the law has significant implications for the operation of democracy both within, and outside, the party – depending on one's perspective. If members are able to take their grievances beyond the party organization to a public forum such as the courts, this may have positive implications for intra-party democracy, political participation and engagement as members' rights can be asserted in a neutral forum. However, this process may also have more negative implications for democracy as a whole, weakening the internal party discipline that is necessary for political parties to convincingly contest elections and that is arguably necessary for the maintenance of responsible party government (see Rose 1969: 416–18; Katz 1986: 43; Katz 1987: 7; Thomassen 1994). Nevertheless, there are some nations that specifically require political parties to adopt the principles of intra-party democracy (Germany, Spain), whereas others mandate parties to observe democratic principles more generally (France, Greece, Italy and Portugal) (see Müller and Sieberer 2006: 440).

Should Political Parties Be Internally Democratic?

Calls for the increased regulation of political parties to ensure that they operate according to the principles of internal party democracy are in part a by-product of, and closely linked to, perceptions that political parties are failing in their democratic function. Consistent empirical evidence across the board in advanced industrial democracies suggests that party membership is in steady decline (Mair and van Biezen 2001; Scarrow 2000), electoral turnout and campaign participation is dropping (Franklin 2004; Wattenberg 2003), and that partisan attachments have significantly weakened (Dalton 2000). The report of an independent inquiry into Britain's democracy, *Power to the People*, found that British citizens no longer wanted to join a political party or to get involved in formal politics (Power Inquiry 2006: 12). Similarly, the Council of Europe's paper, *The Future of Democracy in Europe*, argued that:

> Today, one of the most striking features of European democracies is an apparently widespread feeling of political discontent, disaffection, scepticism, dissatisfaction and cynicism among citizens. These reactions are not, or not only, focused on a given political party, government or public policy. They are the result of critical and even hostile perceptions of politicians, political parties, elections, parliaments and governments in general – that is, across the political spectrum. (Schmitter and Trechsel 2004: 25)

For Mair (2005), this withdrawal is a manifestation of parties' failure to adequately provide a mechanism by which citizens can participate in politics. Similarly, the Power Inquiry (2006: 181) reported that the 'expert and practitioner evidence, the public submissions, and all of the research projects reveal a widespread sense that, at best, the main parties are failing in the basic function of connecting the governed and governors, and, at worst, are serious obstacles to democratic engagement'. In the face of these criticisms, however:

> The ideal of intra-party democracy has gained increasing attention in recent years because of its apparent potential to promote a 'virtuous cycle' linking ordinary citizens to government, benefiting the parties that adopt it, and more generally contributing to the stability and legitimacy of the democracies in which these parties compete for power. (Scarrow 2005: 3)

This view echoes some of the sentiments expressed by the Australian Government's Green Paper on Electoral Reform, *Strengthening Australia's Democracy*, which put forward the proposal that 'political parties should be required to conduct themselves democratically, responsibly and professionally' in order to 'foster a civic culture' (Australian Government 2009: 116). Similarly, former president of the New Zealand Labour Party, Margaret Wilson, has argued that parties ought to be participatory – based on the importance of the democratic *public* functions that they perform. Wilson's views are worth quoting at length:

> … the public function of a political party is to produce the best candidates for election, that is, those candidates who best represent the interests of the party, which includes not only understanding and acceptance of the party's policy, but also an ability to campaign and win the election. Apart from the selection and presentation of parliamentary candidates, political parties are responsible for the formulation of the policy ideas over which the election will be contested. From the public interest viewpoint then, it is important that both processes of candidate selection and policy formulation are conducted fairly. Fairness is a difficult concept when applied to situations that are value laden and heavily contested. By fairness I mean an opportunity for all members to participate in, and influence, the process of decision-making, whether it be on policy or selection of candidates. It is this public function, especially the selection of candidates, that provides the rationale for the internal activities of political parties to be more open to the public, or perhaps more accurately the media. (Wilson 1998: 170)

A similar perspective is advocated by Ewing, who links taxpayer funding with the condition that internal practices conform to socially acceptable principles, invoking the idea of state-sanctioned obligation. Ewing has argued that political parties should adopt democratic practices not simply as a matter of principle, but in exchange for the provision of public funding. In what he terms a 'Charter of Members' Rights', political parties should facilitate:

> Democratic procedures for policy-making and the selection of the party leader, open and inclusive procedures for the selection of parliamentary and other candidates, internal party elections for all nominations to the House of Lords (so long as seats are to be filled by the nomination of party leaders); and fair disciplinary rules and procedures for those who offend against the party rules and practices. (Ewing 2007: 247–8)

Furthermore, Mersel (2006a: 172–3, 2006b) argues that as 'a matter of theoretical consistency', the 'precondition of internal democracy must be included in any thesis concerning the role of political parties in a democracy'. Mersel's reasoning is as follows:

> If the individual in a democracy has a right to equality and liberty, he must also have these rights within the body that represents him and enables him to participate in the democratic game, i.e. the political party … if we see political parties as entities that represent society not by establishing its ideologies but by reflecting and channeling social currents, than we must make sure that the ideologies and politics of the parties are produced by a large and representative group within society. (Mersel 2006a: 172–3)

Mersal's argument relies on two important assumptions about the nature of political parties as organizations. First, they are the primary mechanism by which citizens participate in democratic politics – whether this be directly through joining a party and/or seeking nomination as its candidate; or indirectly through the representation that a party provides for its supporters and voters in the legislature. Secondly, the organizational form of political parties resembles that of the 'mass party'. Both these assumptions may be disputed today, as both the form and functions of political parties are linked to particular normative assumptions about the nature of democracy, and political parties are inherently evolving organizations.

It is debatable as to whether there was ever a 'golden age' of mass parties and membership participation. Indeed, party scholars such as Wilson (1962: 347), Duverger (1954), Schumpeter (1942) and as early as Michels (1962 [1915]), have argued that whilst membership participation and internally democratic party procedures are not necessarily undesirable, they are impossible to achieve in the pragmatic competition for votes. To the competitive theorist who values the primacy of party-based elections, the efficiency and degree of cohesion with which the party can recruit political elites and contest government is paramount. The quick release of policies, and the selection and training of candidates who bring electoral success, requires a hierarchical party organization to maintain the unity of the party position so electors may have a clear choice between parties (Schumpeter 1942). Parties that are organized in a democratic fashion are 'not well armed for the struggles of politics' and are placed at a distinct disadvantage compared to those structured along 'authoritarian and autocratic lines' (Duverger 1954: 134).

Irrespective of these theoretical debates, the organizational development of political parties has largely been a response to pragmatic concerns rather than legal requirements given the lack of legal regulation. In Australia, Canada, the United Kingdom and the United States, there is no legal incentive, or indeed compulsion, to organize the internal affairs of political parties according to democratic principles. Rather, organizational reforms that enhance intra-party democracy in all democracies except New Zealand[68] have been driven by a desire to increase and reinvigorate existing party memberships, by providing members with a greater say in intra-party decisions, such as plebiscites, or in less altruistic circumstances, to circumvent or dilute the voice of party activists. Nevertheless, the law could potentially be used as a mechanism to regulate aspects of parties' internal decision-making processes to reflect normatively desirable democratic principles.

68 Another exception in the Australian State of Queensland, where a party's constitution must set out the rules governing candidate selection and membership, including the requirement that candidate selection contests satisfy the general principles of free and democratic elections – *Electoral Act* 1992 (Qld) (ECQ 2008: 4–6).

The Rights of the Membership and the Application of Administrative Principles

The way in which political parties have been recognized and categorized as voluntary associations has important implications for the rights and powers of the membership in any intra-party dispute. For example, as noted above, the High Court of Australia's decision in *Cameron v. Hogan* (1934) 51 CLR 358 gave Australian political parties the status of voluntary associations. The consequence of this categorization was that a member of a voluntary association could only enforce the rules or constitution of that association, if under those rules, the member had a right of a civil or a proprietary nature. The Court tended to construe these rights very narrowly, severely limiting the membership's ability to mount an action where the party constitution had been breached. However, there has been a distinct trend (observable in the last 30 years) towards the courts applying administrative principles to the resolution of intra-party disputes in Australia, Canada, New Zealand and the United Kingdom, therefore affording party members the rights to procedural fairness and natural justice (Barendt 1998: 150), beyond the terms of a party's constitution.

The practical and political implications of this judicial approach to political parties is that decision making within parties must be exercised according to the rules and constitution of the party. There is no legal requirement that decisions of the party (except in New Zealand with respect to candidate selection provisions – see Chapter 5) be made democratically; indeed, it is entirely possible to have an autocratic party organization – but they must be made fairly and according to the principles of natural justice. As Lord Denning explained of domestic bodies and trade unions in *Breen v. Amalgamated Engineering Union* [1971] 2 QB 175 at 190, 'their rules are said to be a contract between the members and the union. So be it. If they are a contract, then it is an implied term that the discretion should be exercised fairly'.

Questions of procedural fairness and natural justice also arose in the Australian case, *Baker v. Liberal Party of Australia (SA Division)* (1997) 68 SASR 366, which concerned the admission of members to the South Australian branch of the Liberal Party of Australia (Gauja 2006b: 297). The party had rejected the membership applications of some 500 applicants, lodged by an association called the 'Combined Shooters and Firearms Council of South Australia'. Baker was one such applicant. The 500 applications, including Baker's, were perceived by the Liberal Party as constituting a potential takeover threat and compromising its independence. In a press release dated 24 June 1996, the party claimed that 'it would not tolerate any single issue group, particularly the one directed by an outside organisation, attempting to take over a section of the party' (Gauja 2006b: 297). The party further claimed that the South Australian State Executive had the power, under the party's constitution, to reject an application for membership without giving reason.

Justice Bollen of the South Australian Supreme Court accepted the argument that the party could reject a membership application without giving reasons, provided that the application was considered. Although seemingly contrary to administrative principles of procedural fairness, Justice Bollen could not find any:

> … [l]egal fault in the way in which the defendant went about considering the application of the plaintiff. Indeed, it is hard to see how there could have been any such fault. The defendant was empowered by its Constitution to decline any application for membership with or without giving any reason. (at 371)

The plaintiff's argument that she had a legitimate expectation[69] that she would become a member if she complied with the procedure for application was also rejected by the Court:

> The plaintiff no doubt had her own expectations. But the question of legitimate expectation has some element of the objective about it. The plaintiff may have had high hopes. But the only expectation which she was entitled to have in law was that the application would be considered. It was. Mr Manetta suggested that the decision of the Executive was void or voidable. It was not. I do not think that any question of natural justice arises. The executive was not bound to hear the applicant, to invite her to send in more information about herself or, indeed, to do any more than consider the application. (per Bollen J at 374)

Justice Bollen agreed with the defendant's submission that the principles of natural justice that relate to the reasonableness or fairness of the decision do not apply in the case of an application for membership to a voluntary association (at 375). As admission had not yet occurred, no legal relationship existed between the parties and hence there was no proprietary interest to protect. However, the situation would have been different had Baker been a member of the party: 'of course it would have all been different had the plaintiff been admitted to membership and then had her membership purportedly cancelled, that is, been dismissed or struck off' (at 375).

While in this instance the principles of natural justice were beyond the reach of an applicant to a political party, the decision in *Baker* illustrates the close relationship between the principles employed in the adjudication of intra-party disputes and the requirement of procedural fairness applicable to domestic bodies in the realm of administrative law. A similar trend has been observed by Caroline Morris (2008) in the developing case law of the UK courts. In *Lewis v. Heffer* (discussed above), Lord Denning entertained the possibility that the principles of natural justice might apply to intra-party disputes, though he declined to implement them in that particular case. Earlier, in *Fountaine v. Chesterton* (1968) 112 S.J. 690, Justice Megarry had found that the principle of natural justice would apply in a case concerning the expulsion of a member of a political party, unless the constitution displayed a 'plain and manifest

69 As per Justice Mason in *Kioa v. West* (1985) CLR 550 at 582: 'It is a fundamental rule of the common law doctrine of natural justice expressed in traditional terms that, generally speaking, when an order is to be made which will deprive a person of some right or interest or the legitimate expectation of a benefit, he is entitled to know the case sought to be made against him and to be given an opportunity of replying to it'.

intention' that it be excluded (at 691). In *John v. Rees* [1970] 1 Ch. 345, the principle was taken even further by Justice Megarry. In this case, the suspensions of party members were declared null and void in the absence of natural justice being afforded to those suspended by the national executive – even though the executive had a constitutional mandate to take 'any action it deems necessary'.

The New Zealand Supreme Court took a similar approach in a case concerning the expulsion of a member of Parliament from her party, ACT, *Awatere Huata v. Prebble* [2005] 1 NZLR 289, in which it held that:

> The court will enforce the agreement between the members of such bodies, including implied terms importing requirements of procedural fairness [but] associations will typically have wide freedom in their internal arrangements, including the determination of their membership. (at 309)

Political parties could arguably be characterized as performing 'public functions', and as private associations could therefore be subject to administrative review.[70] Although primarily a product of historical jurisprudential development, it seems odd that the justiciability of intra-party disputes continues to be established on the basis of members' rights interests (whether contractual or proprietary) and not on the nature of the power exercised by the political association. As Morris (2008: 423) argues, this approach has created a significant imbalance in power between a party organization and its members, specifically between 'the ability of a party to select its candidates as against the ability of a potential candidate to challenge that decision in law'.

Beyond the issue of applying democratic and administrative principles in interpreting constitutional provisions to resolve intra-party disputes, how should (or does) a court approach a situation in which the party lacks basic constitutional measures that provide for the processes of internal decision making? As we have seen, party registration requirements in common law democracies are generally quite lax in this regard. Although a party must be established on the basis of a written constitution, there are few legislative directives as to what the constitution should actually contain, such as a minimum level of detail for certain intra-party procedures. Hence, a situation where a political party has no, or very few, rules in place to assist a court in resolving any party dispute is actually quite plausible. This lack of constitutional detail can thus pose a significant problem for party litigation and the process of adjudicating such cases.

Burston v. Oldfield [2003] NSWSC 88 (hereinafter *Burston*) presents an example of the New South Wales (Australia) Supreme Court's approach to missing constitutional provisions (see Gauja 2006b: 298). The case concerned a challenge

70 For a discussion of the application of administrative review to private bodies (non-party) performing public functions see *Forbes v. NSW Trotting Club Ltd* (1978) 143 CLR; *R v. Panel on Take-Overs and Mergers: Ex parte Datafin* [1987] 1 QB 815. See also Morris (2008: 423–9) on the applicability of a public law model to political parties in the United Kingdom.

to the order of candidates on the One Nation Party's ticket for the 2003 New South Wales Legislative Council election. The order of candidates (and hence their potential order of election) was contested by two separate meetings of party members claiming to have validly nominated the candidates. The first meeting, that of the State executive of the party, was held in December 2002. Following dissatisfaction within the party as to the decision of the executive, an alternate meeting of all party members was called for 19 January 2003. Although notice of the meeting was sent to all members, less than 28 days' notice was given (as required by the party constitution). Over 70 members attended the meeting, which elected an alternative Legislative Council ticket.

In deciding which of the tickets was valid, One Nation's rules and constitution offered very little assistance to the Court. Although it was agreed between the parties that the constitution was valid and binding, it did not contain any provisions relating to the conduct of State executive meetings, party conferences, or special meetings. As Justice Hamilton noted, 'the Political Party was formed and has proceeded in a very informal fashion'; consequently 'the provisions of the Constitution are exiguous and in some ways more remarkable for what they do not contain than for what they do contain' (at para. 12). To adjudicate the dispute, the Court therefore looked instead to the body of incorporated associations law to determine the validity of the meetings and which took precedence.

Burston was decided on the technical question of whether there was a quorum present at the State executive meeting in December 2002. Applying prior authority of the Australian High Court in interpreting the meaning of a quorum, the Supreme Court held that the State executive meeting was valid (at para. 15). The special meeting of members, although giving expression to the democratic will of the membership, was not provided for in the constitution and therefore lacked binding status within the party (at para. 16).

Although it adjudicated the dispute and therefore effectively determined the outcome of the party's nomination process, the Court was eager to distance itself from any suggestion that it was playing a political role in the proceedings:

> I should add, as I have been at pains to say during the hearing, that this Court is not, of course, engaging in a political process. What the political party does by way of its political activities are entirely within its purview and are not the affair of the Court. The same, of course, applies to all other political parties and, indeed, all other parts of the political process. However, the members of the Political Party have, as is necessary, clothed their existence and operation in legal forms. (at para. 17)

Political parties that are formed without adequate governance structures, regardless of the extent to which they can be regarded as 'democratic', present a real problem and are a significant burden for electoral administrators all over the world. For example, the Australian Electoral Commission expressed its concern that:

> The 'churning' of party registration at the smaller or emerging end of the spectrum involves the AEC in considerable time and effort in seeking compliance with the administrative requirements of registration. This has involved complex challenges in those situations where parties' administrative arrangements are inadequate to properly deal with internal party management issues. In one case there was contention as to the make up of the party executive arising from procedural deficiencies in the conduct of the national conference at which they were 'elected'. This resulted in an application to voluntarily deregister the party that was questioned on the ground that it did not have the support of the party or its 'executive' generally. It also resulted in a considerable amount of correspondence from members on issues that were not within the scope of the AEC's functions. The AEC has, and wants, no role in internal party management matters. It is for the party, or the Courts, to resolve internal conflicts. (AEC 2005: 40–41)

The United States

Unlike political parties in the other democracies analysed in this research, the nature of parties as membership organizations in the United States is distinctly different and hence conclusions from Australia, Canada, New Zealand and the United Kingdom cannot necessarily be generalized to this case. Unlike these democracies, where members join a political party through a process of application to the party itself, party membership in the United States has been described as 'a fiction created by primary registration laws' (Rosenblum 2000: 819; Persily 2001: 765; Garrett 2002: 100–109). For example, the District Court in *Nader v. Schaffer* stated that:

> It is true that, in order to vote in a party's primary, plaintiffs must publicly affiliate with that party. But enrolment in Connecticut imposes absolutely no affirmative party obligations on the voter, in terms of time or money, and it does not even oblige him to vote for the party's positions or candidates or to vote at all.[71]

Furthermore, when it comes to registering partisans, 'the party as such is not consulted. It does not accept the application; it does not vote the applicant into the association; it may not reject the application; and, finally, there is usually no recognized and authoritative procedure by which the party may expel a member' (Schattschneider 1942: 56). American political parties do not have effective control over their membership, and there appears to be 'no formal distinction between member and supporter' (Ranney 1975: 199). Hence cases comparable to *Baker*, *Fountaine v. Chesterton*, *John v. Rees*, and *Awatere Huata v. Prebble*, concerning an application for membership or expulsion from a party, would not arise in the US context.

As political parties do not exist as structured and coherent extra-parliamentary organizations in the United States, the discussion regarding intra-party democracy

71 *Nader v. Schaffer*, 417 F. Supp. 837, 843 (D. Conn. 1976).

is largely redundant in this case. However, one important way in which the state seeks to promote the decentralization of decision making in US parties is through the regulation of candidate selection contests, by mandating and setting the procedures by which party primaries should be conducted (discussed in detail in the next chapter). To the extent that political organizations conduct organized, membership-based activities analogous to political parties in other industrialized democracies, there is little legislation that regulates their internal affairs. Indeed, US courts have stuck down state laws that purport to regulate the internal governance structures of political parties beyond the structure of state primaries or access to the general election ballot (see, for example, *Eu v. San Francisco County Democratic Central Committee*, 489 U.S. 214 (1989)). More recently, the Supreme Court in *California Democratic Party v. Jones* 530 U.S. 567 (2000) reaffirmed the right of political parties to be independent of state interference in their 'expressive associational activities', among them, the candidate selection process (Issacharoff 2001: 274–5).

Conclusion

Should there be legislative provisions to provide for a minimum standard of procedural fairness and democracy in intra-party decision making, given that this is the direction the courts have been taking in Australia and the United Kingdom? On the one hand, documented instances of the abuse of party mechanisms, such as the practice of influencing the outcome of candidate selection contests through 'branch stacking' (discussed further in Chapter 5), and the potential for their reoccurrence can undermine confidence in the political process (Coghill 2001; see also Orr 2001). A lack of intra-party democracy may disenfranchise and alienate party members, in addition to weakening parties' ability to provide a representative channel between the community and the legislature. Conversely, exposing internal party organizations to greater external regulation may threaten political independence and freedom of association in an electoral democracy (Johns 2000, 1999). The logistical difficulties that may arise include the requirement of greater resources to administer democratic processes (staffing and training), the problems encountered by parties in organizing their activities democratically and yet conforming to an election timeframe (Tully 2003: 153), and formulating what might be an acceptable uniform or minimum standard of internal party operation. What does intra-party democracy actually mean?

The theory of party government provides that political parties must formulate policies to present to the electorate, must be cohesive enough to implement them whilst in government, and that parties are held accountable by the electorate in general elections. Intra-party democracy, as mandated by the law, might actually be detrimental to this process and arguably conflicts with democracy at the broader electoral level. Nevertheless, whether or not intra-party democracy is normatively desirable is a question that lawmakers should consider, as judicial decisions in this area have implications for the internal organization of political parties – and therefore this could be a regulatory turn that might just occur by virtue of parties and legislators' own inertia in addressing this important point.

Chapter 5
Regulating Party Candidate Selection Contests

A great deal of the litigation in which political parties have been involved concerns the process of candidate selection. This is not surprising given the importance of obtaining a party's endorsement in order to maximize the chance of election to the legislature, and the fact that the recruitment of political elites is one of the key functions of parties. Therefore, the stakes are high for both organizations and individuals. In this chapter, I compare the different regulatory approaches to candidate selection existing in all the democracies surveyed, the historical and political circumstances that have influenced their adoption, and the litigation that has subsequently arisen. I divide the countries analysed into three broad groupings based on the extent to which we can observe state involvement in selection processes: Australia, Canada and the United Kingdom (no regulation), New Zealand (limited regulation) and the United States (extensive regulation). The second part of the chapter looks at several specific salient debates in particular democracies: branch-stacking in Australia, leadership selections in Canada, and the application of anti-discrimination legislation to parties in the United Kingdom, Canada and Australia.

The Political Importance of Candidate Selection Contests

Candidate selection is the 'process by which a political party decides which of the persons legally eligible to hold an elective office will be designated on the ballot and in election communications as its recommended and supported candidate or list of candidates' (Ranney 1981: 75). There is broad agreement amongst party scholars that candidate selection is one of the crucial functions performed by political parties in representative democracies (Gunther and Diamond 2001; Norris 2006). It is an important arena for internal party power struggles (Schattschneider 1942: 64), often tied to debates over the influence and salience of factions (Ranney 1981: 103); the contest over party candidates has been described as 'even more intense than the struggle over the party manifesto' (Gallagher 1988: 3). Not only is candidate selection crucial for the electoral fortunes of a political party, it also determines the quality of the legislature and government (Morris 2008: 416). Given that most electors will choose to vote for a political party rather than an individual candidate at any given election, candidate selection is potentially a means by which political parties can exercise control over both the composition of the legislature and the behaviour of its elected parliamentarians (through the ever-present threat of non-endorsement at the next election).

Hazan and Rahat (2006: 110) argue that candidate selection is important for three reasons. First, the process 'reflects and defines' the character of a political party and its internal distribution of power. Secondly, candidate selection methods are relatively easy to change. Third, any change in candidate selection methods will subsequently affect both party and legislative politics. Hence, if we accept Hazan and Rahat's argument, from a regulatory perspective, candidate selection is potentially an area where there is scope for effective legislative regulation with a view to influencing the broader character of the party system and the legislature. Nevertheless, with the exception of the United States and Germany, few jurisdictions have attempted to control these processes and candidate selection remains an aspect of legislative recruitment that takes place within political parties – predominantly beyond the realm of legal regulation (Ibid.: 109). Absent legal regulation, selection processes have developed in response to a number of factors: party philosophy and ideology, efficiency requirements (that is, working within the time-frame set by the electoral cycle), and previous disputes within the party that create precedents as to how future selections will occur (Smith and Gauja 2010: 14–17), and the imperative of electoral success (which typically favours measures that allow a central party organization to override lower-level choices by party branches or the membership to secure the 'best' candidates to contest and election).

Democracies with No Overt Legislative Regulation: Australia, Canada and the United Kingdom

Consistent with the liberal notion that parties are private associations largely independent of the state, in the United Kingdom and at the federal level in Canada and Australia, a party is free to determine how it selects its candidates without any external legislative regulation or guidelines. There have been several challenges to candidate selection processes in the courts, but as a general rule, candidate selection is considered an internal matter for the party and can only be adjudicated by the courts to the extent that party members wish to challenge the conduct of the candidate selection contest under the party's own rules and constitution, or in more limited circumstances, if there is an issue concerning natural justice and procedural fairness. However, generally there are no statutory requirements that require candidate selection to be conducted in a democratic manner, a situation that in the face of several candidate selection scandals, has drawn significant criticism. As Johns notes of the Australian context, political 'parties use regulation and the courts to enforce a system which arguably is suited to their own needs, but are reluctant to open themselves to any scrutiny when it comes to the selection of candidates' (1999: 94; see also Jaensch, Brent and Bowden 2004: 47–52; Button 2002; Lawrence 2006).

Australia

Although political parties are defined as organizations whose object or activity is to promote to the election to Parliament of 'candidates endorsed by it', Part XI of the *Commonwealth Electoral Act* 1918, pertaining to the registration of political parties, makes no mention of how this endorsement should occur. Only in one State of Australia, Queensland, does statutory law provide that candidate selection processes must take place according to the general principles of free and democratic elections (ECQ 2008: 5); *Electoral Act* 1992 (Qld) s 73A. Nevertheless, despite the lack of overt legislative regulation, party members have sought to challenge candidate selection outcomes and processes in the Australian courts, which has led to a substantial body of case law on whether candidate selection contests are justiciable, and if so, how they should be conducted.

An example of a high-profile and influential case concerning candidate selection in Australia is *Clarke v. Australian Labor Party (SA Branch)* (1999) 74 SASR 109. In this case, a member of the South Australian State legislature (and prospective candidate) sought to challenge 2,000 new memberships that had been introduced into the party prior to his selection contest in order to influence the outcome of the party vote. Clarke argued that the validation of these memberships by a special convention of the party did not conform to the party's constitutional process. The Supreme Court of South Australia held that the dispute was justiciable due to the 'statutory recognition by the South Australian Parliament of political parties' in the provisions of the *Electoral Act* 1985 (SA).[1] Going beyond the notion that a proprietary or contractual interest might be sufficient to establish a cause of action, Justice Mulligan extended the notion of an interest to something largely intangible that arises from the membership of a political party and as offering oneself as a potential candidate:

> I accept that this 'interest' does not amount to a proprietary interest as discussed in the cases, but it establishes that the plaintiff does have an interest in ensuring the observance of the Constitution and Rules of the SA Branch. Failure to do so may affect him personally, including his livelihood. I accept that this is a sufficient interest to attract declaratory relief. (at para. 92)

This conception of an interest is quite expansive, and arguably takes a pragmatic approach in attempting to reflect the political reality of electoral competition that a significant advantage accrues to those candidates endorsed by a major or established party.

In assessing the constitutional validity of the memberships and the party's validation of them, Justice Mulligan looked to the objectives and rationale of the party as expressed in official party documents. Resolutions of the 1955 and

---

1 *Clarke v. Australian Labor Party (SA Branch)* (1999) 74 SASR 109, per Mulligan J at para. 65.

1979 conferences of the party were analysed to illustrate that 'the Party is a democratic socialist party and, in effect, that its objectives are to be achieved by the democratic process' (at para. 47). It was against these identified democratic values that the court determined the constitutional validity of the party's exercise of power in the resolution of Clarke's dispute:

> The manner of obtaining membership is clear. The fee must be paid to the Sub-Branch which must consider the application for membership at a general meeting. This construction of the Rules also accords with the democratic nature of the party … It provides a safeguard against a group of persons whose interests and motives were contrary to those of the Sub-Branch and the party suddenly joining by merely paying a fee and filling out a form. (at para. 111)

Justice Mulligan also criticized the internal dispute resolution mechanisms of the party, noting that in some instances, the plaintiff's claim was 'not resolved' by the party or the response was 'limited' (at para. 94). The Court regarded the way in which the dispute had been dealt with by the party's executive as unsatisfactory, and noted that the complaint should have been referred to the party's disputes tribunal and resolved by process of conciliation (at paras 94–5). The special convention to amend the rules and constitution of the party was not regarded as an adequate internal dispute-resolution mechanism, despite the defendant's contention that the plaintiff could have attended the meeting to argue his case against the proposed amendments.

The Court granted the plaintiff an injunction restraining the party from convening the special convention to retrospectively amend the rules and constitution to validate the memberships. Although this action would not have been contrary to any express constitutional terms, Justice Mulligan held that:

> Retrospective amendments which prejudice the interests of a member should be regarded as unconstitutional. I think that a relevant interest includes the livelihood of a member. Validation of purported membership of a very large number of persons who are not members and who could influence and dictate policy, executive decisions or selections by constitutional change is of prejudice to valid members. (at para. 47)

There are, however, a number of limitations on the implications of the *Clarke* decision for the organization of political parties. While holding that the proposed constitutional amendments in the *Clarke* litigation were unconstitutional, the court accepted the arguments of the defendants that the party was a voluntary association and therefore may amend its constitution and rules for 'its own purposes' (at para. 142). This proposition was regarded as correct to the extent that any constitutional amendments would have prospective and not retrospective effect (at para. 143).

The significance of the *Clarke* decision lies not only in its approval of the jusiticiability of intra-party disputes concerning candidate selection, but the way in which the court interpreted the Australian Labor Party's rules and constitution in light of democratic principles, namely, 'the establishment of an efficient, effective and fair election process' (at para. 126). This may indicate a trend for the Australian courts to imply and uphold minimum standards of intra-party democracy in party constitutions, particularly when the objective is espoused in the party's constitution and official documents, regardless of the behaviour and management tactics of elected party officials. Far from being exclusively private organizations:

> Certain decisions of a political party's internal process – such as those relating to the selection of candidates for election, for example – are in truth not private matters at all; they are very public, particularly when there are disputes between factions. In such circumstances, a political party may regard it as highly expedient in order to quell faction-fighting that the final decision on the constitutional validity of its internal proceedings be left, not to a domestic tribunal constituted by party members whose impartiality may, however unjustly, be called into question but, rather, to a court whose impartiality is beyond any question.
>
> Judges have called attention to the fact that a modern political party registered under the legislation governing elections is in itself an institution whose internal stability and good governance is important in the democratic process … Accordingly, there is a public interest in ensuring that a registered political party, which is entitled to funding assistance for electoral expenses from public monies, is administered in accordance with a correct construction of its rules. (*Coleman v. Liberal Party of Australia (New South Wales Division) (No 2)* [2007] 212 FLR 271 at paras 47–8)

The United Kingdom

As Morris (2008) argues, the Australian courts have essentially developed a public law approach to candidate selection contests, and one that differs substantially from the recent situation in the United Kingdom, where candidate selection disputes have (for the last decade) been litigated in the field of employment law. Like Australia, there is no provision in the *Political Parties, Elections and Referendums Act* 2000 (UK) (PPERA) that requires political parties to undertake candidate nomination in specific ways, or imposes any statutory obligations upon parties in doing so.

In *Jepson and Dyas-Elliott v. Labour Party* [1996] I.R.L.R. 116, a disgruntled male Labour Party member challenged the party's policy of all-women shortlists for the 1997 general election on the ground that it constituted discrimination in the field of employment – that employment being a Labour Party candidate. Although the application of anti-discrimination legislation to political parties is discussed in greater detail below, the tribunal accepted Jepson's claim that being selected as a Labour Party candidate constituted the conferral of 'authorisation or qualification which is needed for or facilitates engagement in a particular profession or trade' for the purposes of the *Sex Discrimination Act* 1975 s. 13(3). Consequently the affirmative action procedures set in place by the Labour Party were found to be contrary to the provision of the *Sex Discrimination Act*. *Jepson* opened the door for various cases challenging party nomination procedures on the grounds of anti-discrimination legislation.[2]

However, this approach was subsequently overturned by the House of Lords in *Watt v. Ashan* [2008] 2 W.L.R. 17, where Lord Hoffman found that candidate selection did not constitute an 'authorisation or qualification' for the purposes of employment. Candidate selection, according to the House of Lords, was akin to a popularity contest, whereas the processes involved in the selection of an employee were far more objective in nature. Employment law was not, therefore, the correct jurisdiction in which to decide such matters of candidate selection and the House of Lords expressed its view that similar cases should be decided with respect to the laws governing private and voluntary associations 'club law'. This decision marks a return to the pre-*Jepson* position of *Lewis v. Heffer*,[3] where candidate selection disputes are to be decided on the basis of contractual relationship between the party and its members formed by the acceptance of the party's rules and constitution.

Canada

The *Canada Elections Act* specifies that with some exceptions for certain classes of person including sitting members of provincial legislatures, sheriffs, judges and election officers, any qualified elector is eligible to be a candidate in an election (s. 65). Candidates may run as independents (unaffiliated) or be endorsed by a political party. In the case of the latter, the candidate's nomination papers must include the name of the party that endorsed the candidate and an 'instrument in writing', signed by the party leader or a representative, which states that the prospective candidate is endorsed by the party (ss 66(1)(a), 67(4)). This endorsement is usually achieved by way of a nomination contest, but the law as it is currently formulated does not preclude the party's leadership from the common practice of 'parachuting' a favoured candidate into a particular electoral district, without the opportunity of local party members having a say over his or her nomination (Forcese and Freeman 2005: 96).

The Canadian courts have recognized that it may be appropriate to intervene in candidate selection contests where party rules and constitutions fail to provide provisions for the arbitration of internal party disputes over candidate selection. In such cases, 'the Court might be prepared to infer certain basic procedural

2 *Ishaq v. McDonagh* (2000) 45 EOR Discrimination Case Law Digest 5; *Mann v. Secretary of State for Scotland* (15 November 2000, Edinburgh ET); *Sawyer v. Ashan* [1999] I.R.L.R. 609.

3 [1978] 1 W.L.R. 1061 at 1071 per Lord Denning, M.R.

protections, and in the absence of any specific remedial procedure, the courts would undoubtedly use their general jurisdiction to provide the relief to which the parties are entitled'.[4]

Nevertheless, in the most recent case concerning candidate selection in Canada, *Knox v. Conservative Party of Canada* [2007] 286 DLR (4th) 129, the court declined to adjudicate in the nomination processes of the Conservative Party of Canada, and the only remedy for members dissatisfied with the process lay in the provisions of the Conservative Party's constitution and arbitration subject to the provisions of the Alberta *Arbitration Act* 2000 R.S.A. 2000, which were examined in detail in the judgment. Justices Berger, Watson and Slatter held that political parties:

> … Are essentially private organizations … When arranging for the nomination of their candidate in Calgary West, the Party and Association were essentially engaged in private activities, and their actions, in this case, are not subject to judicial review. They are, however, subject to private law remedies that may be engaged. Like many private organizations, the Appellants in this case have constitutions, bylaws and rules. Members are entitled to have those documents enforced in accordance with their terms and the proper interpretation of those terms. The remedies are, however, private law remedies. (at para. 27)

The Court's decision has been interpreted by Geddis (2009: 35) as a refusal to intervene where the Conservative Party's constitution had already provided appropriate protections for candidates and members, rather than a general proposition that parties can structure candidate selection processes in any manner they wish. These developments appear to be compatible with the general trend towards the application of administrative principles of procedural fairness to internal party disputes including, but not limited to, candidate selection contests.

The experience of these three democracies suggests that where there is very little by way of the legislative regulation of candidate selection contests, the courts have been willing to intervene in such disputes, albeit in a limited manner. This intervention has been justified on numerous grounds in the various jurisdictions: to uphold contractual rights between members, to uphold interests based on the importance of candidate selection for the livelihood of the individuals concerned, and similarly as these processes constitute entry into particular professions. However, the common trend across all the democracies surveyed appears to be the willingness of the judiciary to apply principles derived from administrative law, such as procedural fairness and natural justice, to parties' candidate selection contests, regardless of the content (or lack of content) of a party's rules and constitution.

---

4 *Knox v. Conservative Party of Canada* [2007] 286 DLR (4th) 129 at para. 63 per Berger, Watson and Slatter JJ. See also *Cureatz v. Progressive Conservative Party of Canada* [1997] O.J. No. 2309 (Gen. Div.) and *Cameron v. Boyle* [1994] O.J. No. 782 (Gen. Div.).

Limited Regulation: New Zealand

In contrast, section 71 of the *Electoral Act* 1993 (NZ), introduced with the transition to proportional representation, requires that parties follow democratic procedures in candidate selection. The provision reflects the suggestion of the Royal Commission on the Electoral System that candidate selection take place by either a vote of party members or through delegates to a party convention, drawing upon the German experience (see Wallace 1986: 239). The provision is intended to ensure that the 'grass-roots membership of the party takes part in the selection of its candidates (and, by implication, their subsequent ranking on the party list), thus ensuring that the candidates endorsed by the party really are the individuals the party's members wish to see elected' (Geddis 2007a: 80). Far from being a revolutionary measure, it is interesting to note that at the time this provision was inserted into the bill to amend the electoral system (the Electoral Reform Bill) on the recommendation of the Electoral Law Select Committee (which comprised five National Party parliamentarians, four Labour Party parliamentarians and one minor party representative), the provision 'reflected the requirements for candidate selection already included in the constitutions of both the Labour and National parties!' (Jackson and McRobie 1998: 143).

The terms of the Act remain open to interpretation from parties and leave wide scope for a variety of candidate selection procedures. Section 71 of the *Electoral Act* 1993 (NZ) reads:

> Every political party that is for the time being registered under this part of the Act shall ensure that provision is made for participation in the selection of candidates representing the party for election as members of Parliament by:
>
> a. current financial members of the party who are or would be entitled to vote for those candidates at any election; or
> b. delegates who have (whether directly or indirectly) in turn been elected or otherwise selected by current financial members of the party; or
> c. a combination of the persons or classes of persons referred to in paragraphs (a) and (b).

However, as Miller (2005: 110) notes, there has been little attempt to legally enforce that provision in the *Electoral Act* requiring parties to uphold democratic selection procedures. On the one hand, the flexibility of the legislation may be welcomed as providing an overall requirement of democratic organization to which parties should aspire, but are free to implement as they wish. On the other, the provision could be viewed as vague, without any real substance, and exceedingly difficult to enforce. Although this section places a positive legal duty upon parties to structure their candidate selection processes in a certain way, as Geddis (2005: 117) argues, the means of enforcing this provision are uncertain: the Electoral Commission does not have to ensure that a party's selection processes comply with the requirements of the Act before registering a party,[5] nor does non-compliance with this provision constitute a ground for deregistration under section 70.

Nevertheless, despite the introduction of this provision, New Zealand candidate selections are characterized by their diversity – from the relatively centralized procedure of the NZ Labour Party and the small, personality-driven parties, to the more inclusive processes of National and ACT, in which local electorate delegates and individual members have a greater influence (see Miller 2005: 114–15). Rather than proscribing a specific mechanism for selection, a key issue is the balance between the different arms of elements of the party organization in the selection of candidates, a point that was recognized by the Royal Commission on the Electoral System (Wallace 1986: 240–41):

> An important element in the drafting and operation of such legislation would be the balance between the regular members of the party and the central party officials. In the two main New Zealand parties [Labour and National], the central party organizations have some (possibly more in the case of Labour than National) influence in candidate selection. This can have a beneficial effect on the overall quality and representativeness of the parliamentary teams and could be even more significant with the introduction of party lists. We would not wish to prevent such procedures, provided they are acceptable to the party as a whole and provided party officials are themselves chosen by all party members or their representatives.

The only instance of a New Zealand court having to evaluate a party's compliance with the provisions of section 71 occurred in *Payne v. New Zealand National Party* [2008] 3 NZLR 233. In this case, Payne, a candidate who had not been approved for the National Party's nomination, challenged the party's process of vetting potential candidates through the National Party Board and electorate committees before the final candidate is chosen by a selection committee comprising delegates from the party branches within the electorate, or by a universal suffrage of party members in the electorate concerned. The High Court of New Zealand expressed its opinion as to the rationale and intent of section 71:

> Although at first blush there may be a tendency to equate the reference to democratic procedures in s 71 with the principles of natural justice, the origins of the phrase suggest otherwise. The word 'democratic' was, I think, deliberately chosen to capture the notion identified in 'Towards a Better Democracy' and subsequently endorsed by the Electoral Law Committee and by speakers in the House. What the Royal Commission, and subsequent adherents, had in mind was a requirement that the selection of candidates by political parties would be participatory; that members of the party may participate in the selection process, whether directly or through representatives (delegates) themselves elected by the membership at large. (at para. 49)

5 *Electoral Act* 1993 (NZ), ss 63, 67.

However, the Court also added the important qualification that 'the participatory requirement was ... deliberately framed so as to leave scope for the overarching influence of senior officials of the party, provided that they too were democratically elected by the membership' (at para. 52). Hence the vetting of potential candidates could take place by an executive body within the party, provided that it was democratically elected by the membership – a measure that acknowledges some of the realities of practical politics. Overall, the Court was satisfied that the rules of the National Party included:

> ... a comprehensive code for the democratic selection of constituency candidates. The requirement contained in s 71 for participation in the selection process by current financial members of the party from the electorate, or by delegates elected/selected by current financial members of the party, is met. (at para. 64)

A crucial point that is raised by Geddis (2009: 27) is that the enforcement of the duty under s. 71 to follow democratic principles of participation in candidate selection lies with the courts rather than the Electoral Commission or an administrative body established for this purpose. While aggrieved individuals can challenge party processes, the cost and time involved in such litigation is unlikely to make this a particularly effective avenue to force party compliance with the provisions. Furthermore, the High Court's interpretation has left considerable scope for New Zealand political parties to organize selection processes as they wish, acknowledging the political reality that selection decision often need to be made quickly by a centralized body, and may often override majoritarian tendencies within the party to install candidates from minority backgrounds (see Miller 2005: 101).

Expansive Regulation: The United States

As Müller and Sieberer (2006: 441) note, formal legal rules that provide for the process by which party candidates are nominated are relatively rare in a comparative context (see also Hazan and Rahat 2006: 109). Beyond the example of New Zealand provided above, within Europe they exist only in Germany, Greece, Norway and Finland. However, of all Western democracies, the regulation of candidate selection contests is perhaps greatest, and certainly the most historically entrenched, in the United States.

Candidate selection in the United States typically occurs by way of a primary, in which all registered voters in a state vote directly for their preferred party candidate. There are several types of primary: open, closed and blanket. Open primaries are open to all registered voters, regardless of their party or independent affiliation. Closed primaries are limited to a party's registered voters. Blanket primaries allow all registered voters to participate in the primary, but differ from open primaries in that also enable voters to choose candidates across party lines for different offices. It should be emphasized that state laws, and not party rules (as is the case in all the other democracies examined), direct who can become a member of a political party and vote in a party's candidate selection contest. The crucial point to note here is that 'the very fact that political parties hold primaries for the nomination of candidates is a product of state compulsion under laws dating back to the turn of the last century' (Issacharoff 2001: 275). In the US, it is also the state that regulates the waiting period for voters between their registration and being able to vote in a party's primary, which ranges from the same day[6] to 11 months.[7] A political party has no say in the length of the waiting period (Ibid.: 284).

State legislation introduced in the late 1800s began to regulate the conduct of party candidate selection ballots, including the requirement that parties nominate candidates in direct primary elections. By 1910, 22 states had enacted laws establishing direct primaries and by 1916, this had risen to 26 (Miller 2004). These laws were viewed by the state courts as protecting the rights of voters from the corrupt, centralized and 'boss-led' party machines, and due to the parties' central role in elections, the courts were willing to regard them as quasi-state agencies that were therefore subject to the legal regulatory authority of the state (Winkler 2000; see also Lowenstein 2006: 456).

Political parties immediately began to challenge these laws, which they claimed restricted their associational freedoms. However, as the case law shows, the courts have generally upheld the laws that regulated parties and their candidate selection processes for much of the twentieth century, in particular, those that required parties to undertake primaries. In this respect, and unlike the judicial attitude towards political parties that was characteristic of other liberal democracies until the later half of the twentieth century, the US courts have refused to consider political parties purely as voluntary associations. For example, in *Smith v. Allwright* 321 US 649 (1944), which concerned a challenge by African Americans to their exclusion from Democratic Party primaries in the South, the court held that primaries and general elections could not be distinguished as separate political processes.[8] Although primaries were conducted by the Democratic Party, the fact that primaries and elections were 'fused … into a single mentality', meant that the nomination process was regarded as a state function (Lowenstein 2006: 457). This reflects a distinct judicial attitude that political parties form part of the state electoral apparatus, an assumption that for much of the last century remained 'too plain for argument', and has allowed states to mandate the participation of political parties in primaries (Aisenbrey 2006: 607) and expose them to the degree of regulation that we would otherwise reserve for state or public bodies.

6 *Nader v. Shaffer*, 417 F. Supp 837 (D. Conn. 1976).

7 *Rosario v. Rockefeller*, 410 U.S. 752, 760–61 (1973).

8 *Smith v. Allwright* is one of a number of 'white primary' cases in which the state sought to enforce relatively 'open' primaries, or to ensure that parties did not arbitrarily restrict participation in them – see also *Nixon v. Herndon* 273 U.S. 536 (1926); *Nixon v. Condon* 286 U.S. 73 (1932); *Terry v. Adams* 345 U.S. 461 (1952).

From the 1970s onwards, however, we see the US Supreme Court shift its emphasis from upholding state regulatory regimes to the protection of political parties and their associational freedoms. For example, in *Brown v. O'Brien* 409 U.S. 1 (1972), a federal appellate court had intervened in the primaries used to select delegates to the Democratic Party National Convention in 1972 in two states: California and Illinois. Both had been challenged in the party's credentials committee, which overturned the California primary as it had been conducted on a winner-take-all basis, and thus the winner of the Californian primary would be assured of the party's presidential nomination. The delegation elected by the Illinois primary was challenged for under-representing women, minorities and youth (Lowenstein 2006: 457). The appellate court reinstated the California primary but let the decision of the nominations committee on the Illinois delegation stand. This intervention was overturned by the Supreme Court on two grounds: first, insufficient time for adequate consideration of the process, and secondly, the availability of an intra-party forum (the National Convention) to reconsider the decision of the credentials committee. More importantly, the Supreme Court questioned the justiciability of the dispute, the 'public' nature of the credential committee's action and expressed 'grave doubts' about the intervention and its consequences for the party's 'vital rights of association' (Ibid.: 457).

In *Nader v. Schaffer*, 417 F. Supp. 837, 847 (D. Conn. 1976), aff'd, 429 U.S. 989 (1976), the Supreme Court, once again, came down on the side of political parties. In this case, independent voters in Connecticut who wanted to vote in the closed primary of the Republican Party (that is, the primary was only open to registered Republican voters), brought an action against the state to have to primary opened. The Republican Party opposed allowing non-registered voters to participate. The court recognized that although a closed primary burdened voters' rights by disallowing them from participating in a democratic process, or making this right contingent upon a formal affiliation with the political party, it found that the motives of non-Republican voters may not serve the best interests of the party and its role in the democratic process: such voters 'are not interested in nominating the candidate who presents the best chance of winning the general election while remaining most faithful to party policies and philosophies' (at 848). As Aisenbrey (2006: 612) argues, the Court's language suggests an overall concern with protecting the associational rights of a party if it appears that its primary might be 'raided' by independent voters that do not support its cause or have an interest in selecting the best candidate.

The Supreme Court's judgment in *Nader v. Shaffer* is also consistent with the idea of parties and their role in representative democracy that is inherent in the responsible party model of government, a defence for strong parties that gained much currency in the American political science community from the 1950s onwards. This is a specific normative vision of partisan politics that prioritizes a stable, two-party system in which the major parties enjoy maximum autonomy, which, coupled with existing political institutions (for example, the first-past-the-post electoral system) has served to insulate them from political competition (see further Magarian 2003).

The inclusiveness of a party's primary was also at issue in the later case *Democratic Party of the United States v. Wisconsin ex rel. La Follette*, 450 U.S. 107 (1981). In this case, the Wisconsin Democrats acted against the national party's directive in conducting an open primary to elect delegates to the Democratic National Convention (1980), where the national rules specifically called for closed primaries. In reversing the state court's order to seat the delegates at the Convention, the Supreme Court nevertheless held that the 'National Party rules do not forbid Wisconsin to conduct an open primary. But if Wisconsin does open its primary, it cannot require that Wisconsin delegates to the National Party Convention vote there in accordance with the primary results, if to do so would violate party rules' (cited in Lowenstein 2006: 458). Therefore, the interests of both the state and national party were not necessarily seen as incompatible. However, reconciling these two interests would necessarily require a break in the chain of delegation from party members to convention delegates, and thus arguably compromising the rationale of the selection process.

In *Tashjian v. Republican Party of Connecticut*, 479 U.S. 208 (1986), a state's imposition of a closed primary on a party that preferred an open primary was held by the Supreme Court to be unconstitutional. The persuasiveness of this case was of some doubt prior to the Supreme Court's decision in *Jones* (see below) as the circumstances of the case took place in a situation where the political party that controlled the legislature refused to change the primaries in a way in which the outside political party saw as more democratic and competitive. Therefore, *Tashjian* concerned circumstances where the state (and hence the legislator of the electoral regime) was also the dominant political party, and in this situation the Court found that 'the views of the State, which to some extent represent the views of the one political party transiently enjoying majority power, as to the optimum methods of preserving party integrity, lose much of their force' (at 224).

Commentators have agreed with the Supreme Court's decision in *Tashjian* on the grounds that a political party and its leaders should be able to determine the interests that should form the basis of its electoral coalition and support. As Persily and Cain argue:

> [T]he closed primary served one purpose only: to prevent parties from catering to individuals and groups that chose not to identify with a party. To allow such a law would permit the state to define the meaning of party membership, and, more importantly, to substitute its judgment for that of party leaders as to what interests should form the basis of its electoral coalition. (2000: 801)

Arguably, the closed primary guards against the possibility of independent voters 'raiding' the candidate selection process (as was the court's concern in *Nader v. Shaffer*), but the key difference in this case is that the party should be allowed to choose the appropriate method of candidate selection and the degree of inclusiveness of its selectorate – rather than this being mandated by the state.

In a controversial and high-profile 7–2 decision, the US Supreme Court held the structure of primary elections in California unconstitutional in *California Democratic Party v. Jones*, 530 U.S. 567 (2000) (hereinafter *Jones*). The Californian primaries were significant in that they had been changed from a closed primary to a blanket primary through popular initiative in 1996 (Proposition 198), which was supported by a majority of both Democrat and Republican voters.[9] In a closed primary, only members of a political party (that is, those who have declared affiliation with that party when they register to vote) can vote to select its nominees for public office. A blanket primary ballot paper lists every candidate regardless of their party affiliation and allows the voter to choose freely amongst them. Before Proposition 198 was passed, the legislature (controlled by the two major parties) had refused to change the closed primary system, which effectively shut independents out of the primaries (Pildes 2004: 103). Supporters of the proposition argued that blanket primaries, like open primaries, would generate more centrist candidates and better reflect the views and preferences of the median voter (Ibid.), or as Justice Scalia noted, a measure that would 'weaken party hard-liners and ease the way for moderate problem-solvers'.[10] The District Court that first heard the case characterized Proposition 198 as an 'experiment in democratic government', the product of 'change and adaptation' in response to 'different political forces and circumstances'.[11]

Four Californian political parties (the California Democratic Party, the California Republican Party, the Libertarian Party of California, and the Peace and Freedom Party) brought suit against the California Secretary of State, alleging that the blanket primary violated their First Amendment rights of association. Each of the parties had a rule that prohibited persons who were not members of the party from voting in its primary.[12] The Court in *Jones* held that blanket primaries violated the parties' First Amendment right of association and interfered with their constitutional autonomy (at 586). Legal commentators (see, for example, Pildes 2004: 103) argue that broadly read, *Jones* might mean that political parties are free to opt for whatever primary election system they prefer. This ruling is made all the more significant by the fact that this freedom of association appears to trump the democratic will of the people of the state, as expressed through a popular referendum. However, *Jones* needs to be read in light of the Court's latter decision in *Clingman v. Beaver* (see below), which places restrictions on a party's right to choose, based on the preferences of other political parties in the system.

9 According to exit polls, Proposition 198 received support from 61 per cent of Democrats, 57 per cent of Republicans and 69 per cent of independents (figures cited in Pildes 2004: 103).

10 *California Democratic Party v. Jones* (2000) 530 U.S. 570 at 570.

11 *California Democratic Party v. Jones*, 984 F. Supp. 1288, 1303 (E.D. Cal. 1997). Interestingly, the passage of Proposition 198 can also be read as a battle between factions of the same political party for control of, and the best chance of winning a party primary – see Kang (2005: 164–6).

12 *Jones* 530 U.S. 567 at 571.

In making this judgment, the Supreme Court was essentially placing political parties on the same footing as civil society organizations (a crucial point of contention), and just as the latter have the right not to associate with those antithetical to organization's identity, political parties also have the constitutional autonomy to refuse to allow states to implement open primaries in which non-members might be permitted to vote in candidate selection contests.[13] The Court's judgment suggests that although states play a major role in structuring the primary election process, candidate selection process are not public affairs within which the state may interfere, and states must act within the limits of the constitution when regulating internal party processes. As Justice Scalia (author of the majority judgment), argued previously: 'I see no reason why the government should be any more able to tell the Republican Party how to choose its leaders than to tell the Mormon Church how to select its elders' (Scalia 1981; cited in Pildes 2004: 105–6).

The Supreme Court drew a distinction between its judgment in *Tashjian v. Republican Party of Conn.*, in which it held that it is 'too plain for argument' that a state may require parties to use the primary format for selecting their nominees, in order to assure that intra-party competition is resolved in a democratic fashion, and the applicability to the facts in *Jones*: 'what we have not held, however, is that the processes by which political parties select their nominees are, as respondents would have it, wholly public affairs that States may regulate freely'.[14] The Court's judgment appears to suggest that while the state may dictate a certain method of selection process, it cannot dictate who is involved in that selection – the selectorate. Of particular concern to Justice Scalia in this case was the ability for political parties to restrict participation in their primary contests to citizens sympathetic with their interests and persuasions (as per *Nader v. Shaffer*), acknowledging the importance of the party's public representatives:

> In no area is the political association's right to exclude more important than in the process of selecting its nominee. That process often determines the party's positions on the most significant public policy issues of the day, and even when those positions are predetermined it is the nominee who becomes the party's ambassador to the general electorate in winning it over to the party's views.[15]

Justice Scalia went on to add that:

> proposition 198 forces political parties to associate with – to have their nominees, and hence their positions, determined by – those who, at best, have refused to affiliate with the party, and, at worst, have expressly affiliated with a rival. (at 577).

---

13 *California Democratic Party v. Jones*, 530 U.S. 567 at 577.

14 *Jones* 530 U.S. 567 at 572–3. Note that the dissent shared the respondents' view with respect to participation in a state-run election.

15 *Jones* 530 U.S. 567 at 575.

Or per Justice Kennedy, concurring: 'The true purpose of this law … is to force a political party to accept a candidate it may not want and, by so doing, to change the party's doctrinal position on major issues' (at 587). Justice Scalia cited electoral studies in his opinion to support the argument that 'substantial numbers of voters who help select the nominees of parties they have chosen not to join often have policy views that diverge from those of the party faithful' (at 578), and thus, in the majority of the Court's view, jeopardizing the democratic process. Justice Scalia also argued that parties have the right to 'limit control over their decisions to those who share the interests and persuasions that underlie the association's being' (at 574). However, this data and the Court's concern for the practice of 'primary raiding'[16] have not proved entirely persuasive, and the majority judgment has been criticized for its functional analysis, which lacks convincing empirical support 'that the necessary functions of political parties will indeed be substantially compromised by the blanket primary experiment' (Issacharoff 2001: 312).

The Court then went on to consider whether Proposition 198 was sufficiently narrowly tailored to serve or advance a compelling state interest.[17] Of the seven state interests offered by the respondents: producing elected officials who better represent the electorate, expanding candidate selection beyond the scope of partisan concerns, allowing disenfranchised persons the right to an effective vote, promoting fairness, affording voters greater choice, increasing voter participation and protecting privacy, the Court found none compelling (at 582–6).

The reasons of the dissenting Justices in this case, Stevens and Ginsburg, hinged on the notion of sovereignty, and the elected legislature's right to determine how its members are selected – painting quite a different picture of party government and representative democracy to those members of the Court in the majority:

> A State's power to determine how its officials are to be elected is a quintessential attribute of sovereignty. This case is about the State of California's power to decide who may vote in an election conducted, and paid for, by the State. The United States Constitution imposes constraints on the States' power to limit access to the polls, but we have never before held or suggested that it imposes any constraints on States' power to authorize additional citizens to participate in any state election for a state office. (at 590–91)

Justice Steven went further to comment that the majority's conclusion in *Jones*:

> Rests on the premise that a political party's freedom of expressive association includes a 'right not to associate', which in turn includes a right to exclude voters unaffiliated with the party from participating in the selection of that party's nominee in a primary election … In drawing this conclusion, however, the Court blurs two

16 See further Aisenbrey (2006: 609–10).

17 *Timmons v. Twin Cities Area New Party* 520 U.S. 351 (1997) at 358.

> distinctions that are critical: (1) the distinction between a private organization's right to define itself and its messages, on the one hand, and the State's right to define the obligations of citizens and organizations performing public functions, on the other; and (2) the distinction between laws that abridge participation in the political process and those that encourage such participation. (at 591–2)

> In an era of dramatically declining voter participation, States should be free to experiment with reforms designed to make the democratic process more robust by involving the entire electorate in the process of selecting those who will serve as government officials. (at 601)

Given the declining rates of participation and withdrawal from political parties and formal political institutions that has been experienced in the United States (see, for example, Macedo et al. 2005: 21–30), Justice Steven's advocacy of and comments encouraging participation in the political process present a pragmatic policy position that would resonate well with many of today's political scientists, and the attitudes of democratic governments across advanced industrial democracies that wish to reinvigorate citizen interest and participation with a view to strengthening the legitimacy of party government.

The Supreme Court's majority position has drawn significant criticism from legal commentators (Pildes 2004; Persily and Cain 2000: 801; Issacharoff 2001; Magarian 2003; Ortiz 2000; Hasen 2001), particularly for entrenching the position of the dominant party actors. For example, to draw a parallel between civil society organizations and political parties and grant them both equal autonomy from the state ignores the specific social and institutional contexts within which both these political actors operate. Voluntary associations exist in plurality and 'can flourish as long as the state does not impose improper barriers to the formation of new groups' (Pildes 2004: 106). By contrast, the two major political parties have always been protected by the design of the first-past-the-post electoral system, which has operated to restrict political participation in an otherwise 'tawdry reality of extensive regulation' (Issacharoff 2001: 312) and 'state-run, state financed elections'.[18] The role of the candidate selection process (and what form it should take) needs to be evaluated with this broader institutional context in mind. As Pildes (2004: 106) argues:

> The constitutional rights of association appropriate for a civil-society sphere in which a plurality of associations flourish are not necessarily those apt for primary elections between candidates of two dominant organizations. Analysis of what rights parties ought to have depends upon functional judgments concerning the larger purposes of [first-past-the-post] elections, state-mandated primaries, and the sphere of democratic politics itself.

18 Per Justice Stevens (dissenting) in *California Democratic Party v. Jones*, 120 S. Ct. 2402, 2419 (2000).

Indeed, the very fact that mandatory primaries exist implies that, from the time of the Progressive Era, in both law and political practice, an essential distinction between political parties and voluntary associations exists (Persily 2001: 789–90; Pildes 2004: 107). From a functional perspective, while both these organizations operate to link citizens and the state, political parties are the only organization that can create an entire and unbroken linkage chain – from party supporters, to candidates, to legislators elected to office. By contrast, voluntary associations cannot by their nature field candidates for public office and must rely on external strategies, such as lobbying, to achieve political influence. Another way of expressing the distinction is to use the public–private divide (see Chapter 1), in which political parties sit somewhere between these two poles (Magarian 2003: 1956–7). As Issacharoff (2001: 294, citing Sullivan 1988: 1715) argues, as intermediary institutions, political parties 'function both as "conveyor belts for interests and nurturing grounds for values"'. However, as they occupy an ambiguous position in the public-private spectrum, 'an excess of regulation deprives them of their reason for being, and a pure right of autonomy does not reflect the extent to which they serve to provide critical social capital for the citizenry'.

It may be that dissatisfaction with the Supreme Court's position stems from the fact that evaluating the current system of primary elections and its alternatives is an inherently political question, and in evaluating this, we need to consider the role that is to be played by political parties in our system of representative democracy. However, these are arguably political judgements rather than questions for the Supreme Court:

> Any view that constitutional law is necessary to preserve the parties would entail lack of trust in the resilience of parties and in the self-revising capacity of democratic politics itself to decide what kind of parties best serve democracy … The one proper judicial concern in this area is that state legislatures, composed of partisans, might choose or maintain particular primary-election structures as anti-competitive instruments of self-entrenchment. (Pildes 2004: 115–16)

Indeed, *Jones* has been heavily criticized as providing an example of the dangers of this entrenchment – the major parties being the clear winners from the outcome of the litigation (Magarian 2003: 2011). A further example of the Court's deference to the stability of the two-party system is provided in the case *Timmons v. Twin Cities Area New Party* 520 U.S. 351 (1997), which involved a challenge from a minor political party to Minnesota's ban on fusion candidates. A fusion candidacy is one where two political parties nominate the same person as their preferred candidate for election and as Magarian notes, it is a practice that has 'served as an important vehicle for new, small parties to advance their agendas and develop their identities' (2003: 2031). Most states ban fusion candidacies, through 'statutes enacted almost entirely by lawmakers of the two major parties' (Ibid.).

The New Party's challenge to this ban was based on the First Amendment's principle of free association. However, the Supreme Court rejected this argument and upheld the ban on the grounds that the ban was not an infringement upon the party's First Amendment rights, but rather an ordinary electoral provision – parties did have a right to choose candidates but that candidates might be made unavailable by virtue of them having been chosen by another political party. Justice Rehnquist characterized the ban as another feature of the electoral system that minor parties simply had to contend with:

> Many features of our political system – e.g., single member districts, 'first past the post' elections, and the high costs of campaigning – make it difficult for third parties to succeed in American politics. But the Constitution does not require States to permit fusion any more than it requires them to move to proportional-representation elections or public financing of campaigns (at 362)

The Court went on to make the following statement in recognizing states' 'strong interest in the stability of their political systems' (at 366):

> This interest does not permit a State to completely insulate the two-party systems from minor parties' or independent candidates' competition and influence ... That said, the States' interest permits them to enact reasonable election regulations that may, in practice, favor the traditional two-party system, and that temper the destabilizing effects of party splintering and excessive factionalism. The Constitution permits the Minnesota Legislature to decide that political stability is best served through a healthy two-party system. (at 367)

The US Courts have generally upheld closed primaries as constitutional where there is no indication that a political party wants to open its party primary to voters other than members. However, this principle was extended in *Clingman v. Beaver* 544 U.S. 581 (2005) by the Supreme Court in a situation where one party wanted an open primary, but the others in a particular state system did not. In *Clingman v. Beaver*, the Libertarian Party of Oklahoma (LPO) brought suit against the state of Oklahoma to allow it to have an open primary in which not only Libertarians and Independents, but the registered voters of all political parties could vote. This concerned the major parties, who perceived a potential for their voters to participate in the Libertarian primary and by doing so, develop an attachment to it. Worse still, without being required to deregister from the Republican or Democratic parties, such voters might be able to raid the primaries of either of the major parties by voting for a candidate more sympathetic to the Libertarian cause. As Aisenbrey (2006: 615–16) notes, the Supreme Court found the arguments of the major parties persuasive, and the 'potential for reverse party raiding and the burden it would cause on the associational rights of the other political parties – the Democratic and Republican parties in this case – caused the Court to ultimately uphold the Oklahoma statute'.

Clingman v. Beaver raises two main considerations. The first is whether the state should be able to impose a closed primary upon political parties where the party itself prefers an open primary, and in doing so, knowingly accepts the risk that the primary might be raided by interests hostile to the party's own. The weight of legal analysis appears to suggest that this is an internal decision for the party, and the state should not overturn it unless it threatens the associational rights of another political party or parties (see, for example, Ibid.: 629). This was the essence of the Court's reasoning in *Clingman v. Beaver*. The second question is whether the state may limit the number of political parties with which a voter associates. Beyond restricting the number of nominations that a voter may make to one per office, Aisenbrey argues that it should not (Ibid.). While there are fundamental differences between the nature of American political parties as membership organizations with parties elsewhere in the industrialized world, this is still an interesting point of comparison. In Australia, a legislative requirement that members of one political party must not be members of any other for the purposes of party registration[19] was upheld as constitutional by the High Court in *Mulholland v. AEC* (2004) 220 CLR 181. Arguably, this decision would limit the associational rights of citizens to affiliate with whichever and however many political parties they wished. However, the case was heard on the basis of parties' (not voters') freedoms of association and the main issue at stake was the threshold requirement of 500 members, so this exact issue was not argued.

The American jurisprudence surrounding candidate nomination contests has struggled, like other democracies, with the broader problem of the legal regulation of what are essentially intermediary institutions of civil society; 'critical buffers between the individual and the power of the State'.[20] In recent years, the judgments of the Court have sought to uphold the autonomy of these organizations in line with a liberal conception of pluralist democracy. However, without regard to the institutional context and prior regulatory regime in which these actors operate, the Court's decisions have somewhat ironically reinforced the dominance of the two major political players – the Republicans and the Democrats.

'Branch Stacking' in Australian Candidate Selection Contests

Whereas the US courts have seen restricting those who may participate in a party's candidate selection contest as an effective way of preserving the integrity of the ballot, the Australian system – where only party members may participate in party 'preselections'[21] – has thrown up its fair share of problems. The most pervasive of these is 'branch stacking'.

---

19 Section 126(2A) of the *Commonwealth Electoral Act* 1918 prohibits two or more parties from relying on the same member for the purposes of qualifying or continuing to qualify as an eligible political party.

20 *Roberts v. United States Jaycees*, 468 U.S. 609, 619 (1984) per Justice Brennan.

21 'Preselection' is a uniquely Australian term and has the same meaning as candidate selection.

Branch stacking refers to the process of enlisting members in a branch of a political party for the sole purpose of channelling those members' votes towards a particular candidate in a candidate selection contest. Typically, candidate selection contests in Australia take place as closed primaries – open only to members of a political party in a specific geographic branch, which coincides with the electorate in which the candidate will contest public office. The practice of branch stacking is most common within the Australian Labor Party, which as Jones (2001: 4) argues, reflects the fact that the Labor Party's rules require branch members to be enrolled and reside in the electorate in which they vote. Branch stacking will commonly involve the recruitment of people from non-English-speaking backgrounds, the provision of funds to cover membership fees and the falsification of signatures of branch meeting attendance rolls where attendance at a minimum number of meetings is a requirement of eligibility to vote (Jones 2001: 4; Allan 2002).

Pervasive electoral fraud practices in one Australian State, Queensland, led to the establishment in 2000 of an inquiry by the Criminal Justice Commission (the Shepherdson Inquiry) into electoral fraud concerning several candidate selection contests conducted by the Australian Labor Party during the 1980s and 1990s. The Commission's report resulted in the passing of a legislative requirement that political party candidate selection contests be conducted according to the principles of free and democratic elections.[22] Oversight of this regime is entrusted to the Queensland Electoral Commission, which may enquire into and undertake audits of party preselection processes. Parties that breach these provisions are liable to deregistration and consequently the loss of public funding.

Most recently, a Liberal Party preselection for the New South Wales (NSW) electorate of Cook was overturned by the NSW Supreme Court amid allegations of branch stacking: see *Coleman v. Liberal Party of Australia, New South Wales Division (No. 2)* NSWSC 736 (6 July 2007). Although aggrieved candidates were able to find redress through the courts in this instance, intra-party animosity continued after the election and the newly elected member of Parliament was blocked from joining the local branch of his own party (Taylor 2008; Sawer, Abjorensen and Larkin 2009: 139).

Several recommendations have been made to attempt to control the problem of branch stacking in Australian political parties. The first is the introduction of American-style primary contests, in order to widen the pool of participants (Jones 2001: 51–2; Coghill 2001). The second is the supervision of candidate selection contests by an independent body, such as the Australian Electoral Commission. It has been suggested that this would result in 'greater impartiality, accuracy, fairness and accountability' and 'would reduce the power of party factions to influence the outcome of a preselection' (Jones 2001: 50–51). On the other hand, it is argued that such reforms might present an unnecessary and undemocratic intrusion into the private affairs of political parties:

22 Criminal Justice Commission (Queensland) (2001); *Electoral Act* 1992 (Qld) s. 73A.

> AEC involvement in the preselection of candidates for elections conducted by the AEC could be seen as compromising political neutrality. It is also considered improbable that the major parties, the Liberal Party and the ALP, would be amenable to external regulation of their preselection ballots. Further, for the AEC to take on such a responsibility would involve substantial establishment and ongoing costs that would have to be specially resourced.[23]

Despite the difficulties surrounding the integrity of candidate selection ballots in Australian parties, they are generally regarded as matters for the parties themselves to determine. As the Australian Electoral Commission recognized, much will depend on the political will of the parties to adopt different process or submit to the regulation of the state, and only in very exceptional cases of gross corruption of the process (as occurred in Queensland) will state regulation be enforced.

Canadian Leadership Selection Contests

Although leadership selection is not regulated by law in any of the nations surveyed in this book (with the exception of the US to the extent that the state regulates primaries), it has caused a great deal of concern in Canada, where party rules and requirements are used to restrict participation in these votes and has led to calls for the 'professionalization' of the process by bringing in Elections Canada to oversee leadership and nomination races (Forcese and Freeman 2005: 95). In reporting the results of the Canadian Democratic Audit, Cross (2004: 92) has written:

> The most disconcerting aspect is that party rules are being used to dampen public participation in the leadership contest. Canadians would not tolerate obstacles such as poll taxes, 90-day cut-off periods for voting eligibility, and efforts by candidates to freeze the composition of the electorate more than a year prior to the vote in general election contests. Nor would the Charter of Rights and Freedoms probably allow such barriers to democratic participation. However, because leadership contests are widely considered the private business of parties, no one has yet raised a Charter challenge to these practices and it is uncertain whether one would be successful.

What is particularly interesting is that many of these internal practices would be regarded as desirable in order to preserve the integrity of any internal leadership ballots in Australia, the United Kingdom and New Zealand. Cross's views constitute

---

23 Australian Electoral Commission, *Submission to the Joint Standing Committee on Electoral Matters, Inquiry into the Integrity of the Electoral Roll*, 17 October 2000, 59. Cited in Jones (2001: 51). See Orr (2001) for an analysis of the arguments for an against reforming candidate selection processes.

somewhat of a paradigm shift to something similar to primaries in the United States. This presents an example of a law reform agenda driven by a different set of normative principles to maximize participation by actually removing key decisions from the exclusive domain of the parties:

> It is peculiar that party leadership selection is considered a private event of the political parties. Selecting a leader (which often means selecting a premier or a prime minister) is not like the choice of a party president or secretary. The latter are clearly internal party affairs. The importance of the leadership choice, however, goes far beyond the internal interests of the parties. In a democratic audit, one is left with the question of why the rules governing who gets to make this important decision should be left to the parties … (Cross 2004: 105)

It also demonstrates the potential for the convergence of electoral and party law provisions across the globe as democracies learn from the experiences of others and adopt solutions to their own problems based on the principles of institutional borrowing.

Political Parties, Candidate Selection and Anti-discrimination Law

A further theoretical and practical challenge that law makers face is reconciling the relationship between political parties as private organizations free to set their own rules, given the monopoly these organizations have over legislative recruitment, with the application of anti-discrimination legislation and the adoption of quotas and other affirmative regulation measures designed to produce broader equality in representation. Litigation based on racial discrimination in political parties has had a long history in the United States, dating back to the racial segregation policies adopted by the Democratic Party in many southern states following the Civil War. Yet as Orr (2011) notes, US jurisprudence is only of limited applicability to other common law democracies owing to the specific American historical experience and notions of freedom of association that are constructed around collective rather than individual rights. As such, this section focuses on the issue of anti-discrimination in political parties in the UK, Australia and Canada.[24]

Under the provisions of the *Sex Discrimination (Election Candidates) Act* 2004 (UK), parties in the United Kingdom receive limited exemption from anti-discrimination legislation and are able to adopt positive discriminatory measures to achieve gender parity in the election of candidates to parliaments in the UK with a sunset date of 2030. The legislation was enacted after an industrial tribunal found that the Labour Party's policy of adopting all-women shortlists for the 1997 general election constituted direct discrimination against men contrary to the *Sex*

24 There have not yet been any notable cases relating to anti-discrimination provisions and political parties in New Zealand.

Discrimination Act 1975 (UK).[25] The provisions of the 2004 Act preserve the independence of parties, as they are permissive rather than restrictive (allowing parties to take certain measures to achieve gender parity, but stopping short of requiring them to do so). Interestingly, although the passage of this amending Act enabled the Labour Party to once again adopt all-women shortlists for the 2005 general election, which consequently increased the proportion of female MPs in the House of Commons, neither the Conservative Party nor the Liberal Democrats opted to pursue this course of action (Turpin and Tomkins 2007: 541).

Political parties in the United Kingdom are also subject to the provisions of the *Race Relations Act* 1976 (UK), which prohibits racial discrimination in any association of more than 25 people in both their treatment of prospective members and in providing 'benefits, facilities or services' to members (s. 25). The constitution and rules of the British National Party (BNP) have been challenged under this Act. In June 2009, the Equality and Human Rights Commission (the statutory body responsible for administering the Act) requested that the BNP amend its constitution to change the qualifications for membership, which under section 2 were limited to specific ethnic groups – namely 'Indigenous Caucasians'. After a county court order in October 2009, the BNP changed its constitution to read:

> We are implacably opposed to the promotion by any means of any form of integration or assimilation of any indigenous people … including the Indigenous British, which is likely to deprive such people of their integrity as a distinct people or the distinctiveness of their cultural values or of their ethnic or national identities or characteristics.

However, the amended constitution has been criticized by the EHRC as constituting indirect rather than direct discrimination through the repeated use of the phrase 'indigenous British' (Taylor 2010). The court is yet to rule on the legality of this formulation and it appears that the controversy may continue for some time.

Political parties in Australia are exempt from sex discrimination legislation (*Sex Discrimination Act* 1984) and the anti-discrimination laws that apply to associations, excepting party employees. Candidate selection contests do not fall under the ambit of employment legislation, as they are not seen in Australian law as necessary qualifications for the profession of politics – see *Scott v. Gray* [1999] HREOC 15 (HREOC, 3 August 1999). Consequently, and benefiting from an exemption for the *Sex Discrimination Act*, the Australian Labor Party has been able to implement affirmative action measures to increase the number of women selected as candidates in winnable seats. The quotas adopted have increased the presence of women in the Parliament (Sawer et al. 2009: 119–20); however, they have not been supported by all the Australian parties (Ward and Stewart 2006: 148). Similarly, affirmative action programs are protected in Canada by Article 15(2) of

---

25 *Jepson v. Labour Party* [1996] I.R.L.R. 116. See Busby (2003) and McHarg (2006) for further commentary on this case and the legislation that arose from it.

the *Constitution Act* 1982 if they have the objective of ameliorating the conditions of disadvantaged groups. The New Democratic Party (NDP) has used affirmative action measures to select its candidates, and for the 2008 general election the party's conference adopted a resolution that women were to be selected in no less than 30 per cent of seats not currently held by the party. However, in both Canada and the UK, such affirmative action measures have only had a very minimal effect in changing the overall composition of the Parliament (Jones et al. 2007: 194).

Allowing, rather than requiring, affirmative action measures is probably as far as we can expect legislation with cross-party consensus to reach in this area, as the relationship between discrimination (whether positive or negative) and democracy is highly contentious. In abstract terms, discrimination based on race, age and gender could be considered 'anti-democratic', but may be normatively desirable to achieve a more democratic balance of representation in the longer term, both within parliaments and party organizations.

Typically, anti-discrimination provisions have been invoked by unsuccessful candidates contesting party nomination ballots, for example, *Jepson* and in the Australian context, *Scott v. Gray* [1999] HREOC 15. Yet, such cases raise the question of the underlying rationale for the litigation, and whether anti-discrimination legislation is the best means by which to pursue it. For example, a case brought by an unsuccessful nominee against his party under Section Three of the *Charter of Rights and Freedoms* was struck down (*Kenneth Robinson and Beryl Jones v. A.G. for Canada and Dorothy Kirby* (31 October 1988), T-2099-88 (F.C.)). The nominee alleged that his right to qualify for membership in the House of Commons under Section Three had been violated after the party refused to put his name on the list of candidates after the properly nominated candidate withdrew from the contest after nominations closed. Given the importance of candidate nomination in the selection of legislatures, do we want anti-discrimination laws to assist in achieving a distribution of seats in the legislature consistent with a particular conception of representation (mirror representation, and so on)? Or do we want them to provide the opportunity for everyone to participate in politics?

As Orr (2011) argues, the application of anti-discrimination law to the internal disputes of political parties (particularly those concerning candidate selection) tends to construct a false dichotomy between a political party's freedom to associate and individuals' right to equality in opportunities to participate in the political process. Rather, an alternative is to conceive the problem in terms of party competition (see also Issacharoff and Pildes (1998) for a competition-led view of legal oversight in the US context). Rather than forcing individual political parties to accommodate all interests, the competitive space should be open enough to allow a plurality of political parties to form and contest elections. This would require a consistent and coordinated approach to legal regulation and the design of the electoral system that places more emphasis on the maintenance of competition between parties rather than regulating internal processes. For example, it may be more fruitful to consider the effect and appropriateness of registration requirements and gatekeeper provisions, or the overall design of the electoral system (proportional representation systems weighed against majoritarian systems), or even give consideration to establishing dedicated parliamentary seats for minority groups that may not be adequately represented or integrated into the major party groupings.

Despite the limited case law cited, the extent to which anti-discrimination laws should apply to political parties is also a contentious question that has not yet been fully resolved by either the legislatures or the courts. Should anti-discrimination laws apply to who can or can not become a member of a political party? Should they apply to the internal decision-making processes of a political party, including candidate selection? Should we make a distinction between positive forms of discrimination (such as affirmative action provisions) and negative discrimination? Can one or the other be justified? Given the complexity and contentiousness of the ancillary questions that need to be addressed if anti-discrimination laws were to be applied wholesale to parties' internal activities, it is probable that any legislative action in this area will be incremental at best.

Conclusion

As this chapter has demonstrated, there is a substantial variation between democracies in the way in which candidate selection is regulated. This is illustrated in Table 5.1, which summarizes the legislative regimes that apply to selection, key judicial decisions made in this area, and the outcomes for parties of both of these sources of regulation.

These approaches range from no direct legislative regulation whatsoever (Australia, Canada and the United Kingdom), to limited regulatory measures (New Zealand), to extensive regulation (the United States). The variation in these approaches can best be explained by the historical development of the party and electoral systems in each of the democracies concerned. Although the principles of liberalism and voluntary association underpin political relations in each of these states, the reform of the New Zealand electoral system in the 1990s and the introduction of proportional representation necessitated some measure of regulation, whereas concern with the centralization of power and corruption in US parties (which were seen to exercise an important public function) spurred extensive regulation early on in the genesis of the US party system. Interestingly, developments in Australia (the incidence of branch stacking) and in Canada (concerns over leadership selection) have seen a push for the greater regulation of candidate and leadership selection contests in the states. These calls have been made in response to similar arguments concerning corruption, the centralization of power and the characterization of candidate/leadership selection contests as democratic functions too important to be left to a relatively small number of party members to decide.

Furthermore, US courts have sought in recent years to temper the extensive regulation to which parties are subject by emphasizing their autonomy and right to choose those who can participate in their primaries. However, courts in the UK,

Table 5.1 The Legal Regulation of Candidate Selection Contests in Australia, Canada, New Zealand, the United Kingdom and the United States

State	Legislative measures	Key judicial decisions	Outcomes applicable to selection process
Australia	None	*Clarke v. ALP* (1999)	A party must abide by its rules and constitution, read in light of the democratic principles of an efficient, effective and fair election process.
Canada	None	*Knox v. Conservative Party* (2007)	A party must abide by its rules and constitution; possibility of some judicial protection of basic procedural safeguards.
New Zealand	*Electoral Act* 1993 s. 71 – parties must follow democratic procedures in candidate selection	*Payne v. NZ National Party* (2008)	Parties must follow democratic procedures in candidate selection. Wide interpretation by the courts that balances participation with the reality of centralization.
United Kingdom	None	*Lewis v. Heffer* (1978), *Jepson* (1996), *Watt v. Ashan* (2008)	A party must abide by its rules and constitution. Political parties are subject to anti-discrimination legislation.
United States	Various state legislation requiring parties to hold primaries	*Tashjian* (1986), *Jones* (2000), *Clingman v. Beaver* (2005)	State legislation requires that parties conduct primaries. Some judicial support for the proposition that parties should be able to determine the method and selectorate of the primary (open, closed, and so on).

Australia and Canada have been willing to intervene in candidate selection disputes to ensure that the processes outlined in a party's rules and constitution are followed and to provide some basic procedural safeguards in the selection process. Hence we may be witnessing a trend towards convergence in the regulation of candidate selection procedures with some measure of regulation that seeks to guarantee a base level of participation and fairness in the process, without dictating the exact terms upon which it must take place.

Chapter 6
Parties and the Conduct of Elections

The previous three chapters have examined how the law regulates some of the key contours of the electoral contest: from the point of entry (party registration and ballot access) to candidate nomination, the organizational directives (or lack of) that shape the process of policy making within parties and the creation of election platforms and manifestoes. Chapters 7 and 8 analyse in greater detail issues concerning the public and private financing of political parties and their campaigns. In this chapter, I examine some of the miscellaneous legal provisions that influence the conduct and activities of political parties *during* election campaigns, including electoral offences such as bribery, the regulation of broadcasting, advertising and the new media. Overwhelmingly, legislative provisions regulating the conduct of elections are formulated and expressed in terms of individual candidates rather than political parties (Loveland 2006: 244). Nevertheless, many of these provisions have practical implications for the structure and activities of political parties for two main reasons. First, parties are essentially composed of individuals. Secondly, parties as organizations will often take on many of the responsibilities and coordinate the activities that electoral law technically allocates to the individual (for example, submitting candidate nomination forms and coordinating advertising campaigns).

The Maintenance of Fair and Equal Competition During Election Campaigns

There are several democratic values that a state will typically seek to promote when establishing a regime for party regulation: participation and citizen input into party business, an informed electorate and democratic responsiveness (Kang 2005: 138). As we have seen, not all of these principles exist in perfect harmony. A good example is the overarching democratic ideal of competition in elections. There is a crucial distinction between the promotion of competition *between* political parties and the promotion of competition *within* or *through* political parties. Legislation to secure the former will typically focus on creating a reasonably level electoral playing field where a certain number of political parties can compete for the votes of the general public. Legislation to secure the latter (competition within parties) might impose democratic requirements upon political parties' internal decision-making processes to achieve higher levels of participation and responsiveness within these organizations. On aggregate, the rules that constitute the electoral system in any given polity will reflect and facilitate a particular vision of party competition.

While facilitating or legislating for competition *within* political parties is a contentious topic, all democracies in the study purport to regulate their electoral systems so as to provide for competition *between* the parties. Nevertheless, the number of parties that *should* be able to compete (or more importantly, the number that *are* effectively able to compete) is another unsettled question that varies between states and depends on one's normative vision of representative democracy. In large part, this is influenced by the overall design of the electoral system. First-past-the-post systems typically produce a two-party system of competition, whereas proportional representation systems produce a multi-party pattern of competition. Yet, it is also influenced by ancillary legislation and regulations, such as those pertaining to registration (see Chapter 4), candidate selection (see Chapter 5) and party finance (see Chapters 7 and 8). In this chapter, I look at three further areas of the law that indirectly influence the character of electoral (and hence party) competition: electoral offences, election broadcasting and campaign advertising.

Bribery and Other Electoral Offences

If the goal of minimizing voter confusion is partly achieved through the imposition of registration thresholds for both candidates and political parties to discourage non-serious contenders, and if candidate selection contests are in part regulated to achieve more widespread participation in party activities, then criminal offences such as bribery exist to eliminate deception, corruption and achieve a fair and equal contest between those parties that have achieved ballot access. Although the focus of this section is bribery, there are several other electoral offences to which the individuals that make up political parties (members, candidates, officer holders and agents) are subject, including interference to political liberty, intimidating voters, misleading electoral officials, interfering with ballot papers, and so on. Unlike the some of the penalties and offences associated with campaign finance (discussed in Chapters 7 and 8), electoral offences are directed at individuals rather than parties.

In the United Kingdom, political parties, their candidates and their officials are subject to the provisions of the *Representation of the People Act* 1883 (UK), which outlaws several corrupt and illegal practices with respect to the conduct of elections. Bribery, treating and undue influence are all offences described as 'corrupt' acts, where the offender is liable to one year's imprisonment and a fine. Bribery involves the payment of money or the provision of office to an elector in return for a vote (s. 113), whereas treating involves the provision of food, drink, or entertainment (s. 114). A person is guilty of undue influence if they use the threat of violence, damage, or harm to induce a person to vote or not to vote (s. 115). It is also illegal under section 107 to bribe a candidate to withdraw from an electoral contest.

Under section 326 of the *Commonwealth Electoral Act* 1918 (Australia), it is an offence to ask for, receive, or offer a benefit, the effect of which is likely to influence: the vote or candidature of another person, a person's support or opposition towards a candidate or political party, the preferences of a voter, or the order of names of Senate candidates on a ballot paper. The maximum penalty for this offence is $2,000 and/or two years' imprisonment.[1]

One of the more recent cases of alleged bribery involving political parties concerned a payment between two Australian political parties – the Australian Labor Party and the Australian Democrats – in return for the allocation of preferences in the alternative vote for the House of Representatives (see Jones 2001: 18–19). In November 2000, a prominent current affairs programme revealed that Wayne Swan, a Labor member of the Federal Parliament and member of the Rudd government's 2007–2009 cabinet, gave an undisclosed sum to the campaign director of a smaller political party – the Australian Democrats – in the Brisbane seat of Lilley prior to the 1996 federal election. When questioned in Parliament, Swan confirmed that a financial contribution had been made to the Democrats' local campaign, but did not name a figure and denied that the contribution had been made in exchange for preferences (Grattan and Murphy 2000). The allegation was investigated by the Australian Electoral Commission, which in turn consulted the Director of Public Prosecutions for advice on whether Swan's actions might have constituted electoral bribery (under section 326 of the *Commonwealth Electoral Act*) and hence be liable to prosecution. The matter was referred to the Federal Police and during the period of investigation Swan stood down as Shadow Minister of Family and Community Services. None the less, in February 2001, Swan was cleared by the Federal Police of any wrongdoing and no further action was taken in the matter.

Bribes are similarly outlawed by s 481 of the *Canada Elections Act*, which states:

> 481. (1) Every person is guilty of an offence who, during an election period, directly or indirectly offers a bribe to influence an elector to vote or refrain from voting or to vote or refrain from voting for a particular candidate.
>
> (2) Every elector is guilty of an offence who, during an election period, accepts or agrees to accept a bribe that is offered in the circumstances described in subsection (1).

Practices that constitute a 'bribe' include transportation and travel allowances that *induce* rather than *enable* electors to vote (Williams 1928: 279). Hence the practice of party volunteers providing transportation to polling booths for both the general public and the party's supporters (whom the party might be reasonably certain might vote in its favour) are not illegal (*Genereaux v. Cuthbert* (1884), 9 S.C.R. 102). However, offering an elector a ride or a travel allowance on the condition

1 See Orr (2006a) and Hughes (1998) for further commentary on the offence of bribery under Australian law.

that they vote a particular way would constitute bribery (*Cooper v. Slade* (1858) 6 H.L.C. 746; 27 L.J.Q.B. 449).

Laws concerning bribery and other electoral offences are left to individual states to legislate for in the United States, following early cases that held bribery in connections with national elections could not be prosecuted under the federal Criminal Code.[2] Nevertheless, all states have enacted legislation that prohibits acts of electoral fraud, bribery and treating.[3]

The modern offences against electoral bribery in New Zealand originated from the *Corrupt Practices Prevention Act* 1881, which outlawed forms of electoral spending that might compromise the integrity of the electoral process (Geddis 2004). Bribery is classified as a 'corrupt practice' under the *Electoral Act* 1993, and occurs when a person gives money, a gift, employment or office, or any other form of valuable consideration to another in return for the promise to vote (or not vote) (s. 216). The *Electoral Act* also outlaws the practice of 'treating', where votes are secured through the provision of food, drink and/or entertainment (s. 217). These corrupt practices are punishable by a fine of up to $4,000 and/or one year's imprisonment, and a disqualification from voting and standing for public office for three years (s. 224(1)). Other 'illegal practices', punishable by a fine of up to $3,000, include providing any money for any purpose which is contrary to the provisions of the *Electoral Act* (s. 220), the payment to an elector to display a poster or notice on the electors' property promoting a candidate at an election (s. 219(1)),[4] and the publication of election advertisements without due written authorization and the name and address of the person publishing it (s. 221; discussed further below). Political parties are also subject to the provisions concerning unduly influencing voters at polling stations by broadcasting or advertising material provided in s. 197 of the *Electoral Act*.

However, as Geddis (2004) notes, these provisions are rarely invoked. This may reflect one of two possible explanations – that New Zealand appears to be 'relatively free of overt corruption, both in its electoral system and its general processes of governance'. However, it may also reflect difficulties of enforcement and the fact that many of these provisions rely on a measure of self-regulation and proactive referral to the police (see also Geddis 2007a: 126–9). In the United Kingdom, recent investigations of electoral malpractice concerning postal votes occupied a significant proportion of police resources, leading to a common call from both the UK police and the Electoral Commission for an approach to

2 *United States v. Bathgate* (1918) 38 Sup. Ct. 269; *United States v. Gradwell* (1916) 243 U.S. 476, 37 Sup. Ct. 407.

3 For example, s. 18500 of the *California Elections Code* prohibits acts of fraud in connection with votes cast, ss 18520–24 prohibit bribery and treating. Bribery and promising voters' employment is also prohibited by the *Massachusetts General Laws*, Pt. 1, Title VIII: 'Elections', Ch. 56, ss 32, 34.

4 A similar provision also exists in the United Kingdom – see s. 110 of the *Representation of the People Act* 1883. It is also an illegal offence to employ a person for the purpose of canvassing votes (s. 111).

electoral malpractices that centers upon 'prevention rather than prosecution' (UK Electoral Commission 2009: 2). However, given that the financial penalties for such offences are relatively low, this may not constitute a significant deterrent to potential offenders. Overall, occurrences of electoral malpractices by candidates and parties in the democracies surveyed are relatively rare, but where they do occur, they have the potential to become significant media events that undermine the integrity of the electoral process (Ibid.: 1).

A further difficulty of the prosecution of electoral offences is that such prosecutions may be coloured by political motivations, for example, to silence unpopular political parties or opponents. Such criticism was made of the prosecution, initial conviction (which was subsequently overturned) and imprisonment of the former leader of the right-wing anti-immigration Australian political party One Nation. Hanson was convicted under section 408C(1)(d) of the *Criminal Code* (Qld) for 'dishonestly gaining a benefit or advantage' by registering One Nation on the basis of false information. However, the litigation against One Nation was originated by a former disgruntled member, Terry Sharples, who was financially assisted by a group 'Australians for Honest Politics', comprising former and current prominent major party politicians (Head 2003: 265). According to Head, Hanson's conviction and subsequent jailing 'set a dangerous precedent for use against any electoral grouping considered a threat to the political establishment' (Ibid.: 264).

The Regulation of Election Advertising and Broadcasting

All the democracies surveyed in this research place some restrictions upon the advertising and broadcasting of political materials and statements during election campaigns. In doing so, law makers have faced a number of difficult challenges in reconciling this regulation with freedoms of political expression guaranteed in the various national constitutions and bills of rights applicable to these democracies. At issue is the balance between equality of access to this powerful political resource, and the freedom of electoral participants to communicate with the voting public during elections.

Regulating Access to the Media

Political parties' access to the media during the period of an election campaign is regulated in similar fashions in New Zealand and Canada. Both democracies grant registered parties limited rights of access to the broadcasting media for electioneering purposes, providing them with the option to purchase paid advertising time, and an allocation of free broadcasting time. In New Zealand, a sum of money provided by the state is divided between the parties for the purposes of purchasing airtime to broadcast election programmes. The public broadcasters Television New Zealand and Radio New Zealand must also make time available at no cost so that eligible political parties can broadcast opening and closing election addresses.[5] Outside of the election period and these regulations, there is a blanket ban on using the broadcast media for election-related advertising or to broadcast an election programme.[6] In Canada, political parties are given the option of purchasing a share of 6 and a half hours of broadcast time during prime time, which must be set aside by broadcasters and offered to parties at the lowest price the broadcaster charges to commercial entities for the equivalent broadcast time (*Canada Elections Act* 2000, ss 335, 348). Each of the major broadcasters must also provide a further 6 and a half hours of free broadcasting time, which does not need to be allocated in prime time. As part of this allocation, each of the registered parties making a request must be provided with a minimum of two minutes and the remaining time allocated amongst the parties according to the formula used in the distribution of paid time (s. 345).

British political parties are prohibited from purchasing broadcasting time on television and radio, although they can purchase advertisements in the press and on billboards.[7] Eligible parties are granted free broadcast time on the national broadcaster – the BBC – for party-political and election broadcasts. The commercial channels – ITV, 4 and 5 – are also required to air party-political broadcasts. These broadcasts are notably distinct from election advertisements, are listed like television and radio programmes, and are limited in length and frequency (Rowbottom 2006: 77; see also UK Electoral Commission 2001).

When it comes to regulating access to the media, Australia and the United States are the most liberal of the democracies surveyed; neither imposes any limitations on the purchase of broadcasting time on television, radio and in the print media. In 1991, the Australian government attempted to ban the purchase of paid political advertising, and legislated to provide blocks of free air-time to registered parties on the basis of their vote shares at previous elections. The legislation was supported by the smaller parties and independent legislators, subject to the allocation taking place in such a way that encouraged diversity amongst the parties and promoted competition (Sawer et al. 2009: 111). The legislation was struck down in the landmark case, *Australian Capital Television Pty Ltd v. Commonwealth* (1992) 177 CLR 106 (*ACTV*), where the High Court held that the ban contravened the implied

5 In New Zealand, parties' access to election broadcasting is regulated by the *Broadcasting Act* 1989 and the *Electoral Act* 1993.

6 An election programme is defined by s. 69(1) of the *Broadcasting Act* 1989 as 'a program that encourages or persuades (or appears to encourage or persuade) the voters to vote for (or not to vote for) some individual candidate or political party; or advocates support for or opposes a candidate or political party; or notifies that a meeting is to be held in connection with an election'.

7 *Broadcasting Act* 1990 (UK) ss 8(2)(a), 92(2)(a). Following the European Court of Human Rights Decision in *VgT Verein gegen Tierfabriken v. Switzerland* (2002) 34 EHRR 4,which found similar legislation in Switzerland incompatible with Article 10 of the European Convention on Human Rights, the validity of the ban has been thrown into some doubt. See Rowbottom (2006) for commentary on this case.

freedom of political communication found in the Constitution. Free broadcasting time is provided to political parties by the two public broadcasters – the ABC and the SBS – by virtue of their public service charters. During each campaign, a number of election debates between the major party leaders will be broadcast, but these debates are not subject to any regulation. In the US, broadcast stations are required by statute to provide equal access to all candidates (the 'equal time' rule), and to sell political broadcast time at the lowest unit rate that it has charged commercial advertisers in the last 45 days.[8]

Another way in which parties' access to the broadcast media is regulated by the state is through the imposition of blackout provisions, the rationale of which is to give voters time to reflect on the campaigns run without being bombarded by advertising in the last moments before an election. It also eliminates any advantage a party may have in being the last to advertise before voters make their decisions. Both election advertising[9] (except for signs and pamphlets) and the release of surveys are banned in Canada on polling day.[10] In Australia, the blackout period extends back to the three days prior to an election and covers both television and radio broadcasts, but allows press advertisements.[11] In New Zealand, it begins on the day before polling day, and covers only broadcast advertising (television and radio) (Elections NZ 2008). Similar provisions do not exist in the UK or federally in the US.

Equality of Access

All democracies analysed in this research provide their registered parties with access to a mix of public and private broadcasting resources for the purpose of election campaigning. How this access is distributed will usually depend on a formula that takes into account measures of popular support, for example, previous election results and/or the number of seats a party holds in parliament.[12] In Australia and the United States, it may simply depend on the amount of money

8 Communications Act 1934 s. 315; Federal Communications Commission (FCC) Rules ss 73.1941, 73.1942. Until 1987, broadcasters in the US were also required by the FCC to ensure that a diversity and balance of views were presented in the discussion of controversial matters: 'the Fairness doctrine'. The doctrine was repealed after the FCC reported that it was no longer having its intended effect, may have actually been 'chilling' political debate and was potentially a violation of the First Amendment: *Fairness Report* (102 F.C.C.2d 145).

9 Election advertising is defined by the *Canada Elections Act* as 'the transmission to the public by any means during an election period of an advertising message that promotes or opposes a registered party or the election of a candidate, including one that takes a position on an issue with which a registered party or candidate is associated' (s. 319).

10 *Canada Elections Act* ss 323, 328.

11 *Broadcasting Services Act* 1992 (Cth) sch. 2, pt 2, c13A; *Special Broadcasting Service Act* 1999 (Cth) s. 70C.

12 See, for example, the *Canada Elections Act* s. 338.

each political party is able to raise and spend. State-based allocation regimes are criticized on the ground that they are unfair to new parties and challengers to the established parties, particularly those who have not yet contested an election (see, for example, Geddis 2006b: 28–30; discussion below).

However, this criticism is addressed to some measure by the existence of an independent arbitrator for broadcasting allocations in Canada and New Zealand, who has the discretion to alter the formula if he or she deems it to be in the public interest, or if it is unfair to particular parties.[13] In New Zealand, this task is undertaken by the Electoral Commission, and in Canada, it is undertaken by a broadcasting arbitrator, usually appointed by the chief electoral officer after consultation with the parties represented in the House of Commons.[14] Under section 75(2) of the *Broadcasting Act* (NZ), the Electoral Commission will consider several factors when apportioning access between the relevant parties: a party's vote share at the previous election and any by-elections; a party's parliamentary representation; other indications of public support for a political party, such as opinion polls and membership numbers, and finally, the need to provide a fair opportunity for parties to broadcast their political messages to the public during an election campaign.[15]

Apart from the fact that the discretion to award broadcasting time is always subject to subjective criticism and that there is no statutory indication of how these respective factors ought to be weighted, the consultation process privileges the major party actors. The *Electoral Act* 1993 (NZ) has retained the first-past-the-post practice of allowing representatives of the government and the opposition to join the Electoral Commission when it makes its distribution. As Geddis argues, 'the practical consequence is that the nation's two largest political parties – Labour and National – each get to have a representative take an active part in deciding how much access the various parties will receive, while the minor parties have no direct involvement in the procedure' (2007a: 163).[16] A similar criticism has been raised in the UK, where the distribution of party-political and election broadcasts amongst the various parties is determined on an *ad hoc* basis by the BBC and OFCOM (the UK broadcasting regulator) with regard to the views of the Electoral Commission. For example, in 2001, the broadcasters decided that only political

13 *Canada Elections Act* s. 338(5), the *Broadcasting Act* 1989 (NZ) s. 75(2) and the *Electoral Act* 1993 (NZ).

14 *Canada Elections Act* s. 332. The existence of such an independent arbitrator with discretion to alter the funding formula was a key reason why the Reform Party's challenge to the regime under section 2 of the *Charter* failed – see *Reform Party of Canada v. Canada (Attorney General)*, [1995] A.J. No. 212 (C.A.).

15 Electoral Commission, *Decision of the Electoral Commission: Te Kaitiaki Take Kowhiri, on Allocation of Time and Money to Political Parties for Broadcasting of Election Programmes: 2005 General Election*, Wellington, Electoral Commission, 24 August 2005.

16 None the less, under sections 75A and 76 of the *Broadcasting Act* 1989, the Electoral Commission must 'consult' with both the broadcasters and the political parties before it makes its allocation.

parties that fielded candidates in at least one-sixth of the parliamentary seats would be eligible for a broadcast allowance, excluding parties such as the Communist Party and the National Front (Ewing 2007: 179–82). While many small parties (such as the Greens and the British National Party) have unsuccessfully challenged these arrangements, as Ewing (Ibid.: 181) argues, the governing principle is proportionate access, not equal access.

The debate over allocation demonstrates a broad issue at stake over the nature and level of competition in the party system, and the interests of entrenched actors. Smaller political parties complain that the major parties receive too great an allocation of money and time, and are already benefited by a greater proportion of free air-time and media coverage. By contrast, larger parties claim that it is too easy for registered parties to claim access to the broadcasting allocation, therefore diverting resources from 'serious electoral contenders' (Geddis 2007a: 170). An area in which this has caused particular controversy has been the staging and broadcast of political debates.

During the 1988 election, the Green Party of Canada claimed that its constitutional rights had been violated when it was excluded from a televised leaders' debate that included the major parties. The Supreme Court of Ontario failed to grant the Green Party's request to participate, stating that for section 15 of the *Charter* to apply, the Greens must be 'similarly situated with the major parties'. Relying on the decisions of both the broadcast media and the major parties to exclude the Greens on the significance or newsworthiness of their policy pronouncements, the Ontario Supreme Court ruled that the party's constitutional rights had not been violated as the Greens were not similarly situated with the three older parties (Supreme Court of Ontario, Action 32392/88 at 10–11; reported in Courtney 1993: 403–4).

A similar claim was made by an Independent candidate in the United States who had qualified for the ballot in a general election for an Arkansas US House of Representatives seat under the First Amendment of the US Constitution: *Arkansas Educational Television Commission v. Forbes* 523 U.S. 666 (1998). Ralph Forbes sought participation in a televised candidates debate, but was turned down by the state-run station that was organizing it, which had decided to limit the debate to 'major party candidates or any other candidate who had strong popular support' (at 670). Justice Kennedy, writing for the majority of the Supreme Court, dismissed Forbes First Amendment challenge, characterizing the television debate as a 'non-public' forum, due to the fact that the station had provided only selective rather than general access to it (at 679). As such, the station had only a duty to ensure a diversity of views and there was no evidence to suggest that Forbes' political views and manifesto had led to his exclusion (at 682–3).

By contrast, a case launched by two New Zealand incumbent parliamentarians against television network TV3 when it failed to include them as the leaders of two minor political parties (the United Future Party and the Progressive

Coalition) in a multi-party debate was successful.[17] TV3 had used a public opinion poll to rank political parties to determine who should be included in the debate. Unlike the US Supreme Court, the New Zealand High Court ruled that pre-election television debates were conducted very much in the public realm and that TV3's method of selection was unreasonable and arbitrary. It consequently ordered the parliamentarians to be included in the debate (see further Geddis 2007a: 168–9).

Overseeing the Provision of Information to Voters

Another element in the maintenance of free and fair elections is to ensure that voters are not misinformed. This is generally achieved through a combination of regulations prohibiting the publication or broadcast of false and misleading statements, requirements that the publication be authorized or its source disclosed, and common law actions of libel or defamation.

For example, section 199A of the *Electoral Act* 1993 (New Zealand) deems it an offence to publish false statements or influence voters. The *Canada Elections Act* 2000 states that 'no person shall, with the intention of affecting the results of an election, knowingly make or publish any false statement of fact in relation to the personal character or conduct of a candidate or prospective candidate' (s. 91). Similar provisions exist in the United Kingdom[18] and Australia.[19] In 2007, former UK Labour Party councillor, Miranda Grell, was convicted under the *Representation of the People Act* 1983 (UK) for making false statements about another candidate in order to gain electoral advantage. She was fined £1,000, ordered to pay a total of £4,750 in court costs and banned from holding public office for three years (Ahmed 2007; BBC Online News 2007). The conviction was upheld on appeal.

In the United States, redress for these alleged wrongs must be sought by aggrieved candidates through libel laws because, as a general rule, the law seeks to prohibit the censorship or regulation of political comment (UK Electoral Commission 2001: para. 6.11). However, it is extremely difficult for 'public figures' to succeed in civil actions for libel, as the plaintiff must establish that the defendant's comments were made with knowing or reckless disregard for the truth – a very high burden of proof.[20] Consequently, negative or 'attack' advertising has raised significant concerns in US political campaigns, particularly in the publication or broadcast of false or misleading material. To counter this, some states have instituted more creative measures to encourage fair play through creating 'positive examples'. For example, candidates in Texas are encouraged to sign the 'Code of Fair Campaign Practices', in which the candidate pledges (amongst other things) to:

---

17 *Dunne and Anderton v. CanWest TV Works Ltd* [2005] NZAR 577.

18 *Representation of the People Act* 1983 s. 106.

19 *Commonwealth Electoral Act* 1918 s. 329.

20 See *New York Times Co. v. Sullivan* 376 U.S. 254 (1964).

1. Conduct the campaign openly and publicly and limit attacks on my opponent to legitimate challenges to my opponent's record and stated positions on issues.
2. Not use or permit the use of character defamation, whispering campaigns, libel, slander, or scurrilous attacks on any candidate or the candidate's personal or family life.
3. Not use or permit any appeal to negative prejudice based on race, sex, religion, or national origin.
4. Not use campaign material of any sort that misrepresents, distorts, or otherwise falsifies the facts, nor will I use malicious or unfounded accusations that aim at creating or exploiting doubts, without justification, as to the personal integrity or patriotism of my opponent.
5. Not undertake or condone any dishonest or unethical practice that tends to corrupt or undermine our system of free elections or that hampers or prevents the full and free expression of the will of the voters, including any activity aimed at intimidating voters or discouraging them from voting.
6. Defend and uphold the right of every qualified voter to full and equal participation in the electoral process, and will not engage in any activity aimed at intimidating voters or discouraging them from voting.
7. Immediately and publicly repudiate methods and tactics that may come from others that I have pledged not to use or condone. I shall take firm action against any subordinate who violates any provision of this code or the laws governing elections.[21]

Signing the Code is voluntary, but in doing so, candidates may advertise that fact on any of their campaign material. In a similar measure designed to prevent the dissemination of misleading, false or questionable information, the New Zealand Broadcasting Authority has issued the 'Election Programmes Code', which contains standards that apply to the content of election programs (see Geddis 2007a: 165).

Civil law litigation has also been used in cases of political misrepresentation in Canada. In March 2008, Canadian Conservative Prime Minister Stephen Harper filed a $3.5 million lawsuit against his opponents, the Liberal Party, after comments were posted on the Liberal's website alleging Harper had full knowledge of an attempt by Conservative MPs to bribe Independent MP Chuck Cadman in order to secure a budget vote. The suit was dropped in February 2009 after both parties settled the matter, details of which were not disclosed. Such litigation has the potential to be used as a political tool, to cast doubts over the truth of the allegation, in addition to a means of finding civil redress. However, given the expense of such litigation, it is in reality an instrument of regulation that is beyond the reach of most candidates running for elected office.

In Australia, using defamation law as a protection against reputation arising out of false statements made in political advertisements is also problematic, as

21 *Texas Elections Code*, s. 258.001, 'Fair Campaign Practices Act'.

such communications may be protected by a defence of 'qualified privilege'. This defence pertains to statements made to the general public about matters of government, which, by developing and encouraging views upon government, relate to the function of electors in a representative democracy. Although this has not been tested specifically in relation to political advertisements (most cases concern public-interest speech and media reports) – given that the defence covers instances of 'political discussion' relating to the formation of views about government – it is reasonable to suggest that political advertisements pertaining to election campaigns might fall within its scope. A publisher may rely on this defence if the publisher can establish that he/she/it was unaware of the falsity of the statements, that the statements were not published recklessly and that publication was reasonable in the circumstances.[22] A similar defence of qualified privilege exists in the United Kingdom[23] and New Zealand.[24]

In all democracies, election advertisements and broadcasts must reveal the identity of the party or person making the broadcast to the viewing or reading public. This disclosure usually occurs by way of an authorization statement by a candidate or a party's official agent.[25] State regulations in the United States require advertisements to disclose who has paid for the advertisement, and whether it has been authorized by the candidate it seeks to promote or defeat. This strand of regulation goes one step further in Canada, to include the publication and broadcast of survey results, which are also subject to the provision of certain information including the sponsor, sample size, date and margin of error (Forcese and Freeman 2005: 121; *Elections Act* s. 326). The requirement to disclose information about the source and method of surveys was inserted into the *Elections Act* in acknowledgement of the potential for opinion polls to influence voters through what is commonly termed the 'bandwagon effect' (the argument that voters will tend to support the leading party) and past experiences of misleading polls (see Forcese and Freeman 2005: 122–3). The Lortie Commission noted in its Final Report (1991):

> In recent elections, there have been instances of misleading polls, some because of technical errors and others because of partisan misrepresentation. There have even been allegations of fraudulent polls, where the data were said to have to been fabricated to counter a poll showing the opposition in the lead. Such 'bogus' polls and the more common misrepresented poll have been released to the media in many democracies…It is the willingness of the media to report such polls that make them significant and troublesome. (Royal Commission on Electoral Reform and Party Financing 1991: 457; cited in Forcese and Freeman 2005: 122)

22 *Theophanous v. Herald & Weekly Times Ltd* (1994) 182 CLR 104 at 140; *Lange v. Australian Broadcasting Corporation* (1997) CLR 520.

23 *Reynolds v. Times Newspapers Ltd* [2001] 2 AC 127.

24 *Lange v. Atkinson* [2000] 3 NZLR 385.

25 *Canada Elections Act* s 320, *Electoral Act* 1993 (NZ) ss 221, 221A, *Representation of the People Act* 1983 (UK) s. 110, *Commonwealth Electoral Act* 1918 (Australia) s. 328.

It is pertinent to note that election advertising is generally defined to exclude the transmission of debates, speeches, interviews, commentaries and the reporting of news.[26] This provision is necessary so as not to restrict the reporting, comment and analysis of political news events that occur during an election campaign.

Interestingly, the *Canada Elections Act* also bans campaign advertising from outside Canada, and prohibits any attempts by foreigners to influence the Canadian vote (ss 330, 331). Prosecution has twice been threatened against US filmmaker Michael Moore for violating section 331 – once for urging Canadians to vote against the Conservative Party in the 2004 election and again in 2008 for joining an NDP candidate on a campaign visit – however, neither threat came to fruition (see Forcese and Freeman 2005: 123).

Regulating 'New Media'

In recent years, communications tools such as the Internet, mobile/smart phones and email have been increasingly used by both individuals and political parties in election campaigns. The term 'new media' refers to these types of activities, which typically comprise digital, computerized and networked information communications technologies (Flew 2008: 2–3). Yet the use of these technologies in political campaigns remains substantially unregulated.

A key debate concerns whether we might be able to characterize the new media in the same way as the old, and apply existing regulations that pertain to the traditional broadcast media to the Internet. This is what occurred in 2006, when the Supreme Court of Canada ruled that section 329 of the *Elections Act* (prohibiting the reporting of election results until after all polling booths had closed) also covered the Internet and blogs.[27] However, beyond the application of this specific provision, there is an argument that the Internet is more similar to a debate than a broadcast; therefore regulation should remain minimal.

Jurisdictions have typically dealt with the issue in an *ad hoc* way, creating specific legislative amendments when the need arises, usually precipitated by a particular incident. For example, Articles 12320–12323 were inserted into the *California Election Code* by the *California Political Cyberfraud Abatement Act* in 2001. This provisions of this Act are designed to prevent individuals creating websites that look similar to and could be mistaken for those of parties and/or candidates contesting an election, but that could be used to misrepresent or attack their views and candidature. The Act is the only one of its kind in the United States and was passed in response to reports of individuals buying domains similar to the names of candidates or proposition numbers and diverting traffic to white supremacist and other controversial websites.

---

26 See, for example, the *Canada Elections Act* s. 319; *Broadcasting Act* 1989 (NZ) s. 69(1).

27 *R. v. Bryan*, [2007] 1 S.C.R. 527, 2007 SCC 12.

Section 328A of the *Commonwealth Electoral Act* 1918 (Australia) specifically requires paid election advertising material published on the Internet to be authorized. However, the Australian Electoral Commission received a substantial number of complaints relating to the transparency of unpaid advertisements on the Internet, which are not regulated by the provision (Australian Government 2009: para. 10.29). Paid Internet advertisements in the United States are subject to campaign spending limits, and must be authorized by the political party. In 2006, the FEC amended its regulations to include paid Internet advertisements in the definition of 'public communication' after a Columbia District Court ruled that legislation excluding all Internet communication from 'public communication' was impermissible and contrary to the *Bipartisan Campaign Reform Act* 2002.[28]

The relentless pace of technological change is one of the key reasons legislators have been reluctant to impose substantial regulation, for fear of having to significantly change or update regulatory instruments in the near future. Indeed, to keep pace with these developments, regulatory legislation must retain a degree of flexibility. Regulation in this area is also made increasingly difficult by the international/global nature of the Internet, meaning that some offences may transcend national boundaries, issues surrounding freedom of speech and political censorship, and the difficulty of enforcing orders such as the removal of offending material from websites.

Conclusion

Although the style and manner by which electoral campaigns are fought by parties has changed dramatically over time, from personalized local campaigns to the use of television media and the Internet as tools for widespread coverage of parties' and candidates' messages, the issues pertaining to the regulation of parties in the electoral contest remain largely the same. The ultimate aim of any legal regime is to provide for fair competition between the various contestants. There are several ways in which the law seeks to do this: by regulating candidates' interactions with voters so as to eliminate the possibility of corruption or political favours; to regulate parties' access to the media by providing for proportionate shares of media usage; to control how the media is used and what information is provided – for example, by restricting parties' ability to disseminate false or misleading claims about their opponents. In this general area of party law, we see a remarkable similarity between democracies in their general approach to regulation, indicating that the principle of free and fair elections is indeed a universal democratic norm.

28 *Shays v. Federal Election Commission*, 337 F. Supp. 2d 28 (D.D.C. 2004) aff'd, 414 F. 3d 76 (D.C. Cir. 2005).

Chapter 7
The Public Funding of Election Campaigns and Political Parties

In this chapter I present a comparative analysis of the extent to which states support the activities of political parties through the provision of public funding. The first section of the chapter analyses the theoretical explanations provided in the political science literature for the emergence of public funding as a significant resource for political parties, and the consequent impact this has had on parties' organizational capacities. Secondly, the chapter outlines the various comparative regimes that exist to provide public funding for parties' activities in election campaigns. While all states surveyed provide for some support for parties' activities (whether this be financial or in the allocation of goods and/or services), only Canada and Australia provide for the direct and unconditional funding of election expenses.[1] I look at the rationale behind these regimes and some of the criticisms that have emerged, particularly the tendency for public funding regimes to privilege the interests of major party actors. In the third section, I move beyond public financing that specifically relates to election campaigns to an examination of more general sources of income for parties that are sourced from the state, for example, the use of parliamentary funds and tax subsidies on donations for political parties.

Why Public Funding?

The public funding of the activities of political parties is a relatively new phenomenon, which is inextricably linked to the evolution of parties as electoral actors, social attitudes towards the importance of these bodies, and their ongoing participatory and representative roles in modern democracies. Political finance laws and public subsidies also mark a crucial intersection between the regulation of political party competition in the context of election contests, and the potential impact and often unintended consequences that this external regulation might otherwise have for the internal affairs and organizational structure of political parties. There is a substantial body of literature on the consequences of funding regimes for the internal financial organization and management of parties, and in particular, their relationship to

1 Public funding is provided for presidential candidates in the US and in some states, but this is subject to candidates agreeing to abide by expenditure limits.

the state.[2] A common theme amongst these studies is that while public funding was introduced to encourage equality amongst parties in the electoral arena given the high financial cost of representative democracy, it also marks a shift in the resources that political parties are dependent upon. As I will argue throughout this chapter, this changing reliance on different patterns of resources has significant implications for the organizational structure of political parties, not only in their internal financial management, but also in the way in which they undertake campaigning activities and their character as participatory organizations.

In those democracies where it is provided, the public funding of political parties was introduced from around the 1970s onwards, which coincided with the emergence of the electoral professional party (see Chapter 2). Previously, mass parties had relied upon a large individual membership to provide a steady stream of income through the collection of membership dues and fund-raising efforts, and upon donations from affiliated trade unions and other interest groups. What could not be collected as income for the party from its members and affiliates was supplemented by way of volunteer labour. Before the emergence of the mass party, cadre or elite parties (those parties built around prominent politicians with a relatively small social support base) would typically obtain financial support from contributions made by private enterprise or wealthy individuals (van Biezen 2004: 701). These sources of party funding, whether they came from organized interests, or individuals, were both reflective and constitutive of the conception of political parties as private and voluntary associations belonging squarely within the realm of civil society (van Biezen 2008a).

However, party scholars have argued that the growing reliance by political parties on the use of public funds to finance their activities has resulted in a prominent shift in the internal power structure of parties away from the rank-and-file membership or the party's supporters, towards the legislative arm of the party (the party in public office). Nowhere is this organizational adaptation more pronounced than in the 'cartel party' thesis, discussed previously in Chapter 2.[3] Indeed, the cartel party thesis has prompted comparative party scholars to re-examine the relationship between parties and the state. In organizational terms, the evolution of the cartel party has been characterized by an increasing dependence on the state to provide material resources and legitimacy in lieu of those once provided by mass memberships and civil society. This change has suitably been described as the transformation of political parties from private voluntary associations to 'public utilities' (Epstein 1986: 157; van Biezen 2004: 705).

---

2 See, for example, van Biezen (2008b, 2004), Austin and Tjernström (2003), Pinto-Duschinsky (2002); Koole (2001); Nassmacher (2001); Gunlicks (1993); Ewing (2007, 1987); Epstein (1986).

3 Katz and Mair (2009, 1995); but see also Lambert and Jansen (2007); Young (1998); Nassmacher (1989, 1993); Jenson (1991); Panebianco (1988).

From a regulatory perspective, the trend towards parties' utilization of public funds has provided the catalyst for a 'particular conception of democracy and political parties, in which parties are increasingly seen as an essential *public good* for democracy' (van Biezen 2004: 702, emphasis added), which as we have seen in the previous chapters of this volume, has been used by scholars and courts alike to justify the increased regulation of parties' external and internal activities. State funding and the regulation that typically accompanies it may also be used strategically to engineer a particular type of party organizational model. If political parties have now 'transcended the mass membership party' model, conditional state funding could be used 'strategically to encourage the parties to recruit members and engage people in the political process' (Ewing and Issacharoff 2006: 5). Nevertheless, state funding could also be used to structure a pattern of party competition that privileges major parties at the expense of minor parties, by directing resources towards entrenched or established interests rather than new players.

But why have these changes occurred? The political science literature on party financing and the public funding of election campaigns reveals four key motivating factors: public perceptions of political parties as important democratic actors, the increasing cost of democracy, a concern with the equality of party competition in the electoral contest, and a desire to mitigate against the potential negative and/or corrupt influence of private money in politics.

As van Biezen (2004: 702) argues, 'the increasingly prominent role of the state in party funding should be interpreted in the context of an ideational transformation concerning the place of political parties in modern democracy'. In contrast to the public perceptions of parties as divisive factions in the era in which many constitutions were drafted and which marked the emergence of stable party systems, political parties have now become viewed as institutions that are a necessary component of representative democracy (Dalton and Weldon 2005: 933). For example, in introducing one of the most extensive schemes for the public funding of elections of the democracies surveyed in this research, the Australian Joint Standing Committee on Electoral Reform recognized that 'political parties play a vital role in the working of democratic government. Indeed one of the central characteristics of democracy is that there should be parties competing for the right to govern' (JSCER 1983: 152). Similarly, the Report of the Royal Commission into the NZ Electoral System recommended the adoption of public funding of political parties on the ground that 'political parties are too important to be left to starve' (Wallace 1986: 217).

The second justification for the introduction of public funding regimes concerns the increasing cost of electoral democracy and campaigning, coupled with political parties' shrinking income from traditional sources such as membership dues and donations from affiliated organizations. Volunteer labour, in the form of party memberships, has also been declining over the decades as citizens become increasingly disengaged from political parties. As the Joint Committee on Electoral Reform posited:

> Public funding will also relieve all parties new and established from the constant round of fund raising and allow them to concentrate on discussion of issues of local and national concern and development of policy responses to these problems *which is more appropriately the role of political parties*. (JSCER 1983: 155, emphasis added)

When legislating for such regimes, political parties in favour of public funding have relied on a slightly different set of justifications that focuses predominantly on fair and equal competition between political parties in the electoral arena (Gunlicks 1993: 5). For example, in promoting the introduction of public funding for parties' election expenses in Australia in the mid-1980s, the Australian Labor Party relied on three key arguments: that elections should be decided on the basis of policy rather than a party's financial resources, that public funding would encourage equality in electoral competition by narrowing the discrepancy in the resource base amongst Australian parties, and third, that public funding would reduce reliance on private contributions and hence minimizing the potential for political corruption (Orr 2006b: 104).

The salience of these justifications depends in large part, on the political party concerned. Public funding regimes would no doubt benefit social democratic parties such as the Australian Labor Party, which has seen a significant decline in its grassroots membership and contributions from affiliated unions. Public finance would also aid political parties (such as minor or new and emerging parties) that might not be able to successfully tap into the resources of private contributions, may not have links to affiliated organizations, or might not otherwise appeal to wealthy or established interests through a broad political programme (van Biezen 2004: 707). In contrast, public funding regimes have traditionally been opposed by political parties that have always been advantaged by their relatively strong access to private funds and donations. So whilst the Australian Labor Party advocated the introduction of public funding for parties, the Liberal Party of Australia (a conservative party with strong links to business interests) opposed it and instead advocated a system of tax credits (or deductions) for donations to political parties, thereby encouraging a private system of party funding. A similar pattern of opposition/support emerged in Canada and raises potential constitutional questions about the partisan character of the legislation involved (see Feasby 2007). Where public subsidies involve corresponding restrictions on parties' spending and fund-raising activities, they also need to be balanced against associational rights of autonomy – in particular, parties' desire to raise as much funds as they can in order to support their political activities.

A final argument presented in favour of public funding that has been advocated in all the democracies included in this research is the potential of public funding to mitigate the influence of private contributions and their potentially distorting effect on the operation of representative democracy through minimizing corruption. Bound up with this justification is a general concern that private money might come to unduly influence the actions and opinions of political parties and consequently, legislators (see, for example, Forcese and Freeman 2005: 100; van Biezen 2004: 707).

Table 7.1 Direct Public Funding of Political Parties

State	Reimbursement of election expenses	Annual subsidy	Broadcasting allocation
Australia	Yes. $2.25 (AUD) per eligible vote received. $42 million paid in 2004 election.	No	Yes
Canada	Yes. Reimbursement of 50 per cent of election expenses. $24.5 million (CA) provided in 2006 election.	Yes. $1.75 (CA) multiplied by number of votes in previous election. $28 million provided in 2008.	Yes
New Zealand	No	No	Yes
United Kingdom	No	Yes. Parties with parliamentary representation eligible for share of £2 million policy development fund.	Yes
United States	Optional federal funding (also provided in some states) if candidates agree to adhere to spending limits.	No	No

The Public Funding of Parties and Election Campaigns

In this section I outline the various public funding regimes in place in Australia, Canada, New Zealand, the United Kingdom and the United States. Australia and Canada are by far the most generous democracies in the provision of direct public funds to parties, whereas the United Kingdom, New Zealand and the United States prefer to regulate party finance through measures targeting the receipt of private contributions and electoral expenditure. A summary of the main features of direct public funding is outlined in Table 7.1.

Australia

The Australian system of public funding for election campaigns was introduced in 1983 by a newly elected Labor government, and subsequent to an extensive parliamentary enquiry conducted by the Joint Select Committee on Electoral Reform.[4] According to the Joint Select Committee's Report, the rationale of the scheme was to 'assist parties in financial difficulties; to lessen corruption; to avoid excessive reliance upon 'special interests' and institutional sources of finance; to equalize opportunities between the parties, and; to stimulate political education and research' (JSCER 1983: 153–4).

4 *Commonwealth Electoral Legislation Amendment Act* 1983 (Cth). See further Orr (2003).

The provisions of the funding regime are now found in the *Commonwealth Electoral Act* 1918 (sections 287–321A). The system is based on a post-election reimbursement of parties' electoral and campaigning expenses, calculated on the basis of their popular vote for both houses of Parliament. It is important to note that political parties must be registered with the Australian Electoral Commission in order to receive any reimbursement on their election expenditure (see Chapter 4). Nominated party candidates for election to the House of Representatives who receive more than 4 per cent of the formal first-preference vote in a federal election or by-election are entitled to receive public funding. Similarly, parties contesting a Senate election who receive 4 per cent or more of the vote in any given election are entitled to public election funding. The overall funding entitlement is calculated by multiplying the number of formal first-preference votes received by the funding rate, which is reviewed each six months in line with increases in the consumer price index. The current rate (1 July 2010–31 December 2010) is 231.191 cents per eligible vote. Other than election funding and the provision of parliamentary and broadcast allowances (discussed below), there is no ongoing funding directly provided to Australian political parties (for example, yearly allowances).

The regime of public funding of political parties in Australia has been criticized for perpetuating inequality between political actors (see, for example, Young and Tham 2006; Orr 2006b: 115–16; Tham 2003: 120). By virtue of the voting and popular support thresholds that parties must meet and the fact that funding is retrospective, monetary and other resources derived from the state (election funding, parliamentary entitlements and broadcasting allocations) tend to favour the two major and entrenched parties – the Liberal/National Coalition and the Australian Labor Party. As Young and Tham contend, the bigger picture of political finance in Australia is 'one of institutional rules designed to protect the joint interests of the major parties by arming them with far greater war chests than minor parties and new competitors' – although the authors concede that while electoral competition does exist, 'it is largely confined to the major parties, with players outside this cartel disabled by financial disadvantages' (2006: ix). For example, in the 2004 federal election, of a total of $41.9 million that was paid to eligible political parties and candidates, $37.7 million (or 90 per cent) was allocated to the two major party groupings (AEC 2005: 2–4).

Although small political parties may be disadvantaged in the distribution of public funding after elections, this source of income still makes up a significant proportion of their overall funding. As Table 7.2 illustrates, between 2000 and 2003 (one complete electoral cycle), the income provided by the state constituted over 30 per cent of the two minor parties' incomes (the Australian Democrats and the Greens), but only around 18 per cent for those of the major political parties. This suggests that a pattern of inequality is perpetuated in all spheres of party funding, and that these small parties have even greater difficulty in securing funds from private sources than do the major political groupings. It also means that a poor performance in a given election has severe financial consequences for a minor

Table 7.2 Public and Total Funding of Australian Political Parties, 2000–03

Party	Public funding ($AUD)	Total funding ($AUD)	Proportion public funding (%)
Australian Democrats	2,629,249	7,749,674	33.9
Australian Labor Party	24,798,651	132,147,768	18.6
Green Party	2,044,583	6,438,504	31.8
Liberal Party	21,012,402	120,178,248	17.5
National Party	4,850,000	25,140,003	19.3

Source: Sawer, Abjorensen and Larkin (2009: 113).

party, which has less capacity to absorb reductions in party funding. For example, in the 2001 federal election the Australian Democrats polled 7.3 per cent of the vote for the Senate and 5.4 per cent in the House of Representatives and received over $2.6 million in public funding. However, in the next election (2004) the party polled 2.1 per cent in the Senate vote and an average of 1.2 per cent for the House. Consequently the party received only $8,491 in public funding (AEC 2005: 3) and this proved to be a major contributor to the party's subsequent organizational and electoral decline.

As Orr (2006b: 105) notes, it is misleading to use the term 'reimbursement' with respect to the public funding regime in Australia, which actually provides funding (provided that parties have met the vote threshold) by way of right. It is not necessary to prove that actual expenditure has occurred, and this has subsequently raised fears that a political party or organized group contesting an election with minimal campaigning costs might actually be able to profit from an election campaign. The public funding scheme in Australia originally began on the basis of reimbursement, but this was altered after both the Australian Electoral Commission and the political parties found it too administratively burdensome (see Orr 2006b: 105). Beyond concerns that parties might profit at the expense of the public purse from contesting elections, once they have been obtained, there is no restriction placed upon political parties as to how they should use these funds. As Young and Tham note (2006: 14), there is very little public information about how this money is spent, although the bulk of available evidence suggests that it is allocated to electioneering, particularly advertising. This raises a key issue as to whether or not the public funds allocated to political parties ought to be directed in any particular way.

Canada

The *Canada Elections Act* 2000 provides for a comparatively comprehensive regime for the disclosure of parties' financing arrangements, limits on political contributions and expenditures, and the provision of public funding to electoral

Table 7.3 Quarterly Allowances for Registered Canadian Political Parties, 2008 ($CA)

Registered political party	Total paid ($CA)
Bloc Québécois	3,017,092
Conservative Party of Canada	10,439,132
Green Party of Canada	1,289,951
Liberal Party of Canada	8,701,263
New Democratic Party	5,030,293
Total	28,477,731

Source: Elections Canada.

actors (I discuss contribution limits and disclosure provisions in Chapter 8).[5] As in the Australian case, political parties seeking public funds must meet a minimum threshold of electoral support. Candidates can receive a reimbursement of up to 60 per cent of their electoral expenses provided they poll at least 10 per cent of the votes in their electorate. Registered Canadian political parties are eligible for a refund of 50 per cent of their election expenses if they receive at least 2 per cent of the valid votes cast nationally or at least 5 per cent of the valid votes cast in the electoral districts where the party endorsed a candidate.[6] This funding is in addition to an annual subsidy of $1.75 multiplied by the number of votes the party received in the previous election, adjusted for inflation.[7] The Act introducing these measures also limited corporate and union donations (which have subsequently been banned in Canada), but as Lambert and Jansen (2007: 3) note, the public subsidies now provided to Canadian political parties now more than make up for this shortfall.

The total amount of annual funding directed towards political parties in 2008 is shown in Table 7.3. Compared to Australian political parties, Canadian parties fare quite well – bringing in a total of $28.4 million in funding compared to an average yearly income of $18.4 million that was spent on all the Australian parties between 2000 and 2003 (including election reimbursements). The generosity of the Canadian subsidies has been a point of criticism (see, for example, Forcese and Freeman 2005: 115; Cross 2004: 156); however, it is in relation to the limits on donations and campaign expenditure that these subsidies need to be understood.

Table 7.4 illustrates the amount that was reimbursed to party-endorsed candidates at the 2006 election. In addition to the yearly allowances, a further $24 million was added to parties' coffers by the taxpayer to cover election expenses. These subsidies have an impact on the organizational structure of Canadian parties in the sense that they are 'primarily directed at parties' and paid to their central

5 See Feasby (2007) for an excellent analysis of the current provisions and their historical and contextual development.

6 *Canada Elections Act* 2000 s. 435.

7 *Canada Elections Act* ss 435, 435.01.

Table 7.4 Reimbursement of Candidates' Election Expenses by Party Affiliation for the 39th General Election, 23 January 2006

Political affiliation	Reimbursement	
	Number of candidates	Total amount of reimbursement ($CA)
Bloc Québécois	73	2,465,134
Conservative Party of Canada	303	9,665,403
Green Party of Canada	6	51,011
Independent	2	76,002
Liberal Party of Canada	283	8,757,665
New Democratic Party	214	3,534,111
No Affiliation	1	46,280
Total	882	24,595,606

Source: Elections Canada.

offices – thus leaving individual candidates and electoral district associations with a shortfall in their expenditures, and 'concentrating resources within parties and their leadership' (Forcese and Freeman 2005: 115).

There is evidence to suggest that the provision of public subsidies might be turning Canadian parties into 'wards of the state' (Cross 2004: 156). Lambert and Jansen found that although a significant proportion of all parties' revenue is derived from state sources, two of the smaller parties – the Greens and Bloc Québécois – are over-reliant on state sources of funding (70–80 per cent of their total income between 2004 and 2006). This finding mirrors the Australian case with respect to the Australian Democrats and the Greens. However, although this may indicate increased reliance on the state, it could also be interpreted as providing a challenge to one key aspect of the cartelization thesis: that minor parties are prevented from establishing themselves as key electoral and parliamentary actors owing to funding regimes that privilege established players. While in absolute monetary terms this may be the case, in relative terms these smaller parties derive a greater percentage of their income from state sources than do the major players. On the other hand, it could also indicate that these smaller parties may have also become part of the cartel.

Although it is lower than Australia, the electoral threshold that Canadian political parties must meet in order to receive partial reimbursement on their electoral expenses constitutes 'a significant barrier' and in the 2000 general election (when the threshold was set at 15 per cent in an electoral district), a majority of candidates failed to achieve the necessary votes to be eligible for financial support (Feasby 2006: 254). The Canadian legislature has altered the threshold numerous times, but the dominance of the major political parties and the maintenance of the current party system appears to be a significant factor mitigating against expanding electoral competition. For example, prior to the 2004 general election, the candidate threshold was dropped from 15 per cent to 10 per cent of votes in an electoral district, contrary to the Chief Electoral Officer's recommendation that it should be set at 5 per cent. According to Feasby (2006: 256):

> The apparent reason for setting the threshold at 10 per cent was that in the five party system that prevailed in 2003 when the amendments were adopted, the government believed that at that level *most major party candidates would stand a good chance of qualifying for reimbursement.*[8] (emphasis added)

The district threshold for parties was lowered to 5 per cent in 2003.[9] In the 2006 general election, this meant that 882 of the 1,636 registered party candidates (54 per cent) were eligible for reimbursement. However, this is still only a very small majority.

Nevertheless, both the funding regime and the associated threshold have been upheld by the Canadian courts. An unsuccessful challenge to the threshold was attempted following the 1988 general election by a failed New Democratic Party candidate, Barrette, who fell short of the 15 per cent threshold of that time, obtaining only 11.89 per cent of the vote in his electorate.[10] Although the trial judge held that the partial reimbursement scheme was contrary to section 3 of the *Charter* in denying candidates equal opportunities in contesting elections – the threshold 'tends to discourage some serious candidates for election from conducting an effective campaign, for fear of incurring costs that may or may not be subsidized by the government'[11] – this decision was later overturned on appeal. Writing the judgment of the Court of Appeal, McCarthy JA characterized the purpose of the disclosure threshold as to discourage the proliferation of parties and candidates and subsequently claimed that 'no one suggests that that purpose as such interferes with the rights guaranteed by section 3',[12] and thereby felt it unnecessary to examine the threshold in light of that section (see Feasby 2006: 257). Furthermore, McCarthy JA held that the legislation's compatibility with section 15 was the relevant issue for determination:[13]

---

8 37th Parliament, 2nd Session, Standing Committee on Procedure and House Affairs (3 April 2003) at 1210.

9 Bill C-24, *An Act to amend the Canada Elections Act and the Income Tax Act (political financing)* (S.C. 2003, c. 19).

10 *Barrette v. Canada (Attorney General)* (1992) 14 CRR (2d) 166 (Que Sup Ct); *Barrette v. Canada (Attorney General)* (1995) 123 DLR (4th) 623 (Que CA).

11 *Barrette v. Canada (Attorney General)* (1992) 14 CRR (2d) 166 at 182.

12 *Barrette v. Canada (Attorney General)* (1995) 123 DLR (4th) 623 at 625. Section 3 of the *Charter* provides that 'every citizen of Canada has the right to vote in an election of the members of the House of Commons or of a legislative assembly and to be qualified for membership therein'.

13 Section 15 of the *Charter* provides that 'every individual is equal before and under the law and has the right to the equal protection and equal benefit of the law without discrimination …'

> I am unable to see in the 15 per cent threshold for partial reimbursement of election expenses any discriminatory purpose or effect within the meaning of section 15 of the *Charter*. Unsuccessful candidates who do not obtain at least 15 per cent of the valid votes cast are not, in my view, a 'discrete and insular minority'. Nor are they a 'disadvantaged group in Canadian society'. If the 15 per cent threshold discriminates against them, such discrimination is not based on any analogous ground. For the same reasons, the 15 per cent threshold involves no prohibited discrimination against voters who, if they are more fully informed, might vote differently. (at 628)

Commentators have suggested that in light of the Canadian Supreme Court's decision in *Figueroa*, which determined that section 3 is the correct section of the *Charter* by which to determine equality issues in relation to the democratic process, the Court of Appeal's decision in *Barrette* is 'plainly wrong' (see Feasby 2006: 258). However, the legislation has not since been challenged.

New Zealand

By contrast with Australia and Canada, New Zealand has a very limited system of public funding for political parties, which has led to claims that 'the state fails to give adequate support to the election campaigns of political parties, thereby leaving the parties too reliant on sources of private funding' (Geddis 2006b: 30). The direct public funding of political parties in New Zealand is restricted to a broadcasting allocation, which is discussed in further detail below. Comparatively, however, New Zealand election campaigns are relatively cheap events (Geddis 2006b: 13; 2007b: 4). For example, in the 2008 general election, the 21 political parties that were registered to contest the election spent only $14 million between them.

In 1986, the Royal Commission into the Electoral System Report (Wallace 1986) recommended that the direct state funding of political parties be introduced and administered according to a sliding scale based on voter support in the electorates contested. It also suggested that the Broadcasting Corporation should continue to allocate free airtime to parties at elections. It stated that (at paras 8.121–8.122):

> Given the meager resources available to them, New Zealand's political parties are to be congratulated on the manner and efficiency with which they have managed their financial affairs. For the most part, our parties have met their financial needs from small donations from their members and supporters. By concentrating on the establishment and cultivation of large membership bases, the parties have avoided relying on substantial contributions from either the State or a limited number of large institutions or corporations. This has had beneficial effects, both in terms of high political participation by ordinary New Zealanders and in terms of the responsiveness and representativeness of the parties themselves.

> We consider, however, that … the extent to which ordinary party members and supporters can meet the sophisticated and costly requirements of parties in a modern democracy such as New Zealand is severely limited. Our parties should be able to operate not just as electoral machines, but also as vehicles through which ideas may be discussed and sound policies developed. If and when elected to Government, political parties are expected to implement the policies and programmes developed when in Opposition … the tasks of Government have become increasingly complex in recent years. If the parties' policies and programmes are inappropriate or poorly researched, either the quality of Government will suffer or the people may be denied the implementation of policies for which they voted. In view of the functions that they are expected to fulfill, the incomes and expenditures on which our political parties operate are modest in the extreme. While it is no bad thing for them to be lean and hungry, political parties are too important to be left to starve.

The justifications for public funding in the Wallace Report are similar to those advocated in Australia. Rather than acting as a mechanism to combat corruption, public funding would allow political parties to get on with the 'real' functions they perform in modern democracy – not fund raising – but policy development and implementation. The report also acknowledged the organizational changes occurring within political parties that would make their future reliance on traditional sources of income unsustainable. However, it is interesting to compare the normative role of political parties outlined in the Royal Commission's Report (as participatory institutions), with suggestions that the public funding of political parties has the indirect effect of concentrating power in the party hierarchy and insulating the political party from civil society and its grassroots support base, as the cartel party theorists would advocate.

Regardless of whether or not the Royal Commission's recommendations would have instituted a 'form of taxpayer funding that does not encourage the direct, voluntary participation of party members and supporters' (Geddis 2006b: 31), the recommendation for establishing a scheme of public funding for parties was not included in the *Electoral Act* 1993. This was primarily because the Electoral Reform Bill, as it was introduced into Parliament by the National Party for debate before the binding referendum took place, did not include matters considered by the National cabinet to be 'extraneous and contentious' – a category under which the state funding of political parties fell (Jackson and McRobie 1998: 139–40). However, increasing public assistance to political parties is a reform agenda that remains a part of public debate in New Zealand, and has been floated as a potential remedy to the misuse of parliamentary funding for party-political purposes that has become endemic in New Zealand politics in recent years (see Geddis 2007b: 7; NZ Ministry of Justice 2009).

The United Kingdom

Like New Zealand, political parties in the United Kingdom are not provided with any direct state funding, either as an annual subsidy or as a reimbursement for the expenses incurred during an election campaign. The issue of the public funding of campaigns and parties has been debated in Parliament, but has been rejected several times.

In 1976, the Houghton Commission recommended that the public funding of elections and political parties be introduced (Houghton 1976).[14] This funding was to be allocated on the basis of vote share at the previous election, to both national political organizations and to candidates at the constituency level so as to counterbalance any centralization that may occur if money was to flow directly to the national level of the party (Ghaleigh 2006: 39). The minority position advocated the view that parties were an essential part of civil society, distinctly separate from the affairs of the state and hence should be free from its regulation: 'direct state aid would breach the established British constitutional practice that organisation for political ends is a strictly voluntary activity'.[15] Furthermore, the minority regarded it as 'mistaken and possibly dangerous to suggest that any work can be required of a political party' by anyone other than its members, including the state and Parliament.[16]

The second major investigation into party funding and the operation of the electoral system, undertaken by the Home Affairs Select Committee, recommended that no major changes take place in the way in which parties were funded (Fisher 1997: 235). The committee reported in 1994, but could not agree upon a unanimous position as the Conservatives preferred the status quo, while the Labour Party advocated state funding. This outcome is typical again of the pattern of partisan support that has characterized the advocacy and subsequent adoption of direct public funding measures.

The passing of the *Political Parties, Elections and Referendums Act* 2000 (PPERA) marked a substantial revision and consolidation of the British law in relation to the legislative regulation of political parties. While the Act established financial reporting requirements and a disclosure regime that is discussed further in Chapter 8, the Act did not provide for a wholesale system for the public funding of political parties. Rather, the provision of public funds to parties remains *ad hoc* and includes miscellaneous provisions such as an allocation of free broadcasting time, providing free postage to one address per elector to candidates in an election campaign,[17] free access to public buildings during campaign periods[18] and the provision of parliamentary allowances to parliamentary parties and individual parliamentarians.[19]

The case for state funding in the United Kingdom has been, and still is, very much based on a functional analysis of the perceived role of parties in the country's

---

14 Lord Houghton, *Report of the Committee on Financial Aid to Political Parties*, London, HMSO 1976.

15 *Report of the Committee on Financial Aid to Political Parties* at 78.

16 *Report of the Committee on Financial Aid to Political Parties* at 75.

17 *Representation of the People Act* 1983 s. 91.

18 *Representation of the People Act* 1983 s. 95. See Ewing (2007: 178–9).

19 Discussed below, see p. 158–62.

system of representative democracy. The Committee of Standards of Public Life (CSPL) investigated the possibility of the public funding of political parties, but rejected the notion that a 'new system should be introduced whereby the state is obliged for the indefinite future to provide financial support for the political parties' (CSPL 1998: recommendation 36). Rather, the committee advocated bolstering the policy capacity of political parties through the development of an initiative unique to the United Kingdom – the Policy Development Fund – a total pool of £2 million distributed annually to registered parties with parliamentary representation for the sole purpose of policy development. In part, the fund was designed to address the perception that 'the political parties themselves should be one of the major sources of ideas in British politics. They are not always so at present' (CSPL 1998: para. 7.25; see also Ewing 2007: 190–91). More fundamentally, the British experience raises the issue of targeted state support for political parties towards what have been described as functional or 'essential infrastructural purposes', rather than campaigning activities (Ghaleigh 2006: 56).

The Neill Committee on Standards in Public Life also recommended that donations over a certain amount be declared, that foreign donations be banned, that general election spending be limited to £20 million per party (in 1997 they spent over £25 million), that tax relief be provided for donations up to £500, and that provisions be made so unregistered third parties could spend up to £25,000 and registered third parties up to £1 million in a general election campaign (CSPL 1998). While the PPERA implemented many of these recommendations (including a spending cap, the policy development fund and a disclosure regime), there was notably, however, no tax relief granted for small donations. These provisions are discussed in greater detail below, and in Chapter 8.

The United States

Public funding in the United States has traditionally taken a backseat to private money in election campaigns. In 1974, amendments to the *Federal Campaign Act* introduced a system of public funding for presidential primaries and elections in reaction to Watergate; the Presidential Election Campaign Fund to support this expenditure was set up in 1976. However, in receiving state funding, candidates have had to adhere to expenditure limits and as such the scheme has reduced in popularity with the major party presidential candidates. It was not used by either Barack Obama or John McCain in the 2008 presidential election. Furthermore, although Congress has considered public funding for congressional campaigns from as early as the 1950s, reforms have not yet been enacted.

There is, however, some democratic experimentation at the state level. Several states (including Arizona, Maine, Massachusetts and Vermont) have enacted 'clean elections' reforms that provide for public funding of candidates' election expenses provided they adhere to limits on expenditure. Many more states provide for the partial funding of political campaigns and organizations (see Malbin and Gais 1998). In other states, voters have been more reluctant to finance parties' and candidates' election activities. For example, clean elections reforms have been defeated in polls put to the voters in California in 2006 (Proposition 89) and Alaska in 2008. A further obstacle to the implementation of public funding schemes in the US is constitutional. Given the inherent connection that the Supreme Court has found between electoral expenditure and the freedom of speech guaranteed under the First Amendment, any reforms that impose expenditure limits or assist competitors by providing matching state funds to counter private contributions would raise significant constitutional questions.[20]

Political Broadcasting

The legal regulation of political broadcasting was discussed in depth in Chapter 6. Nevertheless, it is useful to reiterate here that the provision of free air-time to political parties on either public or private broadcasters constitutes another important indirect source of public funding for political parties' election and campaigning activities. Research conducted in the United States and the United Kingdom has suggested that the public provision of broadcasting time (or television broadcasts in general) is of the most value to smaller political parties, which in general receive less attention in mainstream news coverage than their major party counterparts (UK Electoral Commission 2001: 26).

Australia, Canada, New Zealand and the United Kingdom provide their registered parties with access to a mix of public and private broadcasting resources for the purpose of election campaigning. The value of this free time may be quite substantial. For example, the value of the broadcasting allocation in New Zealand for the 2008 general election amounted to a total of $3.212 million (Elections NZ 2009: 4). Given that the total expenditure of all 21 registered political parties for the 2008 election was $14 million, the broadcast allowance represents a significant proportion of the total spent (approximately 18 per cent). In the 1997 UK general election, party-political broadcasts were estimated to be worth £20 million each to the Conservatives and Labour, and £16 million to the Liberal Democrats (CSPL 1998: para. 13.18).

Despite the financial value of these broadcasts, the actual impact of public election broadcasting on audiences is more difficult to discern. In Australia, the two public broadcasters (the Australian Broadcasting Corporation (ABC) and the Special Broadcasting Service (SBS)) are required to provide free broadcast time to political parties during an election campaign as part of their public information charters (Orr 2006b: 106). However, given the limited audience reach of these networks – Orr reports that they receive a combined audience share of around 17 per cent – their political impact is arguably limited. In contrast, the audience

20 See, for example, *McComish v. Bennett* (15 January 2010) in which the Arizona Supreme Court proposed an order finding sections of Arizona's state funding laws that relate to matching funds provisions invalid.

share of the broadcasters required to carry party-political broadcasts in the United Kingdom remains above 80 per cent, even with the proliferation of commercial and additional digital channels (UK Electoral Commission 2001: 20). However, research conducted by the ITC (Independent Television Commission) found that when a party election advertisement or programme was broadcast, 57 per cent of viewers switched the channel or turned the television off (ITC 2001). Much of this may have to do with the format and style of the presentation, which is largely the prerogative of the individual political parties and how much they wish to spend on producing the broadcast. In any case, the extent to which party-political broadcasts engage the viewing public is a matter of debate.

Taxation Arrangements

Another source of public funding for political parties are the subsidies that apply by way of taxation provisions that provide credits or deductions against income tax for donations made to political parties up to a certain prescribed amount.[21] Such provisions have the overall effect of encouraging private donations to political parties, but in turn these donations are subsidized by state taxation revenue. Taxation subsidization schemes currently exist in Canada, Australia and the United States, and have been floated as a potential campaign finance reform in New Zealand (see Geddis 2002a: 191–3). They have not secured popular support in the United Kingdom although they were favoured by the reports of the Neill Committee (Committee for Standards of Public Life)[22] and the Electoral Commission[23] (Ewing 2007: 191–4; Ghaleigh 2006: 39–40, 54).

The law in this area is currently undergoing significant revision in Australia, reflecting the change of governing party in 2007. Until recently, contributions to registered political parties or membership fees of up to $1,500 per annum by both individuals and businesses were eligible for income tax deductions.[24] In February 2008, the Australian Labor Party government introduced the Tax Laws Amendment (2008 Measures No. 1) Bill into Parliament, which sought to repeal the tax deductibility of political contributions provision, in line with the party's long-held policy on this issue.[25] Although the tax deductibility regime has always favoured the Labor Party's

21 For a brief global overview of taxation subsidies, see Nassmacher (2006: 449–50).

22 See the report of the Neill Committee (1998) *The Funding of Political Parties in Britain* (Cmnd 4057, 1998), recommendations 38 and 39.

23 *The Funding of Political Parties in the United Kingdom* (1998) (Cmnd 4057) at 6.44ff.

24 *Income Tax Assessment Act* 1997 (Cth) s. 30-15; Australian Taxation Office, Determination 92/114. This level was raised by the conservative Liberal/National Party coalition government in 2006 from the previous cap of $100 per income year: *Electoral and Referendum (Electoral Integrity and Other Measures) Act* 2006 (Cth).

25 Australian Labor Party *National Platform and Constitution 2004*, Article 16.37; JSCEM (1989: 91).

main opposition rival, the Liberal Party, it is interesting to note that the decision to end the tax-deductible status of donations to political parties was publicized by the ALP in rather neutral terms, as part of the 'Government's saving strategy' in the face of the global financial crisis – a measure reported to have saved $31.4 million dollars in 2009–10[26] – and arguably obscuring what might have otherwise been seen as a political agenda to shore up the party's financial position against its closest rival. The Tax Laws Amendment Bill came under significant challenge in the Parliament; an amended version, the Tax Laws Amendment (Political Contributions and Gifts) Bill 2008 – which restores tax deductions available to individuals in their personal capacity but removes the tax deduction available for businesses, companies and sole traders – has been passed by the House of Representatives but is currently awaiting further debate in the Australian Senate.

In Canada, tax credits are provided on contributions to political parties and candidates up to a maximum donation of $1,275. The rationale behind this regime is to encourage smaller contributions from a larger number of sources. Hence there is a sliding scale on the value of the tax credit as a proportion of the contribution: 75 per cent up to the first $400 contributed; 50 per cent for $400–750; 33.3 per cent on amounts between $750 and $1,275.[27] Despite the stated aim of broadening parties' revenue and support bases, Forcese and Freeman (2005: 115) report that there is little evidence to suggest that the tax credit operates as an incentive to donate to political parties:

> Research reports … found that only 43 to 65 per cent of individuals making a political contribution actually claimed the credit. For corporate donors, only 20 per cent of firms claim the credit. It appears contributors generally do not make their donation with a view to tax planning.

A restriction that previously operated to prevent minor parties from issuing tax receipts to donors in the same way as larger political parties came under challenge in the Canadian Supreme Court in *Figueroa v. Canada (Attorney General)*.[28] Employing what Feasby (2006: 244) terms the 'egalitarian model' of political finance,[29] the Court held that the provision was unjustified as 'enhancing the capacity of one citizen to participate in the electoral process in a manner that compromises another citizen's parallel right to meaningful participation in the electoral process' (at para. 50).

---

26 Press Release No. 007, The Honourable Chris Bowen MP, Assistant Treasurer and Minister for Competition Policy and Consumer Affairs, 'Tax Laws Amendment (2008 Measures No. 1) Bill', 13 February 2008.

27 *Income Tax Act*, R.S.C. 1985, C. I (5th Supp.) ss 127(3).

28 [2003] 1 S.C.R. 912.

29 This model, according to Feasby, is 'rooted in the idea that citizens with equal abilities should have an equal ability to participate in the electoral process. As such, the egalitarian model requires that the influence of private wealth be constrained' (2006: 244; see also Feasby 1999).

Other Sources of Public Subsidization of the Political Process

There are several other miscellaneous sources that could be considered as constituting public funding to the political and election activities of parties. For example, the Joint Standing Committee on Electoral Reform conducted in Australia in the early 1980s regarded the service of maintaining the electoral rolls and enforcing the compulsory voting requirement as services provided by the state that, in removing parties' obligation to ensure that people turn out to vote, constituted a partial public subsidization of the political process (JSCER 1983: 145). In the United Kingdom, the cost of providing each candidate with one free postal communication to each voter in his or her electorate was estimated to have cost almost £18 million at the 2001 general election (Ewing 2007: 176–7). Political parties in the United States (although in reality this is largely restricted to the Republicans and the Democrats) receive public grants to cover the costs of their party conventions. In 2004, this sum amounted to US$15 million (Bennett 2009: 113–17).

Indirect Subsidization of Party Activities: Parliamentary Allowances

An increasingly important (albeit indirect) source of funding for political parties is the provision of parliamentary allowances to both parliamentary parties, defined political groupings in Parliament (the government, Opposition, and so on) and to individual parliamentarians. As a general rule, these allowances must be spent on parliamentary activities and not for party-political purposes. However, political parties are increasingly utilizing these funds by concentrating their personnel and resources in the party in public office and in doing so, fundamentally altering the balance between the constituent arms of the political party. As this occurs, we see another example of the potential for regulatory measures that provide for a specific type of funding to both shape and constrain parties' behaviour and their organizational structure.

If we examine the sources of funding that political parties now rely on, it is clear that the income derived from parliamentary duties (which includes parliamentarians' allowances to employ personal office staff) is now a significant source of revenue and in some cases outweighs that received from donations and reimbursements for election expenses. In New Zealand, for example, parliamentary services income[30] for both the Greens and the Labour Party constituted approximately 80 per cent of party income in 2002.[31] Australian federal MPs are entitled to uncapped phone,

30 The figures are based on the Parliamentary Service Commission's formula on Ministers', Leaders' and MPs' expenses, party leaders' funding, and funding for party groups and MPs.

31 For the Greens, income from donations amounted to $86,000 (6 per cent), from election funding (broadcasting allowance) $167,000 (12 per cent), while the parliamentary

travel and photocopy allowances in addition to annual subsidies for printing, postal and electorate costs. They can employ three staffers, with a greater staff allocation available for the Ministry/Shadow Ministry (Holland 2002). Estimates of the total value of parliamentary benefits to Australian party MPs are around $890,000 per annum (Young and Tham 2006: 58). Opposition parties in the UK are entitled to an allocation of 'Short money', designed to enable them to 'more effectively ... fulfil their Parliamentary functions' (see Gay, White and Kelly 2007: 10–12; Kelly 2006), whereas the governing party receives additional remuneration for ministerial duties and to employ Special Advisers.

To understand the implications of the changing sources of party income and their relevance to the organization and distribution of power within political parties, it is necessary to appreciate that certain sources of income have specific conditions attached to them. For example, the income (or income equivalent) derived from election funding usually must be spent on campaigning activities – or is intended to be a reimbursement for such activities.[32] Donations are made to the party organization or its candidates, and as such can be spent by the party in any manner it wishes. However, parliamentary services income, which now constitutes a significant source of income for political parties, is specifically directed to funding the parliamentary activities of a political party and can only be legitimately expended by this arm of the party organization in its capacity as a public agent. For example, the communications allowance allocated to Westminster MPs and associated parliamentary resources 'may not be used for communicating information about your political activities or those of the party to which you belong' (UK Parliament (Dept. Finance and Administration) 2007: 7).[33]

The New Zealand Auditor-General and Solicitor-General have also issued opinions to the effect that 'the appropriations provided for expenses incurred by MPs in their capacity as members do not cover activities by MPs in their capacity as candidates for election'. Specifically, the Speaker of the New Zealand House of Representatives issued a direction in November 2003 that

> ... explicitly excluded 'electioneering material' from the matters that may be funded under the appropriations. 'Electioneering material' is something that is

allowance was $1.1 million (82 per cent). For Labour, $672,000 (9 per cent) was raised from donations, $617,000 (8 per cent) from the broadcasting allowance and $6.2 million from parliamentary allowances (83 per cent). For National, $530,000 was raised from donations (11 per cent), $617,000 from the broadcasting allowance (12 per cent) and $3.9 million from the parliamentary services allowance (77 per cent). Source: Miller (2005: 96).

32 In New Zealand, parties are allocated funds that can only be spent to purchase election broadcasting time: see *Broadcasting Act* 1989, *Broadcasting Amendment Act* 2004, *Electoral Act* 1993.

33 In February 2010, the UK Parliament was embroiled in a serious personal expenses scandal, in which MPs were ordered to pay back over £1 million in wrongly claimed expenses, with criminal charges laid against four MPs. However, this scandal related to personal, rather than party-political gain.

> intended to favour a candidate or party in an election, and is not limited to material that expressly solicits votes. (NZ Office of the Auditor-General 2006: 6)[34]

Although regulations constrain parliamentary expenditure, parties have generally been quite savvy in circumventing these regulations to utilize available staff (see, for example, Ghazarian 2006: 70–71), with the consequence that the bulk of parties' policy research, on a day-to-day basis, is undertaken by parliamentary researchers working for ministers and individual legislators, rather than the broader party organization. Yet, in order to comply with the requirements of public funding, the work that goes into policy is largely disconnected from the party at large and is not integrated into the party's formal policy-making process in order to create the appearance of party-political neutrality. If it occurs at all, integration will usually come at the point where a minister or MP presents a well-researched and essentially complete policy paper to the party conference, seeking ratification rather than input from the membership. Unsurprisingly, such policies attract criticism from members over insufficient involvement, causing confusion and occasionally resentment between these two arms of the party.

The use of parliamentary funding to pay for aspects of individual parliamentarians' and parties' election campaigns caused particular controversy in New Zealand during the 2005 general election, provoking what was termed a 'political tempest' – the Opposition leader and leader of the National Party, Don Brash, going so far as to label these practices as corrupt and demanded that the 'stolen' election be rerun (Geddis 2007a: 151). At the heart of the conflict was the rather murky distinction between the use of public funds by parliamentarians to convey information to the public, and their use for party-political purposes. As the NZ Auditor-General has expressed:

> Advertising and publicity play an important role in the dialogue between members of parliament (MPs), parliamentary parties, and the public that is central to representative democracy. Because of this, taxpayers meet the costs of MPs' and parliamentary parties' advertising. However, while advertising takes place in a political environment, taxpayers do not pay for political parties' activities. (NZ Office of the Auditor-General 2006: 5)

The start of the controversy was in the production of a 'pledge card' by the incumbent Labour government during the campaigning period that listed the Party's election promises to voters, and which was distributed by mail at a cost of $447,000. The costs associated with the production and distribution of the card were met by the Labour Party's parliamentary funding, rather than through its

34 See also section 1.3, *Members' Handbook of Services*, NZ Parliament; Direction of the Speaker of the NZ House of Representatives, 'Direction and Specifications for Travel, Accommodation, Attendance, and Communications Services Available to Members of Parliament', effective from 1 September 2006.

election funds. A complaint that the material produced and distributed by the Labour Party constituted an election advertisement (or activity) rather than parliamentary or governmental information was upheld by the Chief Electoral Officer and the Electoral Commission. As the pledge card had the effect of 'encouraging or persuading or appearing to encourage or persuade voters to vote for a party', it was also determined that the money spent on the card should have been authorized and endorsed by the party secretary, and that the cost of the card should have been included as part of the party's return of election expenses. Significantly, when this amount was added to the party's overall election expenses, this pushed the Labour Party over the permitted threshold amount for the campaign.

However, as Geddis (2007a: 151–2) notes, despite the infringement having been reported to the police, no subsequent prosecution occurred against anyone involved in the matter. After the election, the Auditor-General conducted an inquiry into how parliamentary funds had been used by political parties in the three months leading up to the 2005 general election. As a result of this investigation, the Auditor-General concluded that both political parties and individual members of Parliament had misused over $1.17 million in parliamentary funding on communications that were more properly categorized as party political or electoral in nature, including newspaper advertisements placed by political parties in the last week of the campaign (NZ Office of the Auditor-General 2006: 6, 36). Of these parties, the incumbent Labour Party was found to have committed the greatest abuses of the parliamentary funding system, having spent approximately $825,000 of parliamentary funds inappropriately (Geddis 2007a: 153).

Similar scandals with respect to government advertising and the misuse of parliamentary funds have occurred in Canada and Australia. The propensity of governments to increase their public interest advertising during election campaigns has been a problem in Canada (see Paltiel 1987) and has resulted in several Canadian provinces placing legislative restrictions upon government advertising during election campaigns in order to reduce any partisan advantage (Forcese and Freeman 2005: 131–2). Further, section 321 of the *Canada Elections Act* and federal Treasury Board policy effectively requires government departments to suspend their advertising during election campaigns. Advertising is only permitted under limited circumstances such as health and safety warnings, employment advertising, or legal notices.[35]

Incumbent governments in Australia have similarly been criticized for dramatically increasing advertising campaigns in the lead-up to general elections. For example, Young (2005) reports that in the lead-up to the 2004 general election, the Howard government spent somewhere between $32 million and $40 million in the two months between May and June on advertisements such as 'Help Protect Australia from Terrorism'. Just before the 1998 election, the government spent $28 million on advertisements promoting the government's reform efforts in areas

35 Treasury Board Secretariat, 'Communications Policy of the Government of Canada' (29 November 2004) s. 23; cited in Forcese and Freeman (2005: 131–2).

such as taxation (Cass and Burrows 2000: 453). Commentators argued that the pre-election advertisements had a distinctly partisan flavour, and in July 2008 the Rudd government announced new Guidelines on Government Campaign Advertising that would reduce the budget for such advertisements and have advertising campaigns with a value above $250,000 vetted by the Auditor-General.

One of the underlying principles of the new guidelines is that 'government campaigns shall not be conducted for party political purposes'. Rather, 'the subject matter of material to be communicated to the public should be directly related to the Government's responsibilities'. Advertising is permitted to 'inform the public of new, existing or proposed government policies, or policy revisions'; 'provide information on government programs or services or revisions to programs or services to which the public are entitled'; 'disseminate scientific, medical or health and safety information', and finally, to 'provide information on the performance of government to facilitate accountability to the public'.[36] Given how broad they are, it is difficult to see how these guidelines could narrow down advertising beyond the status quo. Furthermore, the guidelines make no mention of restricting advertising in any given period (for example, in the lead-up to or during an election campaign).

Conclusion: Public Funding and State Control of Parties

Public funding for political parties was introduced, in part, as a mechanism to ensure parties' survival in electoral democracies characterized by increasing campaigning costs and declining party memberships. For parties in Australia and Canada, it has now become a significant source of their income and for smaller political parties it represents up to 80 per cent of the income they now earn. This is consistent with the experience of Green parties in Europe (Nassmacher 2006: 449). In democracies such as the UK and New Zealand, public funding is advocated as a means by which to curtail parties' and parliamentarians' alleged misuse of parliamentary funds. The widespread use of parliamentary funds suggests, somewhat ironically, that even if political parties are not in receipt of direct public funds, they manage to find some way to bill many of their activities back to the public purse.

Does parties' increasing reliance on public money necessarily mean that they are becoming public bodies or public goods? Some scholars argue that the financial regulation associated with public funding will lead to parties 'being defined as public service agencies' (Bartolini and Mair 2001: 340). However, there are no legislative provisions in place in either Canada or Australia that dictate exactly how annual allowances or direct public funding for election expenses should be spent. Nevertheless, public funding has several implications for the functions performed by parties. The nature of parties as participatory organizations is

36 Australian Government, Department of Finance and Deregulation, 'Guidelines on Campaign Advertising by Australian Government Departments and Agencies', June 2008.

arguably dampened as public money replaces the labour and fund-raising efforts once provided by party members and interested citizens. If funds are paid directly to the central party office, this might further exacerbate the party hierarchy and centralize its leadership. This is of particular concern for small parties, whose reliance on public funds constitutes up to 80 per cent of their total income.

There is, however, a possibility that public funding could be tied to activities that encourage greater citizen participation in politics, such as policy development initiatives. For example, a policy development fund of £2 million per year currently exists for political parties in the United Kingdom. However, there is no requirement that parties spend these funds on encouraging citizen involvement in policy making – it may just as easily be spent on employing professionals. This is, nevertheless, an area of party regulation where financial incentives to political parties could be used to encourage parties to fulfil or undertake particular democratic functions, such as facilitate public involvement in political decisions at the party level.

Although public funding was introduced to encourage greater equality between political parties in electoral contests, the experience of public funding in Australia, Canada and the United States suggests that it has been used and structured to privilege the interests of the major parties at the expense of minor and new political parties. The politics behind the introduction and maintenance of such regimes highlights the close and potentially problematic relationship between legislators and the political parties who seek to protect their own interests at the expense of electoral competition.

Chapter 8
The Private Funding of Election Campaigns: Regulating Political Donations and Expenditures

In the previous chapter, I examined the extent to which political parties are directly and indirectly funded by the state. One of the key arguments that emerged was the suggestion that the public funding of political parties has fundamentally altered the way in which political parties campaign, their organizational structure including the strength and role of their membership, and their relationship to civil society. Political parties in receipt of public funding are said to be acting, more and more, as agents of the state.

The same argument, in essence, can be applied to the private funding of political parties, but it is a variant of the debate that has been around far longer. At issue is the extent of influence upon a political actor that money provides. Does the receipt of funds by political parties from their donors mean that political power is being improperly exercised in favour of those donors?:

> The promise of democracy is that each citizen will share equally in political power. However, in the context of a liberal capitalist democracy and its attendant economic inequalities, wealthy individuals and businesses are able to translate their economic power into political power because '(s)ome moneyed people will always attempt to speak louder and will often succeed as a result'. (Young and Tham 2006: 8; citing Murray and Rock 2000: 29)

The argument of undue influence has not only been levelled at individuals, businesses and corporate interests with the financial resources to potentially buy political outcomes, but also to unions (especially in their relationship to social democratic parties) and other associations with particular policy agendas. In this chapter, I document the various ways in which states legislate to control the influence of private money in the electoral process. As we will see, although some common themes emerge, there is also considerable variation between states as to the extent to which private money is seen to be a problem, how it is best regulated, and the relationship between the legislature and the judiciary in balancing such regulation with the freedom of political expression.

As with the debate on the public funding of political parties, another point of interest that will be examined is the potential for legislation regulating private sources of party income to impact upon the organizational structure and internal political and policy processes of parties. For example, is there a relationship between how political parties are financed and patterns of democratic engagement? Can financing laws facilitate a particular normative democratic agenda? That is, will placing caps on political expenditure and lowering allowable donations to political parties force political parties to re-engage with citizens, communities and civil society? This chapter proceeds by examining the regulatory regimes that exist in each of the individual states: Australia, Canada, New Zealand, the United Kingdom and the United States. This is followed by some general observations on common elements and problems in the regulation of private money in elections, and their impact on political parties as electoral actors.

Australia: Transparency and Accountability?

The regulation of the private financing of political parties in Australia relies predominantly upon the financial disclosure scheme established under Part XX of the *Commonwealth Electoral Act*. Unlike the regulatory regimes of comparable common law nations, there is no legislative restriction placed on the amounts that may be donated to Australian political parties or their expenditure during election campaigns.[1] As Graeme Orr argues, 'Australian society in most respects is more regulated and socialized than the US. In political finance law, however, Australia is decidedly *less* regulated than not just the US, but other comparable common law democracies', including all those examined in this book (2007: 74). Interestingly, Australia stands alone as not even placing a ban on foreign donations, which are currently regulated in the same way as domestic donations. On one hand, Australia's system of minimal regulation of private funding can be viewed as a 'democratic virtue', preserving the liberal ideals of freedom of political association and speech (Young and Tham 2006: 34). However, relatively high disclosure thresholds threaten to undermine transparency and consequently the accountability that this minimalist regulatory regime attempts to achieve.

The key source of federal regulation stems from disclosure obligations imposed upon parties, their associated entities, third parties, candidates and donors. The federal financial disclosure scheme was introduced to 'inform the public about the financial dealings of parties, candidates and others involved in the electoral process' (AEC 2008). It requires candidates, registered political parties and their associated entities, donors and certain other people to lodge annual or election period financial disclosure returns with the Australian Electoral Commission.

1 Note, however, that there is an exception for anonymous donations, the threshold for which is now $10,000. See *Commonwealth Electoral Act* 1918, s. 306. Legislative provisions of the various states have also sought to exclude certain classes of persons or groups from making donations to political parties; for example, casinos are banned from donating more than $50,000 to registered political parties in Victoria (Orr 2007: 74; 2006b: 113). See *Electoral Act* 2002 (Vic), Part 12, Division 3.

The financial disclosure scheme was established in 1983, along with the system of public funding for elections advocated by the newly elected Labor government.[2] Prior to this, Australian political parties and candidates were subject to antiquated laws that prescribed strict expenditure limits on candidates, which for all practical purposes were either repealed or fell into disuse as parliaments failed to increase the caps on candidate expenditures in line with inflation (Orr 2007: 74). Currently, there are two streams of federal disclosure provided for in the *Commonwealth Electoral Act* – election returns and annual returns.

Candidates, unendorsed Senate groups and Senate groups endorsed by more than one registered political party must disclose donations and electoral expenditure incurred (this category applies to everyone but political parties). Election returns submitted to the Australian Electoral Commission (AEC) must show the total value of donations received; the total number of donors; all individual donations received above the disclosure threshold (currently $10,900); the details of donations including the date on which each donation was received; the amount or value of each donation; the name and address of the donor, and the electoral expenditure (mainly advertising, printing and direct mail costs) incurred between the issue of the writ and polling day. People or organizations making donations to candidates in excess of the disclosure threshold ($10,900) must also lodge a donor return.

Registered political parties and their State or Territory branches and associated entities are also required to lodge an annual return with the Australian Electoral Commission.[3] Returns lodged with the AEC for each financial year must show the total value of receipts and payment; the total value of debts as at the end of the financial year, and all individual donations received above the disclosure threshold, including the amount or value of the donation; and the name and address of the donor.

Donors must disclose gifts totalling more than the disclosure threshold made to a registered political party. From 2006–07, third parties (people other than registered political parties, candidates, Senate groups and donors, and including associated entities) who incur political expenditure in excess of the disclosure threshold are also required to lodge an annual return.[4] Multiple receipts received on the same day from the same source are considered to be a single receipt and should be reported if their sum exceeds the threshold. This includes receipts from related entities and bodies corporate.

Receipts to be reported include donations or gifts received as well as membership subscriptions, public election funding, income from investments,

---

2 See Cass and Burrows (2000) for a comprehensive historical overview of the development of political finance regulation in Australia.

3 The category of 'associated entities' includes trade unions affiliated with the Australian Labor Party.

4 Consequently, as a result of these amendments, third parties are required to lodge annual returns rather than the election returns they previously completed. See *Commonwealth Electoral Act* 1918 (Cth) ss 314AEB, 314AEC.

borrowed money and other revenue. Gifts are broadly defined to include any transfer or gift of property or services for which no payment, or an inadequate payment, is received. These may be in cash (for example, money or cheque), or 'gifts-in-kind'.[5] Volunteer labour does not need to be disclosed as a receipt as it is excluded from the definition of gift in the Act. The donation of unpaid time by a person is volunteer labour where it is provided by an office-holder of the party or by a party member, or by any other person where that service is not one for which that person normally receives payment.

The disclosure of information (details of gifts and donations) is subject to a minimum threshold below which disclosure is not required. The financial disclosure scheme was amended with effect from 8 December 2005 to increase the threshold to 'more than $10,000' by the conservative Liberal/National government. Previously the disclosure threshold stood at only $1,500.[6] This amount is indexed with effect from 1 July each year based on increases in the consumer price index. Currently (1 July 2010–30 June 2011), the disclosure threshold amount is $11,500. The 2006 increase in the disclosure threshold proved to be very controversial and sparked significant criticism from political scientists, lawyers and electoral commentators for the 'astonishing level of non-disclosure' that such high disclosure thresholds permitted (see for example, Young and Tham 2006: 19).

Some illumination of the rationale behind the legislative change can be garnered from an examination of the digest that accompanied the Bill.[7] The Digest stated that the proposed increase had 'long been Liberal Party policy' and that arguments put forward by Liberal Party senators included the fact that the threshold was introduced 20 years ago, originally set at $1,000 and has since been eroded by inflation; that it was much too low when it was originally set, and that the $1,500 threshold 'adds nothing to Australia's democracy other than unnecessary red tape'. An attempt to increase the threshold to $3,000 in 2004 failed, and was thwarted on the grounds that three parliamentarians, Senator John Faulkner, Michael Danby MP and Laurie Ferguson MP regarded the proposal as having 'no policy merit and will only diminish the transparency of the disclosure laws and allow further donations to parties and candidates to go undisclosed' (Griffith and Drabsch 2007: 18).

The *Electoral and Referendum Amendment (Electoral Integrity and Other Measures) Act* 2006 (Cth) also made provisions to increase the threshold at which the prohibition against anonymous donations and loans sets in. Before the Act's passage through Parliament, political parties could only accept sums of less than $1,000 from anonymous donors. Now this threshold has been raised to $10,000 and has been criticized on the ground that 'political parties can legally accept

5 *Commonwealth Electoral Act* 1918 (Cth) s. 287.

6 Section 305A of the *Commonwealth Electoral Act* 1918 (Cth) was amended by the *Electoral and Referendum Amendment (Electoral Integrity and Other Measures) Act* 2006 (Cth).

7 *Electoral and Referendum Amendment (Electoral Integrity and Other Measures) Bill* 2005 (Cth), Commonwealth Parliamentary Library Bills Digest No. 95/2005–06.

larger sums without knowing the details of the donor', a practice that 'potentially renders the whole notion of disclosure thresholds meaningless' (Young and Tham 2006: 24).

Administering Disclosure Regimes

Funding disclosure regimes have significant implications for the staffing, organization and professionalization of political parties. One of the key implications of this scheme for the internal organization of political parties is that each political party must appoint an agent in order to administer the regulatory scheme.[8] For parties that are organized in more than one place (for example, multiple States and Territories) – each State or Territory branch must appoint an agent and lodge disclosure returns.

The agent receives public election funding for endorsed candidates and Senate groups, and lodges financial disclosure returns for the party or State or Territory branch. To be eligible for appointment as an agent, a person must be at least 18 years of age; not have been convicted of an offence under the funding and disclosure provisions of the Act, and have signed a consent to the appointment and a declaration of eligibility for appointment. Only natural persons, and not corporations, may be appointed as an agent. A person may have multiple appointments but each appointment must be made separately.[9]

Disclosure regimes that are too onerous also raise a difficult problem in the management of, and compliance with, these regimes where political parties are poorly organized, whether this is because they are relatively young, lack resources, or may be experiencing high levels of intra-party conflict that impinge upon the everyday management structure of the political party. From the Australian Electoral Commission's perspective:

> Internal party management issues also give rise to concerns about the integrity of the financial disclosure scheme. Where a party is not properly organized, or is subject to competing cliques that may or may not communicate with each other, there must be real doubt as to whether the financial disclosure returns are complete and accurate, and indeed whether a compliance review of the record will result in returns that meet the disclosure objectives. A requirement for all new parties to be registered as a company, or as an incorporated association under State or Territory law, would provide a legal framework to assist parties to deal with governance issues of this nature. (AEC 2005: 41)

Australia's federal system of government also creates complications in the effective operation of disclosure laws. Disclosure thresholds currently apply separately to each registered political party. In Australia, it is common practice for each party

8 *Commonwealth Electoral Act* 1918 (Cth) s. 288.

9 *Commonwealth Electoral Act* 1918 (Cth) s. 290.

to register as a separate and distinct entity at different levels of government. As Young and Tham (2006: 21) observe, the consequence is such that a major party that registers at the national level and in all the Australian States and Territories will have the cumulative benefit of nine disclosure thresholds rather than one.

Public Inspection

Election disclosure returns are made available for public inspection 24 weeks after polling day on the Australian Electoral Commission website. Annual disclosure returns are similarly made available for public inspection from the first working day in February. These returns are on the public record, and parties and their associated entities may be subject to a compliance audit by the Australian Electoral Commission. This public disclosure and the ability for individuals to inspect details of the parties' income and expenditure forms a key part of the enforcement and regulation of political finance in Australia.

These returns are subject to further scrutiny through media reporting. Nevertheless, whether the media actually reports details of party donations in a timely and meaningful way for promoting equality in democratic discussion and facilitating an informed electorate is open to debate. For example, in a study of media coverage and reporting of funding disclosures for Australian parties from 2001 to 2004, Tennant-Wood found that:

> With the exception of single issues that have specific policy and political implications … it is only during the brief period of election campaigns, when political reporting increases across all media, that the issue of funding is broadly raised as part of that increased attention to political parties. The internal dealings of the parties remain otherwise largely unaddressed in the public forum. (Tennant-Wood 2004: 6)

Indeed, media organizations are major contributors to Australia's two largest political parties, bringing into question the media's ability to actually police or report the funding activities of the parties in a critical manner. This begs the important question that 'Given that it is the responsibility of the media to report the facts, how might political patronage influence such facts?' (Ibid.). Nevertheless, there are some examples of the media exposing dubious or questionable corporate funding to political parties. For example, in 2001, the *Sydney Morning Herald* exposed the 'cash for visas' affair, which revealed that the then Immigration Minister Philip Ruddock had received funding for his 2001 election campaign from a wealthy Lebanese businessman, allegedly in return for residency visas for Lebanese immigrants (see Ibid.: 9–10; Orr 2007: 82–4). Similarly, in the UK, the parliamentary expenses scandal was originally broken by the broadsheet newspaper, *The Daily Telegraph.* This scandal culminated in criminal charges being brought against four MPs in early 2010.

Transforming Canadian Political Finance: For Partisans or Participants?

Unlike the Australian system, which provides public funding for political parties in return for their compliance with a disclosure regime, the Canadian system of campaign finance regulation combines not only a disclosure regime and some state financial support, but imposes limits on both campaign expenditures and contributions, and regulates the sources from which political parties may receive donations.

Like Australia, Canadian political parties' finances are regulated in part by a system of financial disclosure. Political parties are required to disclose details of donations and expenses received both on an annual basis and after an election campaign. The documents must provide the name and address of contributors giving more than a total of $200, the donation amounts and the dates on which they were received, and the details of any loans provided to the party and non-financial contributions, such as the supply of goods and services (*Canada Elections Act*, s. 403.35). With the exception of electoral district associations spending less than $5,000, all financial returns (donations and expenses) must be professionally audited (s. 435.33). Under s. 429 of the *Elections Act*, political parties must also submit returns of all monetary expenses incurred (paid and unpaid) and non-monetary contributions within six months from the date of the election.

From 1974, Canadian political parties have faced maximum limits on the election expenses that they can incur. This amount is calculated by multiplying $0.70 by the number of electors in each district that the party is fielding a candidate (s. 422). The amount is indexed for inflation. What is considered to be an election expense is limited to both monetary and non-monetary costs incurred 'used to directly promote or oppose a registered party, its leader or candidate during an election period' (s. 407). Examples of expenses include advertising, the conduct of election surveys and the cost of securing a meeting space and providing food and drink. It generally does not cover expenses for fund raising or personal expenses such as travel (see Forcese and Freeman 2005: 103–4).[10]

The Canadian legislation also places limits on the amounts that donors can contribute to political parties, and prohibits donations from several sources. The contributions that corporations and unions could make to parties were reduced substantially in 2003 by amendments to the *Canada Elections Act*, and they were altogether abolished in December 2006 by virtue of the *Federal Accountability Act*. Prior to this, corporations and unions could donate to either individual candidates or electoral district associations. However, they could not donate to national political party organizations or party leadership candidates. The Act also prohibits donations from foreign sources – only Canadian citizens and permanent residents may make contributions to registered political parties, electoral district associations and candidates.

10 While expenditure limits in party nomination contests are regulated by separate legislation, leadership contests are currently unregulated.

The limit on individual donations to political parties was also reduced by the Act from $5,000 per annum to $1,000. The definition of contributions, as it applies to individuals, corporations and unions, includes goods and services that are provided to a political party free of charge. Political parties must appoint a financial agent for the purpose of receiving donations, approving expenses and holding the party to account for its financial affairs. Under the *Elections Act*, an agent may not knowingly accept a contribution that exceeds the limits set in the Act (s. 405.2(3)), keep the donation if it was known that it came from an illegible person or entity (s. 404(2)), or keep the donation if it exceeds the amount that the donor may donate (s. 405.4).

In response to concerns that the new provisions might encourage a culture of circumvention,[11] the Act explicitly prohibits any attempts at circumvention of both the eligibility provisions and the donation limits (s. 405.2(1)), colluding with others for this purpose (s. 405.2(1)(b)) or concealing one's identity (s. 405.2(2)). Furthermore, it is an offence to make a donation to a party if it comes from the resources of another, and was given to the contributor for the purpose of making the donation (s. 405.3).

On both occasions that substantial revisions to campaign finance legislation in Canada have occurred, reforms to the public funding of elections and parties followed political scandals that shook public confidence in the Canadian system of government. In promoting the adoption of the 2003 (Bill C-24) amendments during the Bill's second reading speech, Prime Minister Chrétien advertised the legislation as changing the way 'politics is done in this country' and as 'a bill that addresses the perception that money talks, that big companies and big unions have too much influence on politics, a bill that will reduce cynicism about politics and politicians' (cited in Feasby 2007: 524). Previously, the Lortie Commission had argued against restrictions on corporate donations:

> Canadian organizations with a stake in the political future of the country should not be prevented from supporting parties and candidates who share policies and values, provided the public has full opportunity to be informed about these financial activities. (Royal Commission on Electoral Reform and Party Financing 1991: 450)

However, the salience of this argument comes down to who (or what) should be viewed as an appropriate participant in the electoral process, and whether this should be restricted only to individual members of society, or also include organizational and corporate identities. Cross makes a contrary case to the Lortie Commission's findings:

> The democratic interest in citizen participation in the electoral process lies solely with voters. Corporations, trade unions, foreign entities and other organizations

11 Forcese and Freeman (2005: 112); Cross (1994: 258).

> or associations have no such protected interest. There is no compelling democratic or legal reason why these groups should be permitted to participate as independent expenditors. (Cross 1994: 258)

The impetus for these reforms can also be understood in terms of partisan politics and opportunistic responses to political scandals. Traditionally, the Liberal Party was dependent on large individual and corporate donations, the NDP on funding from trade unions and the Conservative Party, the Bloc Québécois and the Canadian Alliance were financed through smaller, more populist bases (Feasby 2007: 517). By banning corporate and union donations and reducing the amount individuals could contribute to political parties, the *Accountability Act* – originally introduced by the Conservatives but passed with the support of all parties – has had an adverse effect on the Liberal Party (Ibid.: 537–8).

The Transformation of Canadian Party Organizations

It has been argued that the changes to the Canadian system of campaign financing have forced political parties to widen their support base, and seek a more 'grassroots' approach to political funding. For example, Vice-Chairman of the Liberal Party, Daryl Fridhandler, is quoted as saying: 'I see the whole new financing regime as something that is absolutely going to drive things more towards the grassroots. We will definitely be broadening the target' (Forcese and Freeman 2005: 107). It was also widely thought that amendments to the Canadian party financing regimes would disadvantage the NDP by banning donations from unions – a key source of the party's financial support. In 2003, the year before unions contributions were initially capped, unions donated significantly more to the NDP in anticipation of the new limits (Jansen and Young 2005). Nevertheless, Jansen and Young argue that changes to the way in which the party is regulated have brought about a restructuring of (rather than a break in) the party-union relationship, which continues to be based on workers' strong ideological affiliations with the party and the involvement of union members in the party organization.

The role of the courts According to Feasby, the approach that the Canadian Supreme Court has taken in cases such as *Harper v. Canada (Attorney General)*,[12] in which the Court upheld third party expenditure limits, and *R v. Bryan*[13] in which it dismissed the suggestion that legislation prohibiting the early transmission of election results infringed the appellant's freedom of expression, suggests a deferential approach to the legislature, which, given the partisan nature of electoral laws and Parliament's inherent conflict of interest in regulating the political process will 'constrain the Court's ability to rectify abuses and may even invite manipulation of the rules that govern the democratic process' (2007: 451–2). This

12 [2004] 1 S.C.R. 827.

13 [2007] 1 S.C.R. 527.

begs the issue of what is the appropriate role for the courts to play in adjudicating matters that go to the heart of the electoral process (and hence the heart of democracy) in a nation. In *R v. Bryan*, the Supreme Court stated that 'we must be particularly careful not to usurp Parliament's role in determining the rules of the electoral game most appropriate for Canada as a whole' (at para. 58). However, both Feasby and Pildes argue that in certain circumstances, constraining partisan interests or those that serve to favour or entrench the interests of incumbents should serve as legitimate functional grounds for judicial review of the constitutionality of legislation (Feasby 2007: 543–5; Pildes 2004: 154).

New Zealand: Legislative Uncertainty

Perhaps the best way to describe the current legislative regime for the regulation of political finance in New Zealand is 'in a state of flux'. By international standards, New Zealand political campaigns and their financing have attracted relatively little attention for the most part of the twentieth century. As previously noted, when contrasted with other developed Western democracies, New Zealand election campaigns emerge as relatively cheap events. Prior to the 2005 general election and the subsequent flurry of legislative reform, Geddis (2004: 596) argued that it was 'debatable' whether election financing was even a problem that needed to be addressed in New Zealand:

> The evidence is rather that the political parties are at present able to raise enough money to run campaigns that adequately communicate their messages to the voters. Even though the amounts that the various parties spend in each election campaign are quite divergent, there seems little evidence to indicate that this fact had had any negative impact on the overall competitiveness of the electoral process.

Judicial challenge did not seem to be a concern or controversy either – as New Zealand did not have a written constitution or legislative bill of rights until 1990, there was no governing law by which citizens could question the legality of finance restrictions in a manner similar to the United States, Canada or Australia (Ibid.).

Expenditure limits and disclosure requirements for election expenditure and large donations were first introduced to regulate the financial activities of political parties in 1995 with the *Electoral Amendment Act (No. 2)*. Prior to this, limits on candidate expenditure were imposed, but in keeping with the reluctance of New Zealand's first-past-the-post electoral laws to recognize the existence of political parties, no specific rules applied to parties' fund raising or expenditure (Geddis 2007a: 137). The 1995 amendments implemented the suggestions of the Report of the Royal Commission on the Electoral System, *Towards a Better Democracy*, which recommended that limits on candidates' campaign expenditure should be retained, indexed to inflation, and extended to the national campaigning activities of political parties. The Report did not propose any restrictions on donations to political parties, but registered parties were required to appoint an auditor to prepare annual statements of income and election returns showing expenditure during the campaign period (see Chapter 8 of the Report; Atkinson 2003: 206).

Overall, the regime provides registered political parties with some direct public subsidies in the form of a broadcasting allowance (discussed previously). Like Australia and Canada, there is also a disclosure scheme in place to encourage the transparency of political donations. However, the main instrument on which the regulation of party finance in New Zealand relies is limitations on the campaign spending of participants in the electoral contest.

Yet there has been some uncertainty in electoral finance regulation in recent years, with two significant amendments to electoral legislation passed in the last three years. In 2007, the governing NZ Labour Party passed the *Electoral Finance Act*, partly in response to the $1.3 million campaign by a third-party actor, the Exclusive Brethren, in support of its main rival, the Nationals, at the 2005 election. At its substance, the Act placed a limit on what non-party actors could spend in order to promote their point of view. However, the Act came under widespread criticism from commentators, including the Electoral Commission, who claimed that it was impossible to interpret, and that it was so confusing that it had a 'chilling effect' on public participation during the election campaign (Catt 2008).

In 2008, the Labour Party lost government and the new incumbents, the Nationals, promptly passed the *Electoral Amendment Act* 2009. The *Amendment Act* repealed the *Electoral Finance Act* 2007 to establish 'an interim electoral finance regime pending completion of a comprehensive review of electoral finance law'. The Act reinstates the election expenses provisions that governed the 2005 general election; retains the provisions in the Electoral Finance Act 2007 that relate to donations to political parties and candidates, and reinstates the general rules that governed the publication of campaign advertisements that were in force for the 2005 general election. In 'Stage 2', the government will undertake a considered process involving all parliamentary parties and the public to further examine the reform of electoral finance law. The Stage 2 reforms will be enacted in 2010 for the 2011 general election.[14] In April 2010, the Minister for Justice introduced the Electoral (Finance Reform and Advance Voting) Amendment Bill, which is currently before Parliament. Hence the discussion of New Zealand campaign finance law incorporates this somewhat confusing passage of events, but may change in 2011.

Limits on Total Election Expenses

Each political party is limited to spending $1 million, plus $20,000 for each constituency seat contested by a candidate representing the party.[15] This maximum

14 Electoral Amendment Bill 2009 No. 15-1, Explanatory note, General policy statement, 1.

15 *Electoral Amendment Act* 2009 s. 206B(1).

limit only includes spending on what are deemed 'election expenses', that is, an expense incurred by or on behalf of the party in respect of any election activity (s. 206A). Specifically, this includes expenses that are incurred in the three months immediately preceding polling day in respect of any election activity (the election period);[16] the reasonable market value of any materials given to the party free of charge or below market value, and the cost of any printing or postage in respect of any election activity, whether or not the expenses in respect of the printing are incurred by or on behalf of the party.[17] An 'election activity' is defined by the Act (s. 206) as an activity carried out by a party (or with its authority) that encourages or persuades voters to vote for the party or not to vote for a party. Such activities comprise advertising of any kind, radio or television broadcasting, and the publishing, issuing, distributing of material, or displaying addresses, notices, posters, pamphlets, handbills, billboards and cards.

Election expenses do not include travel, the conduct of surveys or opinion polls (unlike Canada), voluntary labour, the allocation of broadcasting time and money under the *Broadcasting Act* 1989, or the election expenses of individual candidates.[18] The fact that no restrictions on spending apply before an election period inevitably means that the 'actual amount spent by each party on its overall election campaign almost certainly will be significantly greater than the "election expenses" it incurs' (Geddis 2007a: 139). Exceeding the election expenses limits imposed by the Act constitutes is a criminal offence.[19] Each registered political party is required to submit a public return of all its expenditure following an election, which must be independently audited.[20] Once submitted, the return is available for public inspection and may be published by the Electoral Commission.[21]

Despite these statutory requirements, political parties have been prepared to flaunt the expenditure limits without prosecution. During the 2005 election, the NZ Labour Party used its parliamentary funding to produce a pledge card that was subsequently found to be a misuse of those parliamentary funds (see previously, pp. 160–61). When the cost of this pledge card was added to the party's existing electoral expenditure, it pushed the total to $2.8 million – almost half a million dollars above the allowable limit of $2.38 million. As Geddis reports, although contrary to the provisions of the *Electoral Act*, the police declined to prosecute the matter (2007a: 141).[22]

---

16 Note that if an election activity occurs before and within the three months immediately preceding polling day, the expenses must be apportioned so that a fair proportion of those expenses is attributed to the carrying on of the activity in the three months immediately preceding polling day. See *Electoral Amendment Act* 2009 s. 206C.

17 *Electoral Amendment Act* 2009 s. 206A(b).

18 *Electoral Amendment Act* 2009 s. 206A(c).

19 *Electoral Act* 1993, s. 206D.

20 *Electoral Act* 1993 ss 206I, 206L.

21 *Electoral Act* 1993 s. 206Q.

22 Labour's main electoral competitor, the Nationals, spent a total of $2.1 million – 95 per cent of its permitted limit.

Donations

There is no limit on the amount that can be donated to political parties in New Zealand. The exception is overseas and anonymous donations. Under s. 207I of the *Electoral Act*, both anonymous donations and those from overseas are permitted but may not exceed $1,000 (s. 207I). If a donor wishes to make a donation anonymously to a party that is in excess of $1,000, he or she may do so through the Electoral Commission, who will forward the donation to the party (s. 208A). The limit of these types of donations that a party can receive during an election campaign is 10 per cent of its maximum spending limit (s. 208B). It is an offence to disclose the identity of a donor under s. 208A to the party (s. 208F). This provision was inserted as the Justice and Electoral Committee expressed concern when drafting the legislation that some donors would withdraw their funding if they could not donate anonymously, so some provision was necessary to preserve this opportunity to ensure that political parties would have adequate funds to survive (Geddis 2008: 228).[23]

Rather than taking the Canadian route and establishing limits on donations and their sources, the 'supply side' of the electoral contest in New Zealand is for the most part regulated by the requirement that political parties disclose the sources of their funding. In addition to the modest restrictions on the amount and types of donations that parties are able to receive, s. 210 of the *Electoral Act* 1993 also requires political parties to submit an annual return of party donations received in the previous calendar year. Details of donations or contributions from a single source (including cumulative donations) in excess of $10,000 must be disclosed (providing the donor's name, address, the amount of the donation and the date), as well as details of anonymous, or overseas donations exceeding $1,000 (date, amount, and excess amount paid to the Electoral Commission) and details of donations made through the Electoral Commission (date, amount, interest accrued). This return must be independently audited,[24] and separate returns must be submitted for donations received from the same donor exceeding $20,000.[25] As with those returns disclosing parties' expenditure, these returns are made available for public inspection.[26]

The ongoing problem of 'contributions' – that is, donations that are derived and pooled together from various sources and are either given directly to the party, or through an intermediary (for example, a trust) – are addressed by the *Electoral Act* through the partial identification of these contributors. A donation

23 Although anonymous donations do not pose any theoretical problems if the identity of the donors is not known to the parties', the actual reality that political parties have no idea who is funding their campaigns is much more dubious (Geddis 2007a: 142). See also Hager (2006: Chapters 14 and 15).

24 *Electoral Act* 1993 s. 210A.

25 *Electoral Act* 1993 s. 210C.

26 *Electoral Act* 1993 s. 210F.

that is funded from contributions must be disclosed as such. The total number of contributions under $1,000 must be disclosed. For contributions over $1,000, the name and address and total amount of the contribution must be disclosed (s. 207C). If a donation is transmitted by another party, he or she must reveal the identity of the donor if this is known. Where a transmitter does not disclose, or is unable to disclose the identity of the donor, then the donation must be treated as an anonymous donation (s. 207E).

The United Kingdom: The Centrality of Disclosure

The *Political Parties, Elections and Referendums Act* 2000 (UK) (PPERA) establishes the legislative regime for the regulation of political donations in the United Kingdom. The scheme provides for the quarterly reporting of donations and loans to registered political parties, and on a weekly basis during a general election for the UK Parliament. Prior to this, political parties were not subject to any disclosure laws or controls on donations, and although campaign spending limits were enforced – these applied only to candidates in an election, effectively ignoring political parties, 'the main players and biggest spenders in general election campaigns' (Ewing and Ghaleigh 2007: 56; see also Ewing 1987). The reforms in 2000 were enacted partly in response to the changing nature of patterns of political donations, and several high-profile political scandals that saw donations used as a means to assert political influence.

The disclosure regime in the United Kingdom aims to meet two main objectives: to prevent or deter corruption, but also to give voters the opportunity to make an informed choice at the election in light of parties' sources of funding. This much was acknowledged by the Committee on Standards in Public Life when it asserted that disclosure regimes 'may have a bearing on the response of other potential donors and it may impact upon voters' intentions' (CSPL 1998: para. 6.7).

The threshold for disclosure for donations, goods and services provided without charge or on non-commercial terms and loans is £5,000 for donations to a central party, or £1,000 for donations to one of the party's accounting units (for example, a constituency branch). Donations from impermissible or unidentified donors must be disclosed for amounts above £200. Therefore the maximum amount under which any donations need not be disclosed is £200 (s. 50). Parties must report donations over the threshold amount whether they are made as a single sum or in aggregate over the calendar year, even if they have been made to different sections of the party (ss 54(5)(b); (7)(b); 62(12)). Parties must provide the value of the donation and the name, address and other relevant details of the donor, and are also under an obligation to report any donations that were subsequently returned due to the impermissible status of the donor, or if the donor could not be identified.

The requirement that political parties disclose details of loans and similar financial transactions was introduced in 2006 by the *Electoral Administration Act*

2006 (UK), which amended the PPERA (s. 71F). These amendments came as a result of the loans for peerages scandal that embroiled the Labour Party in 2005 (see Ewing and Ghaleigh 2007: 71).

The UK scheme imposes some regulations on which entities political parties can accept donations from. Any donation over £200 must come from a 'permissible source'. The party has the legal responsibility of checking whether a donation comes from a permissible source within the scope of the PPERA rules before accepting it. Permissible sources include individuals registered in a UK electoral register, UK companies, registered political parties, trade unions and building societies. Foreign donations are thus indirectly banned by the PPERA as they do not fall within the categories of permissible sources (see Ewing 2007: 91–2).

Ewing and Ghaleigh argue that the disclosure legislation has not been effective in eliminating extremely large donations from politics and elections in the UK: 'it remains the case nevertheless that large donors have opportunities that are not available to less well-heeled or politically disinclined individuals, and that these opportunities arise only by virtue of their donations or prospective donations', including membership of such mechanisms as exclusive access clubs (2007: 68, 69). It has also not helped to curb campaign spending, with the 2005 general election the most expensive on record, with Labour spending £17.9 million, the Conservatives £17.8 million and the Liberal Democrats £4.3 million. Jones and colleagues (2007: 195) estimate that with approximately £10 million spent by the parties in the constituencies, the total amount spent would have exceeded £50 million.

One of the key issues in increasing the financial regulation of political parties in the UK, as in Australia, is the ability of political parties, particular smaller parties who do not have the resources to employ professional staffers and accountants, to be able to successfully implement and follow reporting requirements. In recognition of the onus that is placed upon political parties, the UK Electoral Commission is able to provide assistance for registered parties (either a grant or the provision of non-financial benefits such as computer software) with a view 'to helping them to meet, or to reducing, the expenses falling to be initially incurred by them in order to comply with [the requirements of the Act]' (*Political Parties, Elections and Referendums Act* 2000 (UK) s. 36).

Campaign Finance Laws in the United States: Regulation vs. Constitutional Freedoms

Campaign finance laws in the United States can be characterized as an ongoing battle between legislative initiatives that seek to regulate campaign expenditure and impose limits on contributions, and the role of the Supreme Court in upholding the freedoms of political expression contained in the First Amendment of the US Constitution. Representing a 'tussle' between the legislative and judicial arms of government, 'in large measure, effective political finance regulation has proven impossible because the Supreme Court has defined campaign spending to be a form of political speech given nearly absolute protection by the First Amendment' (Katz 2007: 79). Another factor complicating party control is the fact that campaign finance rules traditionally centre on the financial independence of candidates and treat elections as if they 'were not party activities at all' (Rosenblum 2000: 830). The Supreme Court's latest ruling on the *Bipartisan Campaign Reform Act* in *Citizens United*, discussed below, is a perfect illustration of these observations. All in all, US campaign finance laws have been described as 'bizarre and incongruous' (Persily 2006: 219) and it is impossible to discuss the legislative regime without also examining the Supreme Court's interpretation of it.

The design of campaign finance law in the United States is heavily influenced by the Supreme Court's view that free speech under the First Amendment is a paramount feature of democracy and should be protected, subject only to certain public interests. In protecting freedom of speech, the Court has struck down legislation that purports to limit expenditure but has been more sympathetic to legislative measures that regulate contributions – the latter being regarded as a more dangerous corrupting influence.[27] The Supreme Court has held that the only government interest sufficient to uphold the limitations on expenditure is in preventing corruption or the appearance of it. Interestingly, providing a level playing field for all candidates for election or trying to limit the spiralling costs of election campaigns were not considered sufficient reasons to limit political expression.[28]

The main instrument regulating campaign finance at the national level is the *Bipartisan Campaign Reform Act* (BCRA), enacted by Congress in 2002. The primary target of the Act was 'soft money' to political parties – a practice whereby political parties would circumvent regulation by spending funds that fell outside the ambit of federal regulations (such as donations in excess of the proscribed federal limits) on supposedly non-federal activities such as 'party building' and voter mobilization. The BCRA expressly disallowed this through section 323, which prohibits national political parties from receiving or transferring to another political committee funds that do not comply with federal laws concerning source and contribution limits, and disclosure requirements (Briffault 2006). The soft-money prohibitions of the Act were upheld by the Supreme Court in *McConnell v. FEC* 540 U.S. 93 (2003).

The Act contains further regulations on both donations and expenditures by political parties to their candidates. For example, individuals are able to contribute $2,400 to an individual candidate per election and $30,400 to a national party in a year. National political committees may give $42,600 per year to Senate candidates and $5,000 per year each to House and presidential candidates (2009–10 contribution limits). However, these transfer limits are effectively meaningless as party spending on election campaigns occurs through coordination with the

27 See the *Colorado* cases, discussed below.

28 *Buckley v. Valeo* 424 U.S. 1 (1976) at 14; see also Altman (2002: 1004).

candidate (coordinated expenditure) or independently (independent expenditure). The independent expenditure that a party can make is not limited by legislation, but there is a cap on coordinated expenditure. Originally set in 1974, it has been adjusted for inflation and varies with the population of a state. For example, the limit for Alaska, Hawaii and North Dakota is $87,300 and for California (the most populous state) it is $2,392,400. Contributions from corporations, labour organizations, national banks, government contractors, or foreign nationals are prohibited.[29] Contributions made in the name of another are also prohibited. A disclosure regime is also in place under the BCRA. Any person who spends more than $10,000 on electioneering communications within a calendar year must file a disclosure statement with the FEC. This statement must identify the person making the expenditure, the amount, the election to which it was directed and the names of certain contributors (s. 434(f)(2)). Disclosure regimes also exist at the state level in the US, although the ability of these regimes to produce more competitive elections and reduce the impact of large contributions on the political process is questionable (see Schultz 2005).

The Supreme Court has ruled on the constitutionality of campaign finance laws with respect to political parties on several occasions. These have predominantly concerned the provisions set by the *Federal Election Campaign Act* 1974 (FECA) – the *Bipartisan Campaign Reform Act*'s predecessor, which established limits on the campaign contributions that individuals, political parties and political action committees could make. The main issue that the Court has had to tackle has been how best to balance First Amendment freedoms against governmental interests.

The Court in *Buckley v. Valeo* 424 U.S. 1 (1976) upheld the regulatory provisions with respect to disclosure requirements and individual contributions set out in the FECA on the grounds that they served a compelling interest in preventing corruption, but as they applied to independent expenditures by individuals and groups, campaign expenditures and those made by a candidate from his or her personal funds, they were unconstitutional. State-imposed limits on spending were seen by the Court as violating the First Amendment, representing 'substantial rather than merely theoretical restraints on the quantity and diversity of political speech'. This was because expenditure was *essential* to political debate:

> A restriction on the amount of money a person or group can spend on political communication during a campaign necessarily reduces the quantity of expression by restricting the number of issues discussed, the depth of their exploration, and the size of the audience reached. This is because virtually every means of communicating ideas in today's mass society requires the expenditure of money. The distribution of the humblest handbill or leaflet entails printing, paper, and circulation costs. Speeches and rallies generally necessitate hiring

29 However, see the Supreme Court's ruling in *Citizens United* with respect to independent expenditures by corporations, discussed below.

> a hall and publicizing the event. The electorate's increasing dependence on television, radio, and other mass media for news and information has made these expensive modes of communication indispensable instruments of effective political speech.[30]

However, restrictions upon contributions were not seen as offensive to the First Amendment. The Supreme Court held that, in contrast to expenditure limits:

> ... a limitation upon the amount that any one person or group may contribute to a candidate or political committee entails only a marginal restriction upon the contributor's ability to engage in free communication ... The quantity of communication by the contributor does not increase perceptibly with the size of his contribution, since the expression rests solely on the undifferentiated, symbolic act of contributing ... A limitation on the amount of money a person may give to a candidate or campaign organization thus involves little direct restraint on his political communication, for it permits the symbolic expression of support evidenced by a contribution but does not in any way infringe the contributor's freedom to discuss candidates and issues.[31]

However, the Act's characterization of a contribution was problematic, as it essentially treated all money spent by an individual or organization in coordination with a candidate as though it were a direct contribution, and therefore subject to the limits set by the Act (Briffault 2000: 625). Beyond the difficulty of establishing what type of spending constitutes a contribution, the decision has been criticized for its inconsistency (Bennett 2009: 68–9). Indeed, both parts of the decision (relating to expenditure and contributions) have come under fire. Striking down expenditure limits has arguably fuelled a spending race in American politics, drowning out the speech of individuals and less resourced groups. Furthermore, in his dissent in *Buckley*, Chief Justice Burger argued that individual contributions and expenditures should also be protected under the First Amendment, given that 'contributions and expenditures are two sides of the First Amendment coin'.[32] Nevertheless, despite criticism, the Supreme Court's decision in *Buckley* continues to be the foundation upon which judicial analyses of the constitutionality of party finance laws are constructed.

In *Colorado Republican Federal Campaign Committee v. FEC (Colorado 1)* 518 U.S. 604 (1996), the FEC sued the Colorado Republican Party for exceeding the prescribed campaign contribution limits imposed by the *Federal Election Campaign Act* (FECA). The party argued that its spending constituted 'independent expenditures' rather than 'contributions'. The Court agreed, and held that a political party could make independent expenditures, that the Republican Campaign

30 *Buckley v. Valeo* 424 U.S. 1 (1976) at 19.

31 *Buckley v. Valeo* 424 U.S. 1 (1976) at 20–21.

32 *Buckley v. Valeo* 424 U.S. 1 (1976) at 241.

Committee's expenditure was independent, and as such the limitation upon it, characterized according to the *Buckley* decision, violated the First Amendment and was hence unconstitutional. In doing so, the Court accepted the party's argument that it was making an independent expenditure rather than a contribution (see Magarian 2003: 2023–31). The Supreme Court managed to avoid the party's broader claim that the party expenditure provisions were unconstitutional, including limits on coordinated expenditures (Altman 2002: 1003). However, this issue arose again in *Colorado II*, with respect to the question of whether a state could impose limits on coordinated expenditure with the substantial interest of preventing corruption. By a small majority (5–4), the Supreme Court upheld legislative limits on the total expenditure a political party could make on its candidates' campaigns.[33]

In *Colorado II*, the Federal Election Commission argued that a party's expenditures in coordination with its candidates essentially constituted contributions, and that allowing this expenditure 'would induce individual and other non-party contributors to give to the party in order to finance coordinated spending for a favored candidate beyond the contribution limits binding on them' (at 2361). In opposition, the party argued that the practice of coordinated spending was so fundamental to the activities and structure of the party that it could not function without it, and that a party is in a unique position to spend in such ways that promote candidates (see Altman 2002: 1012). The party's arguments have considerable resonance with the way in which a political party organization is commonly thought of in other liberal democracies, as a body that seeks to elect its candidates to public office, and in doing so would ordinarily expend funds for that purpose and in coordination with the individual concerned. These arguments were rejected by the majority of the Court, which concluded that political parties should be treated in the same manner as all other political actors in the restriction of coordinated expenditures.

The question then became whether the legislative provisions were 'closely drawn' to serve the 'sufficiently important government interest in combating political corruption' (at 2366).[34] The Court held that the state's motivation in limiting coordinated expenditure so as to close the possibility of circumventing contribution limits was legitimate and upheld the provisions as constitutional:[35] 'if suddenly every dollar of spending could be coordinated with the candidate, the inducement to circumvent would almost certainly intensify' (at 2368).

It is a consequence of the unique loose organization of political parties in the United States and the construction of elections in political finance laws as contests between individuals rather than acknowledging the role and importance of political parties, that has led to a line of rather confusing and questionable precedent that fails to recognize the true nature of political parties

33 *Federal Election Commission v. Colorado Republican Federal Campaign Committee* 121 S. Ct. 2351 (2001) (*Colorado II*).

34 Quoting *Nixon v. Shrink Mo. Gov't PAC*, 528 U.S. 377, 387–388 (2000).

35 *Colorado II*, 121 S. Ct. 2351, 2371 (2001).

as campaigning organizations and the intimate relationship between parties and their candidates. This much was acknowledged by the dissenting members of the Supreme Court in the *Colorado II* decision (Justices Thomas, Kennedy and Scalia) and in an earlier Eighth Circuit decision: *Missouri Republican Party v. Lamb* 227 F.3d 1070 (8th Cir. 2000). The Court in *Lamb* recognized that political parties and their candidates were 'virtual alter egos' and the speech or political expression of one cannot be separated from the other (at 1071). Commentators (see, for example, Altman 2002) have thus criticized the Court's decision in *Colorado II* as failing to recognize the place of political parties in American representative democracy.

Katz has documented the negative effect of the 'independent expenditure' requirement on the campaigns run by the major party organizations during the 2004 presidential campaign. In the two months before the election, the Democratic National Committee spent $88 million to oppose President Bush, but only $4.5 million to support Senator Kerry, a 'slant towards negativity' that was repeated in the pattern of Republican spending on campaign advertising. In order to avoid undertaking coordinated (and therefore legally limited) expenditures, it is easier for a committee to produce negative messages against their opponents without directly consulting with candidates than positive statements in support of a particular approach or principle (Katz 2007: 77–8). This example serves to illustrate the crucial intersection between electoral law and the actual functioning of democracy. What sort of a representative democracy do these provisions ultimately facilitate? One that is based on reasoned debate on key policy issues, or a more negative and cynical approach in discrediting one's opponents?

Citizens United

In January 2010, the US Supreme Court overturned provisions of the BCRA and FECA that prohibited corporations from undertaking independent expenditures on election advertising. The decision overturned the Court's previous decision in *Austin v. Michigan Chamber of Commerce* 494 U.S. 652 (1990), which held that political speech could be limited or banned based on the corporate identity of the speaker. In *Citizens United v. F.E.C.* 558 U.S. (2010), the majority held that although the 'government may regulate corporate political speech through disclaimer and disclosure requirements … it may not suppress that speech altogether' (at 1–2). Overall, the impact of the decision will be to allow corporations to play a greater role in election campaigns, either by funding the campaigns of interest groups and other third-party actors, or undertaking election advertising themselves in support of or opposition to a particular candidate.

Citizens United was a group that had produced a movie critical of the Hillary Clinton presidential nomination campaign (*Hillary: The Movie*). The movie was to be screened and television advertisements shown promoting it during the 2008 election season with the use of corporate funds. A federal district court found that using corporate funds to advertise the film violated sections of the BCRA, which prohibited corporations from using general treasury funds to make independent expenditures that advocated the election or defeat of a candidate through any form of media in an election campaign.[36]

On appeal, there were two main issues before the Supreme Court. First, whether *Hillary: The Movie* could properly be characterized as an electioneering communication that falls within the scope of s. 441b. Secondly, whether the legislation prohibiting corporations from making independent expenditures during election campaigns violated the First Amendment right of free speech. On the first issue, the majority found *Hillary* to be an election communication that fell under the scope of the BCRA, citing broader issues that were at stake in the case: 'the Court cannot resolve this case on a narrower ground without chilling political speech … It is not judicial restraint to accept an unsound, narrow argument just so the Court can avoid another argument with broader implications' (at 12).

Furthermore, the majority held that the BCRA's prohibition on independent corporate expenditures constituted a ban on free speech, which could not be upheld on governmental interest grounds. Justice Kennedy, writing for the majority, stated:

> By suppressing the speech of manifold corporations, both for-profit and non-profit, the Government prevents their voices and viewpoints from reaching the public and advising voters on which persons or entities are hostile to their interests … When government seeks to use its full power, including the criminal law, to command where a person may get his or her information or what distrusted source he or she may not hear, it uses censorship to control thought. The First Amendment confirms the freedom to think for ourselves.[37]

In reaching this conclusion, the Court rejected the argument that corporations should be treated differently in the context of electoral and constitutional law because they were not natural persons (at 26). This was a key point with which the dissenting justices disagreed:

> In the context of election to public office, the distinction between corporate and human speakers is significant. Although they make enormous contributions to our society, corporations are not actually members of it They cannot vote or run for office. Because they may be managed and controlled by nonresidents, their interests may conflict in fundamental respects with the interests of eligible voters. The financial resources, legal structure, and instrumental orientation of corporations raise legitimate concerns about their role in the electoral process. Our lawmakers have a compelling constitutional basis, if not also a democratic

---

36 2 U.S.C. 441b (2000 edn). The BCRA amended 441b (s. 203) to prohibited electioneering communications as well.

37 *Citizens United v. F.E.C.*, per Kennedy J at 38–9, 40.

> duty, to take measures designed to guard against the potentially deleterious effects of corporate spending in local and national races.[38]

In light of this decision, corporations may now use their funds to incur independent expenditures in election campaigns – for example, by producing advertisements in direct support or opposition of particular candidates. This now places US corporations in a position similar although arguably superior to corporations in Australia, Canada and the United Kingdom, which may incur political expenditure as 'third parties' in election campaigns with respect to both candidates and policy issues, but which are subject to disclosure requirements and spending limits in the UK and Canada.[39] Previously, under the provision of the BCRA, US corporations were restricted to intervening in campaigns only on policy issues. The majority did not see any increase of corporate money in elections as a threat to democracy:

> The appearance of influence or access … will not cause the electorate to lose faith in our democracy. By definition, an independent expenditure is political speech presented to the electorate that is not coordinated with a candidate … The fact that a corporation, or any other speaker, is willing to spend money to try to persuade voters presupposes that the voters have the ultimate influence over elected officials.[40]

The Supreme Court upheld other elements of the BCRA, including the requirement for disclaimers and disclosure.[41] When contributing funds to an advertisement, or advertising themselves, corporations must be identified. The Court also upheld the ban on corporations donating directly to candidates or political committees, and that of corporate and union 'soft money'.

Nevertheless, the decision raises a number of fundamental issues and implications for the structure of electoral democracy in the United States. First, if corporations are to be treated as political actors for the purposes of free electoral speech, how do we ascertain the 'voice' of the corporation? Should shareholders have a say in what speech and advertising the company engages in? A number of corporate governance issues thus arise, which have interesting parallels with the internal governance struggles that take place between party members and their leaders in both political parties and political associations in democracies outside the US. Secondly, the *Citizens United* ruling redefines the financial balance of corporations with respect to political parties in the electoral contest. While the former are now free to spend an unlimited amount with respect to independent expenditures in election campaigns, the latter are severely restricted in their use

38 *Citizens United v. F.E.C.*, per Stevens J at 2.

39 This was also the situation in New Zealand prior to the repeal of the *Electoral Finance Act* 2007.

40 *Citizens United v. F.E.C.*, per Kennedy J at 44.

41 BCRA 2 U.S.C. 441d(d)(2),(3).

of soft money (see the opinion of Justice Stevens, 20–21). Driven out of business by financial regulations, could we see a situation where the effective or functional role of political parties is becoming obsolete in American politics?

Patterns of Regulation and Emerging Issues

When comparing the regulation of private money in election campaigns and the financing of political parties across democracies, several elements appear as common mechanisms of state regulation: the disclosure of parties' income and expenditure; limits on total income by capping donations, and limits on total expenditure and regulation of specific forms and sources of political contributions. These elements are illustrated in Table 8.1.

Table 8.1 Regulating the Private Financing of Political Parties

State	Disclosure Regime?	Contribution Limits?	Expenditure Limits?	Sources Regulated
Australia	Yes. Donations in excess of AUD$10,900 to be disclosed.	No	No	No
Canada	Yes. Donations in excess of CA$200 to be disclosed.	Yes. $1,000 for individuals.	Yes. $0.70 multiplied by the number of electors in each district contested.	No donations from corporations, unions and foreign sources.
New Zealand	Yes. Donations in excess of NZ$10,000 to be disclosed.	No	Yes. $1 million for each national party, plus $20,000 for each constituency seat contested.	Limit on foreign donations.
United Kingdom	Yes. Amounts over 5,000 pounds to be disclosed (200 pounds if from a non-permissible source)	No	No	Foreign donations indirectly banned.
United States	Yes. Donations in excess of $200 to be disclosed.	Yes. $2,400 to an individual candidate and $30,400 to a national party.	Generally no. Optional limits upon receipt of public funding.	Contributions prohibited from corporations, labor organizations, national banks, government contractors and foreign nationals.

Of the states analysed, Australia and the United Kingdom have the most *laissez-faire* approach to regulation, relying only on disclosure regimes. Canada and New Zealand apply expenditure limits; whereas the United States has developed a regime that focuses more on limiting contributions to parties and encouraging transparency in advertising due to its unique experiences with First Amendment litigation.

Effective Disclosure Regimes

My analysis confirms previous findings that disclosure is the most common way of regulating parties' finance (Johnson 2008: 325). All democracies in this study rely upon a disclosure regime as a part of their overall approach to the regulation of parties' finances. As Bauer (2007: 38) observes, although a modest measure, financial disclosure is for the most part widely supported by electoral participants and legislators, even where limits of income and expenditure are opposed (see also Garrett 2005). Arguably, this is the approach that requires the least effort and monetary expense on the part of the state, as it is parties that must bear the administrative costs of collecting data for the purposes of the disclosure returns and once they are made public, they are effectively policed by the media and interested citizens who report on the party's spending activities. Nevertheless, the threshold at which disclosure is necessary varies among the democracies – ranging from \$200 in Canada to approximately US\$10,000 in Australia, New Zealand and the United Kingdom. While generally lauded as appropriate mechanisms for the deterrence of corrupt conduct through publicity, disclosure regimes have been criticized for their complexity, numerous loopholes and the administrative burdens they impose upon both political actors and electoral administrators. Furthermore, disclosure works by providing information on the donations concerned to a political party's opponents and the general public, but this only operates in a 'retroactive manner' (Geddis 2007: 142) and relies on there being a 'complete' reporting scheme assuming that everything is declared and that this is enforced.

A common problem that plagues any attempt to regulate donations to parties centres on the ambiguity as to what actually constitutes a 'donation' for the purposes of disclosure. As Geddis (2008: 229) argues, is there any practical difference between paying a membership fee and giving a donation to a political party? Furthermore, parties have now found creative ways in which to sell political access and thereby avoid the disclosure and maximum limits imposed by disclosure regimes. Political parties now commonly sell access to senior politicians either directly through events such as dinners or networking opportunities, or indirectly through fund-raising events organized or outsourced to intermediaries. As Young and Tham (2006) argue, the contributions raised from such events are unlikely to be identified as gifts, donations, or contributions as they do not meet the definition under electoral law.

It is crucial to the success of disclosure laws that there is an institutional regime composed of various political actors (parties, the media, electoral regulators, and so on) that can effectively translate political disclosures into transparency and enforcement mechanisms. A key role is played by the media in this regard in analysing and disseminating the information contained in disclosure returns to the public. However, as previously noted, media organizations might not always be willing to report such results for a myriad of reasons: the organization may offer partisan support to a particular political party; it may be a contributor, or the story might not be regarded as having enough commercial interest. There is also a particular relationship between the media and political parties that has been described as confrontational rather than informative, possibly fostering a culture of cynicism in system of political finance and in politics more generally:

> The media is a commercial enterprise that is governed by profit like all other private sector businesses. In my experience it is the way in which the media uses information about the internal activities of political parties, that has led to a desire to exclude them from party meetings and conferences. The feeding frenzy in which the media involve themselves during candidate selections provide obvious examples of the media's tendency to seek the conflict and dissention rather than to explain and inform on the process … I do not believe the public interest is best served under such an arrangement. (Margaret Wilson, former Chief of Prime Minister's Office and NZ Labour Party President, 1998: 170)

If the media can't or won't investigate, it may be necessary for state-funded bodies to undertake the investigation and disclose the information to the public in order to guarantee some minimum level of active enforcement. Failing to actively investigate disclosure returns encourages a culture of non-compliance, and may even lead to the legitimization and institutionalization of such a culture. Another major concern for electoral administrators is certain parties' interpretation of the finance laws that is not in the spirit of the democratic contest: 'there has been an unwillingness by some to comply with disclosure; some have sought to circumvent its intent by applying the narrowest possible interpretation of the legislation'.[42]

Associated Entities and Third Parties

Another challenge to the effective regulation of campaign finance is the existence and operation of what could be termed 'associated entities'. Such entities are associated with, or have a close relationship to registered political parties and may be used as investment vehicles, or to advocate a particular political agenda that is sympathetic to the party. As Young and Tham (2006: 18) note, these entities are not necessarily established in order to avoid transparency (they may be able to appoint a board of

42 Australian Electoral Commission, *Funding and Disclosure Report Following the Federal Election Held on 3 October 1998*, para. 2.

directors more skilled in financial management, or donors may feel more comfortable donating to an organization that is at arm's length from the party). However, they may also be used as a vehicle for expenditure where leaders can otherwise avoid the normal decision-making processes internal to the party. In most cases, such entities will be subject to similar disclosure requirements that apply to political and third parties, but they may not be scrutinized as carefully by the media.

A further difficulty for electoral administrators and legislators in how best to legislate for the participation of third parties in the electoral contest, and how their financial activities ought to be regulated. Third parties and pressure groups have always featured prominently in the American electoral contest. Although political action committees (PACs) are regulated under the BCRA, '527 organizations' (so named after the section of the US Internal Revenue Code that they are created under) do not fall under the scope of regulation if they advertise on political issues rather than seeking to endorse or disparage a particular candidate. Consequently, they are becoming an increasingly important source of influence and electoral expenditure during the electoral cycle (see, for example, Boatright 2007; Bauer 2007: 46–9). 527s are required to disclose contributions and expenditures over a certain amount, yet there have been significant problems with the disclosure regime, much to do with the capacity of the IRS to process and adequately scrutinize the sheer number of disclosures that have been submitted. Like the United States, third-party actors in Australia are subject to disclosure requirements (under s. 314 AEB of the *Commonwealth Electoral Act* 1918), which are the same disclosure requirements that apply to political parties.

There are limits imposed on total expenditure that can be undertaken by third parties in the United Kingdom under the PPERA (sections 85–100) and were also previously in force in New Zealand. The *Canada Elections Act* 2000 was amended in 2000 to place restrictions on the level of third-party advertising, which is capped at $150,000 (of which no more than $3,000 can be used to promote or disparage an electoral district candidate). The previous cap of $1,000 on third-party spending was held to be contrary to the freedoms of expression under the *Charter*.[43] However, general restrictions on third-party advertising were upheld by the Supreme Court in *Harper v. Canada* [2004] 1 S.C.R. 827, which concerned a challenge to the provisions of the *Canada Elections Act* by Stephen Harper, the then head of the National Citizens Coalition (NCC). Although the Court conceded that third-party limits were an infringement of the freedoms of expression provided for in the *Charter*, they were acceptable under section 1 as demonstrably justifiable in a free and democratic society. The Court held that unregulated third-party spending would:

> Lead to the dominance of the political discourse by the wealthy. Second, it may allow candidates and political parties to circumvent their own spending limits through the creation of third parties. Third, unlimited third party spending can

43 *Somerville v. Canada (Attorney General)* [1996] 8 W.W.R. 199 (Alta C.A.).

> have an unfair effect on the outcome of an election. Fourth, it can erode the confidence of the Canadian electorate who perceive the electoral processes as being dominated by the wealthy.[44]

Generally, the campaigning activities of 'third' parties now fall within the ambit of the various electoral provisions, and they are treated in much the same respect as political parties. For example, any election advertising made by third parties is subject to the same authorization requirements that political parties must also adhere to and they must also register with a relevant electoral authority. However, whereas the expenditure of third parties is limited in the United Kingdom and Canada, it is not in the US, Australia and New Zealand. The imposition of expenditure limits upon third parties was trialled in New Zealand at the 2008 election (a maximum of $120,000). However, the ambiguity surrounding what actually constituted expenditure for the purpose of the limit was so confusing for both third parties and electoral administrators that this legislation was repealed in 2009 (Trevett 2009).

Conclusion

Despite some similarities in the way in which private money flows to parties are regulated (for example, the baseline requirement that parties' incomes and expenditures be subject to public disclosure), there are some key differences between democracies which reflect historical idiosyncrasies that make uniform regulation difficult. The approaches of Australia and the United Kingdom are comparatively *laissez-faire*, while New Zealand and Canada buttress their disclosure requirements with limitations on party expenditure. Canada, the most regulated of the Commonwealth states, also imposes limitations on individual contributions or donations to political parties and bans donations from several sources including foreigners, trade unions and corporations. The United States relies predominantly on a combination of contribution and expenditure limits, although the latter have been subject to severe constitutional scrutiny by the Supreme Court.

These diverse regulatory regimes say much about the nature of the party systems in each of the democracies surveyed, and in particular, parties' relationship to other actors. In the United States, for example, elections are barely regulated as though political parties are present at all, instead centring on individual candidates. Recent legislative efforts to outlaw the use of soft money by parties and a corresponding willingness of the Supreme Court to allow election expenditures by a diverse range of political actors (now including corporations) could be said to increase the number and diversity of actors and voices in the electoral market-place – but correspondingly decrease the relative importance of political parties as electoral actors. At the same time, Canadian laws that prohibit unions from

44 *Harper*, 2004 SCC 33 at para. 79.

making contributions to political parties would be considered a source of outrage in Australia, the United Kingdom and New Zealand – where the labour parties' continued relationship with the trade unions in all of these countries has been a defining characteristic of the party system and the pattern of political competition since the late nineteenth century. By the same token, the constitutional right of free speech in United States jurisprudence is so pervasive that campaign expenditure limits such as those proscribed in Canada and New Zealand may well be struck down by the Supreme Court if implemented in the United States.

Nevertheless, all democratic societies are faced with the common challenge of reconciling the freedoms of the participants in the electoral process to solicit, donate and expend funds however they wish with their equality in the electoral contest. The regulatory regimes of a majority of the states in this research appear to favour the former goal – that of electoral freedom – through 'hands off' approaches to party finance, and the lax enforcement of disclosure regimes and expenditure limits. However, whether or not this preference for participant freedom is due to concern with the integrity of the democratic competition or the protection of incumbent interests is open to debate.

Chapter 9

Parties in Parliament: The Independence of the Legislature

Political Parties and Elections has documented an increasing (although not always consistent) programme of electoral and intra-party regulation, pointing towards the acknowledgement of parties as important political actors in elections. However, in the legislative arena, the law's conception of the 'proper' place and role of political parties remains influenced to a large degree by the doctrines of parliamentary sovereignty and legislative independence. As I argued in Chapter 2, the recognition of parliamentary parties and state support for their activities, particularly in Canada and the United Kingdom, has been an important catalyst for the evolving legal status of the extra-parliamentary party organization. None the less, as this chapter will demonstrate, there continues to exist a fundamental tension between the practical reality of political parties in Parliament, and the constitutional design of representative legislatures based on the Westminster model, where Parliament is composed of independent constituency representatives. Nowhere is this tension more apparent than in the potentially competing mandates or demands that parliamentarians face from their constituents and party organization. This chapter examines how the law has dealt with, and attempted to reconcile, these dual responsibilities.

The unique way in which political practice has evolved in the United States has meant that this tension is not as significant as in the other democracies analysed in this research. Unlike Australia, Canada, New Zealand and the United Kingdom, legislative party groups in the United States are largely independent from, and are not directly responsible to, the extra-parliamentary party organization. As Rosenblum (2000: 828) notes, 'officials are concerned with their own political positions and constituencies, not with the party; their campaigns are largely financially independent of the party; and they are candidate-, not party-, centered'. As such, the scope of this chapter is confined to an analysis of the four parliamentary systems: Australia, Canada, New Zealand and the United Kingdom. The first part of this chapter examines judicial attitudes towards the appropriate role of a parliamentarian, particularly an MP's relationship with their nominating party. The second part of this chapter examines laws that seek to prevent MPs from changing party allegiance once elected to Parliament and evaluates the experience that New Zealand has had in implementing them, drawing broader conclusions about the character and consequences of these laws and their potential application to other democracies.

Elected Representatives and the Westminster Parliamentary Tradition

The constitutional design of representative democracy in the United Kingdom and its former colonies is rooted in Burkean conceptions of the role of the parliamentarian as an independent representative (or trustee) of their electorate rather than a party delegate. Despite changing party systems and the modification of electoral laws to accommodate political parties as formal actors in electoral and parliamentary processes (see Gauja 2008), the common law has held a relatively consistent view of the representative role of a parliamentarian over the last century.

The 'proper relationship' between a parliamentarian and their electorate was first considered by the English Court of Appeal in 1909. The court expressed a strict disapproval with the concept of a political mandate, a position that stands in stark contrast to the importance of the concept in the model of party government that is prominent today:

> To deliver an opinion is the right of all men; that of constituents is a weighty and respectable opinion, which a representative ought always to rejoice to hear; and which he ought always most seriously to consider. But authoritative instructions; mandates issued, which the member is bound blindly and implicitly to obey, to vote, and to argue for, though contrary to the clearest conviction of his judgment and conscience; these are things utterly unknown to the laws of this land, and which arise from a fundamental mistake of the whole order and tenor of our constitution. Parliament is not a congress of ambassadors from different and hostile interests; which interests each must maintain, as an agent and advocate, against other agents and advocates; but parliament is a deliberative assembly of one nation, with one interest, that of the whole; where, not local purposes, not local prejudices ought to guide, but the general good, resulting from the general reason of the whole.[1]

If a member of Parliament is not bound by the wishes of their electorate, despite having been elected by a majority, they certainly cannot be bound at common law by the wishes of the party they represent. This line of reasoning was later applied in the 1980s by the UK courts in two key cases concerning party discipline and the delivery of election promises at the local council level.

Policy and Election Promises Made by Parties

According to the decisions in *Bromley London Borough Council v. Greater London Council* [1983] 1 AC 768 and *R v. Waltham Forest London Borough Council; ex parte Baxter* [1988] 2 WLR 257, parliamentarians are required to take individual

1 Per Farwell LJ in *Amalgamated Society of Railway Servants v. Osborne* [1909] 1 Ch. 163 at 197 (Court of Appeal).

responsibility for their actions and at all times consider the 'public interest' when voting or contributing to legislative debates. MPs should not consider themselves bound by policy documents or previous promises made by the party, even if the electorate has endorsed them by voting for the party in a general election. As Denning MR commented:

> It seems to me that no party can or should claim a mandate and commitment for any one item in a long manifesto. When the party gets into power, it should consider any proposal or promise afresh – on its merits – without any feeling of being obliged to honour it or being committed to it. It should then consider what is best to do in the circumstances of the case and to do it if it is practicable and fair.[2]

Blind deferral to party policy is considered a breach of a representative's duty to consider the interests of all in his or her electorate, irrespective of majority opinion:

> The rigid adoption of policy simply as a matter of political commitment to a section of the local government electorate and without regard to the purpose for which the statutory powers are given by itself demonstrates a breach of the fiduciary duty. That duty is owed not simply to all electors, but to the whole body of ratepayers, including a large and important number who have no voice at all in electing local councillors.[3]

Bromley v. GLC [1982] 1 All E.R. 129 concerned the implementation of a Labour Party election promise of an overall cut of 25 per cent across all London transport fares. As McAuslan (1983: 16) notes:

> Cuts of this nature had been a central plank of the election manifesto of the London Labour Party, and it might have been reasonable for that party, when it obtained a majority in the G.L.C. [Greater London Council], to think that it had a mandate to carry its policies out.'

However, the Court of Appeal was not convinced that the Labour Party had such a mandate and held that the party's manifesto was 'subject to an overriding limitation to do what was practicable and fair, as determined by a court, and to hold the balance fairly and reasonably' (Ibid.). As Lord Diplock pronounced:

> In neither case [majority or minority party] when the time comes to play their part in performing the collective duty of the [Greater London Council] to make choices of policy or action in particular matters must treat themselves as irrevocably bound to carry out pre-announced policies contained in election

2 *Bromley v. Greater London Council* at 777 per Denning MR.

3 *Bromley v. Greater London Council* at 793 per Oliver LJ.

> manifestos even though by that time, changes of circumstances have occurred that were unforeseen when those policies were announced and would add significantly to the disadvantages that would result from carrying them out.[4]

This line of precedent reveals a conception of the place of political parties that arguably contrasts with their role as electoral actors presenting policy alternatives to the electorate in order to form government. Although citizens will typically vote for a political party rather than an individual candidate, once a parliamentarian enters the legislative chamber, party considerations take a back seat to constituency interests, and the more ambiguous 'national interest', or in Lord Denning's words, to do what is 'practicable and fair'. This arguably complicates the chain of accountability central to the model of responsible party government, whereby parties formulate policies, present them to the voters at elections, and once in office act as a cohesive and disciplined body to implement them. However, the courts' conception of democracy could also be said to embrace a view of politics that extends beyond majoritarian interests, or those of the 'winning' political party, to protect the more general interest of the public at large and any minority groups that may have not had their preferences granted at the last election, but who still deserve to have a government govern with respect to their well-being. It also guards against a position where parties may be forced to carry out their policies even if economic circumstances have changed, or they are later found to be unworkable.

However, the House of Lords' decision in *Secretary of State for Education and Science v. Tameside Metropolitan Borough Council* [1976] 3 All E.R. 665 departs from this reasoning in some respects. While upholding previous authority that legislators cannot be dictated to vote or act in any particular way by a third party, the House of Lords in *Tameside* suggested that political parties may have a duty to carry out the policies for which they were elected. This case concerned a Conservative council that planned to carry out its election promise to retain selective-entry grammar schools. The policy was controversial and contrary to the views of many education professionals. The Secretary of State, dissatisfied with the Conservatives' policy and plans, acted under his powers to give directions to a local education authority that he was satisfied was acting unreasonably, and ordered the Conservative council to implement its predecessor's plans to scrap selective-entry grammar schools – to the detriment of its own election promises.

This order was challenged and struck down by the English Courts (including both the Court of Appeal and the House of Lords), which held the policy was not unreasonable and further placed great emphasis upon the existence of the ruling party's mandate to implement its election manifesto unimpeded by the bureaucracy. For example, Lords Dilhorne and Salmon regarded the Conservative Party as having obtained a mandate from the electorate not to implement the policies of its predecessors, but rather to preserve grammar schools.[5] Lord Wilberforce further

---

4 [1982] 1 All E.R. 129, 165.

5 *Tameside*, [1976] 3 All E.R. 665 at 688, 698.

held that 'In voting for this change in May 1976 the electors must have accepted if not favoured, some degree of improvisation … The Secretary of State … failed to take into account that it was entitled – *indeed in a sense bound – to carry out the policy on which it was elected*'.[6]

The key distinguishing feature between *Tameside* and *Bromley* appears to be the 'reasonableness' of the election promise or the policy in question, and the change in economic and social circumstances that might occur in the period between when the policy is promised, and when it is to be implemented.

Crossing the Floor

In the United Kingdom, and presumably in the other democracies surveyed in this research (although it has not been tested in the courts),[7] if a parliamentarian crosses the floor on an issue and votes against the wishes of their party, they cannot be expelled or forced to resign from Parliament, even if the MP has taken a pledge or signed an agreement to do so (Oliver 2003: 133; Cowley 1996: 219; also see Orr 2002; Tardi 2007). As Donaldson MR ruled in the context of local council representation:

> What would be objectionable would be a provision that a member had forthwith to resign his membership of the council if, in the absence of a conscience situation, he intended to vote contrary to group policy. This would fetter his discretion and make him a mere delegate of the majority of the group.[8]

Similarly, the Court of Appeal in *Conservative and Unionist Central Office v. Burrell (Inspector of Taxes)*[9] held that 'once elected members of the House of Commons [parliamentarians] become representatives of the constituency for which they have been elected, not delegates of the local constituency associations which may have put them up as candidates' (per Lawton LJ at 252). As noted, a difficulty with this legal conception of representative democracy is that it bears little semblance with the reality of party politics, where constituents vote for parties rather than individuals, and parliamentarians overwhelmingly vote along party lines (see Cowley 1996: 221). The law's rather creative response to reconciling the latter of these tensions has not been to alter the basic conception of the role of the representative as a trustee for the electorate, but to include party discipline and unanimity as a legitimate consideration in choosing how to vote. As the majority in *R v. Waltham* found:

6 *Tameside*, [1976] 3 All E.R. 665, 684–685 (emphasis added). See further McAuslan (1983: 14–15).

7 Note the exception of New Zealand between 2001 and 2005 – see further below.

8 *R v. Waltham* per Donaldson MR at 261.

9 [1982] 1 WLR 522.

> I can see no reason why a councillor should not vote in favour of a resolution contrary to his own intellectual assessment of the merits, taken in isolation, in order to secure unanimity of vote, provided he retains an unfettered discretion in the council chamber. There is nothing, in my view, morally or legally culpable in voting in support of a majority which he has considered, and rejected, in his arguments providing he considers all the available options and that he considers that the maintenance of such unanimity is of greater value to the ratepayers than insistence upon his own view.[10]

> Party loyalty, party unanimity, party policy, were all relevant considerations for the individual councillor. The vote becomes unlawful only when the councillor allows these considerations or any other outside influences so to dominate to exclude other considerations which are required for a balanced judgment. If, by blindly toeing the party line, the councillor deprives himself of any real choice or the exercise of any real discretion, then his vote can be impugned and any resolution supported by his vote potentially flawed.[11]

Therefore, legal precedent suggests that members of Parliament are effectively free agents – immune from any attempt to mandate their voting in the legislature in favour of their party or electorate. It would appear that subsequent to the decision in *R v. Waltham*, a voter cannot hold their elected representative legally accountable for voting along party lines in breach of their duty to their constituency. Similarly, neither a political party nor its members nor supporters can hold its parliamentarians legally accountable for failing to abide by party policy or election promises. This position consequently has implications for the internal organization of political parties, necessitating the creation of extra-legal and intra-party means by which to hold parliamentarians to account to the party and its platform. The most common of these measures is the candidate selection contest, which sitting members of Parliament may be subject to (see Chapter 5). For example, in the 1970s, leftist activists in the UK Labour Party successfully challenged the party's rules to provide for the mandatory reselection of all parliamentarians in the life of a Parliament. This measure, as Jones and colleagues (2007: 194) argue, was 'widely regarded as a device to make MPs more beholden to leftist activists in the constituencies than to the party whips in Westminster'. However, this requirement was overturned again in the 1990s when the party agreed that reselection would only be necessary if requested by a ballot of local members. Although mandatory reselection of parliamentarians is a norm of formal party practice in Australia and New Zealand, the influence MPs have over the internal decision-making processes of their parties all but guarantees their reselection.

---

10 *R v. Waltham* at 264–5 per Stocker LJ.

11 *R v. Waltham* at 265 per Russel LJ.

Party Hopping Laws

With the exception of New Zealand (discussed in detail below), parliamentary party groupings and individual parliamentarians are generally free from legal interference – in that their members are free to cross the floor and vote against a party's majority position or platform, or even switch party allegiance without being forced to resign from Parliament. Nevertheless, the practice of 'party hopping' does have the potential to significantly alter the balance of representation in the legislature.

In the United States, party defections between 1947 and 1994 (where of the 20 members changing sides in this period, 16 switched from Democrat to Republican) incrementally assisted the Republicans in gaining the control of the Congress in the 1990s (Nokken 2000: 421). In a 'celebrated reversal of the trend', control of the Senate reverted to the Democrats in 2001, when Jim Jeffords (a Republican Senator from Vermont) switched to the Democrats when the Senate was split between the two parties and voted with the Democrats to choose the chamber's leaders (Janda 2009: 6–7). In Canada, former MP Belinda Stronarch switched her allegiance from Conservative to the Liberal Party in 2005, enabling the Liberal government to survive a vote on budget amendments that might have otherwise brought it down. Stronarch was offered a place in the Ministry immediately upon joining the Liberals' ranks.

Arguably, such pivotal events and other instances of party hopping have the potential to destabilize legislatures and party systems. They may even be viewed as anti-democratic – as acts that render voters' party preferences as expressed through general elections meaningless (Kelsen 1929: 42–3; Manin 1997: 211–14). For these very reasons, several nations (including India, Israel and Portugal) have in place laws and regulations to control or prohibit party hopping by requiring parliamentarians to surrender their seats if they change sides (see, for example, Janda 2009; Miskin 2003). In Canada, following Stronarch's defection, a private members' bill was introduced by Conservative MPs (C-208), which required a by-election within 35 days in any riding where an MP defected from the party through which they were elected. One of the co-sponsors of the Bill, Helena Guergis, argued, 'When voters elected that person they made the decision based on what they campaigned for and what party they were representing … If they're not going to continue to get what they voted for, then they should have the right to have what they want' (CTV News Online 2005).

However, the Bill has not yet progressed through the legislative process.[12] On the flip side, anti-party hopping laws could also be construed as fundamentally incompatible with the democratic parliamentary freedoms of independent

12 The Canadian province of Manitoba has passed legislation requiring MPs who cross the floor to sit as Independents, preventing them from joining another political party (s. 1, *Elections Reform Act*, S.M. 2006, c. 15, Schedule E). However, the legislation cannot stop MPs voting with a rival party (see Tardi 2007).

thought and association, and have also been interpreted as a more disingenuous means by which to protect the interests of the established or entrenched parties (Janda 2009: 21; Geddis 2006a). Consequently, established liberal democracies tend not to restrict the party associations of their legislators. A notable exception is the experience of New Zealand in the transition to a proportional representation electoral system.

New Zealand's Electoral Integrity (Amendment) Act 2001

The tension between parliamentarians' independence and their election on a party platform caused particular difficulties in New Zealand after the transition to multi-member proportional representation and the introduction of party list voting, which entrenched the role of parties (not individual parliamentarians) as the unit of interest aggregation. As Stockley (2004: 134) notes, since the introduction of the reforms in 1996, it has been presumed that parliamentarians will vote with their party unless they advise otherwise.

As in Australia and the UK, several parties in New Zealand require candidates to ratify their commitment to the party cause.[13] For example, Labour candidates must sign a pledge to 'vote on all questions in accordance with the decisions of the Caucus of the Parliamentary Labour Party' (NZ Labour 2003). The effectiveness of such pledges was tested by the New Zealand Parliament's Privileges Committee after the Alliance Party list parliamentarian Alamein Kopu decided to leave the party but refused to resign her seat. The Alliance Party, which governed in coalition with Labour between 1999 and 2002,[14] required candidates to resign their seat in Parliament if for whatever reason they left the party. In ruling the pledge to be unenforceable on the ground of public policy, the committee upheld the common law's refusal to regulate the decisions of parliamentarians, or uphold any document that purported to do so. However, in this instance, the committee was faced with the added difficulty of reconciling its decision with the fact that the actions of a parliamentarian in leaving the party through which they were elected might destroy the proportionality of the New Zealand Parliament. The Privileges Committee considered this predicament, but held that in the absence of any statutory intention to the contrary, the principles of freedom and independence should prevail over that of proportionality:

> The balance that, in my view, has been struck between these two principles under the current statutory regime is that while the principle of proportionality dominates the process by which Members are appointed to Parliament, the

13 For example, the Constitution of the Australian Democrats requires that if MPs elected subsequently resign from the party, they must also resign their parliamentary seat (Article 11.2). Interestingly, there is no mention of this in the constitutions of the Canadian parties (see Tardi 2007).

14 The Alliance is a small leftist party that gained parliamentary representation between 1996 and 2002. Although currently registered, it holds no seats in the NZ Parliament.

> statutory scheme supports their freedom and independence once elected. Thus in law an Alliance MP retains the freedom to cross the floor and vote with the opposing political forces notwithstanding the fact that this would be in breach of both the Alliance nomination pledge and the principle of proportionality … There may be legitimate questions of whether this is a desirable legislative policy. If so, that question needs to be resolved by Parliament.[15]

To counter this problem, but contrary to the common law tradition of representation, the New Zealand Parliament passed the *Electoral (Integrity) Amendment Act* 2001. The Act was initiated by the Labour/Alliance government elected in 1999, which in the aftermath of the Kopu resignation was 'determined to stop defections' (Palmer and Palmer 2004: 140). Indeed, 'party hopping' was perceived to be a significant problem during the period of transition to proportional representation: during the 44th parliament (1993–96), 14 MPs defected from their parties, while a further 11 defected during the 45th parliament (1996–99) (Malone 2008: 51).

Containing provisions contrasting with the constitutional norms of representative democracy in New Zealand, there was significant doubt over the legislation's consistency with the *New Zealand Bill of Rights Act* 1990 and despite the determination of the governing coalition to pass legislation that would in essence enforce party discipline, the Act passed through Parliament subject to 'serious criticism' and required 'heavy amendment in order to secure enough votes to pass' (Palmer and Palmer 2004: 140). Under the Act, an MP who notified the Speaker of having resigned from their party was also deemed to have resigned from the Parliament. Section 55D of the *Electoral Act* 1993 also contained a provision to declare a seat vacant if the Parliamentary Leader of a party served notice on the Speaker that he or she 'reasonably believes that the MP has acted in a way that has distorted, and is likely to continue to distort' party proportionality in the Parliament (Stockley 2004: 134). However, the MP must be given prior notice and an opportunity to respond, and two-thirds of the party's MPs must agree with the serving of the notice.

The implications of this legislation for party organization are significant and diverge considerably from the traditional position of the common law. As Geddis (2006a: 25–6) notes, the legislation sought to sever 'any direct link between each individual representative's right to sit in Parliament and the voting decisions of the electorate at large, by effectively transferring the legal "ownership" of each MP's seat' to the party who nominated him or her, and constituted a 'sea change in New Zealand's conception of the "proper" role of an elected representative'. With the intent of maintaining proportionality within the Parliament, the Act formalized and institutionalized party discipline, holding MPs legally accountable to their parliamentary parties with significant sanctions. This arguably strengthens party accountability if individual parliamentarians are not able to depart from already

15 Question of Privilege: Contention as to Resignation of Mrs Alamein Kopu MP, McGrath JJ, 10 September 1997, p. 5.

formulated policy positions. Their actions did not necessarily have to amount to crossing the floor: 'if there is a cumulative number of particular actions or a continuing pattern of conduct designed to embarrass the political party, to harm its reputation not only in Parliament but also with those who voted for it', then the leader can form a reasonable belief that proportionality is distorted and request a seat be declared vacant.[16] Therefore, the legislation could stop rebel MPs from hijacking policy decided by the party and endorsed by the voters. It could not, however, serve this function if all MPs agreed on a policy position (as it is the MPs who initiate and approve the notice, not the party members or voters), significantly reducing accountability to the extra-parliamentary party organization and the general public. As the legislation treats political parties as homogenous entities, it has also been criticized as unworkable in practice, particularly in a situation where there is an irresolvable split within a political party – a situation that is not uncommon in party politics (Geddis 2006a: 41–3; Geddis 2002b).

Currently, this legislation is more notable for its theoretical rather than practical application, as there was little attempt to enforce it. The legislation was not invoked in the defections of Jim Anderton from the Alliance in 2002 and Tariana Turia from Labour in 2004 (Miller 2005: 125). It was, however, used by the Act Party to force the resignation of one of its MPs, Awatere Huata, from Parliament (*Awatere Huata v. Prebble* [2005] 1 NZLR 289, SCNZ). Huata was suspended from the Act Party after public accusations and subsequent charges being laid relating to her misappropriation of public funds. She challenged the party's notice to expel her, arguing that she would continue to sit in Parliament as an Independent but still vote with the Act Party, and therefore she would not be distorting the proportionality of Parliament for the purposes of the legislation. The New Zealand Supreme Court disagreed in what could be interpreted as a very technical line of reasoning that simply equated the concept of distorting proportionality with a parliamentarian's party membership status (Geddis 2006a: 45). Regardless of the way in which she would vote (which was deemed to be irrelevant), the Court held that the very fact that she was sitting as an Independent would change the balance of representation in the House by reducing the overall number of Act parliamentarians in the legislature. By linking parliamentary and party membership status in this way, Geddis (2006a: 45–6) has argued that the legislation transfers enormous power to the party hierarchy (as they determine who is/is not a party member) to also determine whether MPs may continue to serve in the Parliament if there is a disagreement, or if the MP has become a political liability.

Given the *Electoral (Integrity) Amendment Act*'s rocky passage through Parliament and uncertain application, the legislation was unsurprisingly subject to a sunset clause and expired in September 2005. Attempts to reintroduce the legislation in December 2005 were aborted after a majority of the Justice and

16 Per Gendall J, *Huata v. Prebble and Shirley,* High Court, Auckland, Civ 70/4/03, 19 February 2004.

Electoral Committee voted to reject the amending bill.[17] Advice received from the New Zealand Solicitor General indicated that a bill to reinstate the party-hopping provisions may have infringed the constitutional freedoms of association and expression protected by the New Zealand Bill of Rights Act.[18] The Attorney General (Arnold 2005) noted that:

> … the importance of political parties in the current electoral and parliamentary system must be considered in light of the established Burkean view of members' independence, under which dissent from members' parties is not only tolerated but accepted as an element of the democratic process. (at para. 34)
>
> In summary, the Bill does not protect what I have described as 'legitimate dissent' in the House by an individual member concerning his/her party or its policies. Rather, it accords to the party and its leader a very wide discretion. The question is whether that means that the limitation on rights contained in the Bill is not 'proportionate', and therefore that the Bill is not BORA [Bill of Rights Act] consistent. (at 42)

None the less, according to information obtained by the author in an interview with senior Labour Party parliamentarians in 2008, reinstating the anti party-hopping laws remains on the agenda of the NZ Labour Party.

Conclusion

The most significant practical consequence of the judicial decisions relating to the behaviour of legislators is that they guarantee the autonomy of both the parliamentary party and individual parliamentarians from decisions of the party organization in any matters that can be applied to the legislative arena. If parliamentarians are to represent their constituencies, which are typically defined by electoral law in geographic rather than party terms, they must remain independent in their deliberations and cannot take orders from third parties or external bodies. This includes voting in Parliament in accordance with party policy, even if it has been formulated with the involvement of the membership and approved by the electorate. At face value, this approach appears to be fundamentally inconsistent with the chain of accountability between voters and legislators that is established in the model of responsible party government.

---

17 Electoral (Integrity) Amendment Bill 2005 – see Malone (2008: 73).

18 New Zealand Crown Law Office, Attorney General, Legal Advice, Consistency with the New Zealand Bill of Rights Act 1990: Electoral (Integrity) Amendment Bill 2005, 3 November 2005. However, despite expressing grave concerns the Attorney General advised that subject to the NZ Supreme Court's decision in *Awatere Huata v. Prebble* the 'better view' is that the Bill is consistent with the Bill of Rights Act (at para. 48).

While in most cases, the accountability of parliamentarians must be secured by political (extra-legal) means such as regular elections and candidate selection contests, some nations legislate to require MPs who change their party alliance to resign from Parliament. Such legislation was adopted by New Zealand during 2001–2005 in the transition to proportional representation in order to protect the proportionality of Parliament as determined by voters' preferences for particular political parties rather than individual candidates. Nevertheless, the legislation expired in 2005 and was subject to many criticisms, including that it contravened basic liberal principles of freedom and association and expression, could not adequately deal with intra-party splits, protected established parties and gave a great deal of power to the party leadership to decide the fate of individual parliamentarians if they voted against the party line.

Chapter 10
Conclusion

Political Parties and Elections presented a comparative analysis of the way in which the law regulates the activities of political parties as electoral actors in five common law democracies: Australia, Canada, New Zealand, the United Kingdom and the United States. The basic pattern that has emerged in all of these democracies over the last century is an increasing trend towards the regulation of parties' activities, particularly with respect to their financial affairs and, to a lesser extent, how they make 'important' internal decisions, such as choosing candidates for public office. In part, this regulation has been driven by a desire to eliminate corruption and centralization in party politics, and create a fair and equal playing field for all electoral participants. However, regulation has also developed in tandem with legislative measures that acknowledge political parties as official actors in the electoral process and that bestow upon them significant state resources and public subsidies. Many of these measures (for example, public subsidies for campaign expenses and gatekeeper provisions) are not equal in their application, and tend to privilege the major parties and entrenched interests. The increasing field of regulation to which parties are now subject has also been driven by more than a century of judicial decisions that have largely reflected shifting social conceptions of the place of political parties in democratic society: from private entities to organizations performing important democratic (public) functions.

The central argument of the book has been that the similarities and differences between the various regimes can best be understood as the product of, or inherently connected to, lawmakers' own visions of representative democracy and the place of parties within it. However, despite a general trend towards increased regulation and some convergence between the democracies, these laws are by no means the product of a consistent normative vision – either across time or between the various actors that influence the development of the law. As I noted in Chapter 1, there are many areas of law that can potentially influence the behaviour of political parties, many different legislators who formulate these laws, numerous judges who interpret them, and various executive agencies and electoral commissions that apply and enforce them. Taken together, what we are left with is a body of law resembling a patchwork quilt of decisions and statutes, that is characterized by its *ad hoc* and fluid nature, and that bears the marks of a battle between different sets of law makers – whether this is a battle that is fought along partisan lines or one that takes place between the arms of government, notably between the legislature and the judiciary.

Indeed, one of the characteristics of the relationship between politics and the law, and one of the key difficulties in regulating the activities of political parties is the immense conflict of interest that arises when political parties essentially legislate for their own existence. What we have seen is electoral reforms that privilege some party types over others, for example, prohibitions on certain sources of party funds – such as corporations or labour unions – that have historically favoured certain parties, or constituted a significant source of their income. Other laws that are enacted, such as gatekeeper provisions that require a certain level of electoral support before a party may gain registration or ballot access, may privilege major party players at the expense of minor parties or new competitors. For the most part, such laws are left unchallenged as on the surface they apply to all parties equally. However, upon deeper analysis, inequalities in the application of the law to different political parties may become apparent. In this sense, politics and the pattern of dominant interests play an important part in shaping the law.

Beyond the partisan battle is another that has been forged between the legislature in formulating party laws, and the decisions of the judiciary in interpreting them. In rare instances, the courts have used their power of constitutional review to strike down legislation that has a clear partisan bias (for example, *Tashjian*). In other instances, the courts have interpreted statutory provisions in such a light so as to reflect a different set of normative political values to those of the Parliament (for example, cases dealing with the delicate balance between freedom of political communication and expression and campaign financing laws). Where there is no legislation that seeks to control the behaviour of parties, courts have occasionally adapted common law principles in other areas of law (for example, contract, employment and administrative law) to resolve intra-party disputes and shape the internal workings of political parties according to a particular conception of their role in representative democracy. However, there is considerable variation here between democracies as to the extent to which courts will look into what have traditionally been considered parties' internal matters, with more willingness to do so in Australia and the United Kingdom and less in Canada and the United States.

As the legal status of political parties is still evolving, so too is opinion as to the body of law that is most applicable to them. In Canada and the United States, the internal affairs of political parties are not interfered with by the protection of Charter and First Amendment rights. In Australia and New Zealand, interference has been justified on the basis of legislative recognition and subsequently principles of administrative law have been applied. By contrast, contract and employment law have been the main mechanisms to resolve party disputes in the United Kingdom. What this illustrates is a pragmatic approach by the courts to attempt to adjudicate disputes and solve existing political problems with only a limited repertoire of tools available in the absence of any statutory or explicit constitutional directions. In acting creatively, courts can indeed act as political institutions.

I noted in Chapter 1 that the law plays a crucial role in regulating politics and in legitimizing election processes and government decision making once a party assumes office. What appears to be reasonably consistent across the party laws of all democracies analysed here is an underlying conception of representative democracies as reflecting majority values and an associated concern for the integrity of the electoral process within a context of limited competition. Although the threshold is always a matter of degree, courts have been willing to uphold gatekeeper requirements that demand parties have sufficient electoral support to demonstrate the seriousness of their purpose and limit the number of electoral participants so as to avoid voter confusion. However, a careful consideration of appropriate thresholds (seats contested, minimum membership numbers required and electoral results) is necessary to ensure that electoral law provisions do not unduly discriminate against minor players to the continued benefit and dominance of the major players – thereby depriving voters of a longer-term electoral choice. The Green Paper on electoral reform commissioned by the Australian government in 2009 recognized that the current electoral arrangements in Australia should seek to accommodate a number of competing interests, among them accessibility:

> From the perspective of ensuring representation, it might be argued that registration and nomination systems should be accessible to a broad range of parties and candidates, and should not of themselves present an unreasonable barrier to persons who wish to stand for election to Parliament. (Australian Government 2009: 116)

Reforms to electoral laws that encourage greater participation and a plurality of interests that move away slightly from the majoritarian system may do something to address the problem of decreasing public engagement in, and satisfaction with, formal political institutions. In this respect, New Zealand is an interesting case as it is an example of a polity in which such electoral reforms were actually undertaken in response to citizen disaffection with majoritarian electoral processes. With the transition to MMP in 1993, political parties now occupy a central place in New Zealand's electoral legislation. The *Electoral Act* 1993 imposed key regulatory requirements, both internal and external, on New Zealand's political parties. In some respects, this is illustrative of a legislative regime that has been implemented with a reasonably clear and coherent vision of the place of parties within the framework of representative democracy. However, even this relatively comprehensive legislative scheme is subject to judicial interpretation and the practical reality that such provisions actually need to be actively enforced.

The relationship between political parties and the law is dynamic. The law both constitutes, and is constituted by, political parties. We have seen how parties can influence the law, but in regulating political parties, the law also has important implications for structuring the functions that they perform. For example, by controlling the flow of money to political parties, the law can indirectly affect the level of engagement parties have with civil society and individuals, both in seeking contributions and volunteer labour. This has important flow on effects for the function of political parties as participatory organizations. However, the law also needs to take into account the fact that political parties are adaptive organizations, and as the nature of politics and patterns of political behaviour change – so must the law. An excellent example of this is parties' use of associated entities, third parties and creative fund-raising activities to avoid expenditure limits and disclosure obligations. Another is the continued use of a minimum number of financial members as a threshold for party registration in Australia, Canada and New Zealand – a measure of popular support that is becoming outdated as the number of citizens joining political parties declines across the globe.

There is no doubt that in all democracies surveyed, political parties have become formalized actors in the political process. Although their constitutional absence is a reminder of parties' traditional role in civil society, they are now subject to significant statutory regulation as 'public entities'. With this regulation comes significant benefits such as public funding, access to electronic broadcasting and the right to print party affiliations on ballot papers. However, this regulation as the product of legislative instruments remains at best ambivalent towards the internal processes of political parties, preferring to regulate parties' intersection with the operation of the broader electoral system rather than their internal organization. This raises the important question of whether, given the public benefits that they accrue, political parties should be expected to conduct their internal affairs consistent with public expectations, which may include an adherence to democratic principles in intra-party decisions.

The claim that political parties have attained legislative recognition as political actors in the electoral arena does not of itself justify legal intrusion into parties' internal affairs. In this sense, the public–private distinction is misleading, circular and unhelpful. However, underlying this public–private reasoning is the normative policy consideration that political parties now play an important role in our society and representative democracy, and as such their activities ought to be regulated. The justification for regulating political parties must flow from their functions, not necessarily their status. However, in turn it is necessary to determine what these functions are (or what they should be) and develop regulatory measures that seek to facilitate them.

If we see parties as promoting citizen participation in politics, then the external enforcement of parties' rules or the regulation of the content of these rules may be seen as desirable. Whether or not intra-party democracy is desirable is a continuing topic of contention and it is debatable as to whether or not democratic decision-making processes should be imposed upon political parties externally (either by the courts or the legislature). Nevertheless, we run into trouble when electoral legislation (in particular, registration requirements) do not require parties to formulate a set of rules that enumerates how they are run on a daily basis and the procedures by which binding decisions are made. In this situation, intra-party disputes (without a written constitution outlining the governance structure of the party) cause concern and can become a real headache for the courts that must adjudicate these matters. As I have shown with respect to the case law in Australia and the United Kingdom, if political parties don't provide these rules themselves, the courts will apply existing legal principles in order to fill in the gaps. This has seen a trend towards the application of administrative principles, usually reserved for public bodies, to the internal affairs of political parties. It is also an extremely costly way for litigants to resolve what at their core are essentially political disputes.

If it is the electoral function of parties or that of interest aggregation that is the primary concern, then it will be worthwhile prioritizing regulations that enhance fairness, transparency and accountability to the public. As Turpin and Tomkins (2007: 507) argue, 'the free choice of the electorate may be impaired if the competing parties have unequal opportunities of making their policies known to the people'. Nevertheless, not all enforcement can, or should come from the state. Some may be brought about by self-regulation in compliance with the logic of electoral competition, but where this fails, there is a *prima facie* case for state regulation to achieve normative democratic goals. As it currently stands, political parties (as entrenched actors) in all the democracies surveyed in this research tend to benefit from this dual system of treatment that regulates their activities within the electoral arena (for example, laws pertaining to the design of electoral systems and the provision of public funds), but also protects their associational autonomy and freedom with respect to their intra-party affairs.

In Chapter 5, I examined the legal regulation of parties' candidate selection contests. This is one of the most heavily litigated areas in party administration, given the importance of achieving a party nomination for having any hope of gaining election to the legislature. Australia, Canada and the United Kingdom do not have any statutory provisions that regulate their candidate selection contests in any particular way. Disputes that may arise are resolved by the parties themselves, or the courts, whether this be through administrative principles (Australia), or employment law or contract (United Kingdom). It is often a costly and electorally damaging exercise, and as the case of pre-selection battles in Australia demonstrates, left unregulated it may also have a detrimental effect on the overall integrity of, and trust in, the democratic process. New Zealand employs a limited system of regulation, requiring parties to uphold democratic principles in the selection of their candidates. However, the terms of the provision are very wide and open to interpretation, meaning that there is actually significant diversity amongst the parties in their candidate selection procedures. The United States, by contrast, provides for a comparatively expansive system of regulation – opening party contests up to registered voters and making them in effect, public events and subject to judicial and legislative regulation. Interestingly, party primaries have been floated as a reform option in Australia but at the suggestion of the parties themselves – not as a state-imposed measure.

The question that then arises is where should the impetus for regulation of parties as electoral actors lie? Should these decisions be made by legislators, by the judiciary, or by the parties themselves? Unlike many democracies that have explicitly provided for political parties in their constitutional documents, Australia, Canada, New Zealand and the United States have typically omitted political parties from their constitutions, instead relying on convention and arguably taking parties for granted and acknowledging their existence only when need occurs, often in a very *ad hoc* fashion. This has left a substantial gap in the regulatory regime for courts to potentially fill. In arguing the importance of the common law in the overall scheme of party law, I also acknowledged the central importance of judges as both law makers and political actors. Recalling the US Supreme Court's decision in *Bush v. Gore* 531 U.S. 98 (2000) and the outcome of this decision on the 2000 presidential election, Nelson (2005: 87) argues that issues surrounding the Court's conception of political parties 'go to the very core of the operation of our constitutionally framed democratic representative government. In the contemporary context, the institutional and political significance of what the Supreme Court says and has said about political parties can hardly be exaggerated'. However, as with the possibility that parties might make laws to serve their own interests, the democratic legitimacy of judicial decision making is also questionable on the grounds that this decision making should lie in the hands of elected officials who at least can be held accountable through general elections, rather than non-elected judges (Avnon 1995: 285). As Justice LeBel of the Canadian Supreme Court wrote in *Figueroa*:

> In suggesting that the motive behind the legislation may itself be illegitimate, the Court risks unduly expanding the scope of judicial review of the design of the electoral system. I would sound a note of caution against blurring the distinction between the respective roles of the Court and the legislature in dealing with a question which, while it certainly has legal dimensions, is also profoundly political. Within certain boundaries, which it is the responsibility of the judiciary to delineate, balancing competing democratic values and choosing between the various species of democratic electoral systems primarily fall within the domain of political debate and of the legislative process. Those boundaries should be viewed as fairly broad. They allow for a good deal of latitude within which the people, through their elected lawmakers, may choose rules and institutions that enhance certain aspects of the democratic right to meaningful participation and diminish others. (at para. 182)

Yet, the appropriate role of the judiciary is a question that has been around for a very long time, and is no closer to resolution. On one hand, Justice LeBel's approach could be interpreted as representative of a school of thought that respects the democratic authority of the legislature; on the other, it could be regarded as characteristic of a 'disturbing tendency toward unreflective deference' (Feasby 2007: 542).

It is impossible, or indeed undesirable, to escape normative arguments and considerations in the context of the legal regulation of political parties. Yet, adopting a comparative and interdisciplinary method combining both law and politics to analyse the regulatory regimes that already exist uncovers these normative assumptions and reveals the patterns of interactions between the various political actors, that together, shape the character of the law and guide its continuing evolution. There are important findings and conclusions for both branches of social inquiry. As Müller and Sieberer (2006: 435) argue, 'party law is the domain of academic lawyers. Political scientists, while interested in the substance of party regulation in some selected fields, in particular with regard to elections and party finance, have not devoted much attention to party law as such'. Nevertheless, taking a 'legal approach' and carefully analysing all aspects of the way in which the law impacts upon political parties (incorporating both statute and case law) reveals important institutional constraints upon the organization of parties and the way that they interact and compete with one another in the party system. It also reveals another institutional mechanism that can be used (and indeed manipulated) by party actors in order to gain electoral advantage.

Conversely, the political sciences, particularly the body of party scholarship that has developed over the last century is the source of an important set of analytical tools that can be used to evaluate the impact of regulatory regimes upon political parties both as institutions and political actors. In particular, political science brings to the fore the importance of a functional approach to party regulation. Rather than seeking to regulate political parties on the basis of their legal status (an approach that is plagued by uncertainty, disagreement and circularity), we need to approach regulation by thinking through what we want political parties to do in society or what we want them to be (that is, their functions and their character). This could be achieved in part, by the courts utilizing a more developmentalist and dynamic approach to legal reasoning given the transformation of parties over the last century and their absence from original constitutional documents, and through a more considered approach to future legislative reform that acknowledges the democratic functions of parties and the normative assumptions underlying otherwise seemingly innocuous legislative provisions. A third option might be to put propositions concerning electoral laws to the people, thereby addressing the concern that as these provisions are largely contained in ordinary legislation and are typically not subject to any specific entrenchment provisions, they might be used or manipulated for partisan purposes. This functional approach will not eliminate disagreement, but will at the very least acknowledge the inherently political nature of law making and bring the functional questions and debates concerning to role of parties in modern democracy out into the open where they can be deliberated and answered in a more transparent way than currently exists.

Bibliography

AEC (Australian Electoral Commission) (2009a) 'Minute: The Meaning of "Obscene" Under the *Commonwealth Electoral Act* 1918', 5 August 2009 (Canberra: Australian Electoral Commission).

—— (2009b) 'Party registration decision: Australian Sex Party', <http://www.aec.gov.au/Parties_and_Representatives/party_registration/Registration_Decisions/austsp.htm>.

—— (2008) 'Financial Disclosure', <http://www.aec.gov.au/Parties_and_Representatives/financial_disclosure/index.htm>.

—— (2005) *Funding and Disclosure Report Election 2004* (Canberra: Australian Electoral Commission).

AEO (Australian Electoral Office) (1977) 'AEO Referendums to be held on Saturday May 21, 1977 – Arguments for and Against', 28 March (Canberra: AEO).

Ahmed, M. (2007) 'Labor Rising Start Found Guilty of Smearing Her Election Rival', *Times Online*, 22 September <http://www.timesonline.co.uk/tol/news/politics/article2507836.ece>.

Aisenbrey, M. (2006) 'Party On: The Right to Voluntary Blanket Primaries', *Michigan Law Review* 105: 603–29.

Aldrich, J. (1995) *Why Parties? The Origin and Transformation of Political Parties in America* (Chicago, IL: The University of Chicago Press).

Allan, L. (2002) 'ALP Modernisation, Ethnic Branch Stacking, Factionalism and the Law', *People and Place* 10(4): 50–58.

Altman, A. (2002) 'Party Poopers: The Supreme Court Overlooks the Party, in *Federal Election Commission v. Colorado Republican Federal Campaign Committee*', *Saint Louis University Law Journal* 46: 1001–34.

APSA (American Political Science Association Committee on Political Parties) (1950) 'Toward a More Responsible Two Party System', *The American Political Science Review* 44(3). Part 2, Supplement: 1–96.

Arnold, T. (2005) 'Electoral (Integrity) Amendment Bill', Legal Advice to the Attorney General, Australian Ministry of Justice, published November 5 <http://www.courts.govt.nz/bill-of-rights/bill-list-2005/e-bill/electoral-integrity-amendment-bill.html>.

Atkinson, N. (2003) *Adventures in Democracy: A History of the Vote in New Zealand* (Dunedin: University of Otago Press).

Austin, R. and M. Tjernström (2003) *The Funding of Political Parties and Election Campaigns* (Stockholm: IDEA).

Australian Government (2009) *Electoral Reform Green Paper: Strengthening Australia's Democracy* (Canberra: Commonwealth of Australia).

Avnon, D. (1995) 'Parties' Laws in Democratic Systems of Government', *Journal of Legislative Studies* 1(2): 283–300.

Banning, L. (1989) *After the Constitution: Party Conflict in the New Republic* (Belmont, CA: Wadsworth).

Barendt, E. (1998) *An Introduction to Constitutional Law* (Oxford: Oxford University Press).

Bartolini, S. and P. Mair (2001) 'Challenges to Contemporary Political Parties', in L. Diamond and R. Gunther (eds) *Political Parties and Democracy* (Baltimore, MD: Johns Hopkins University Press).

Bauer, R. (2007) 'Not Just A Private Matter: The Purposes of Disclosure in an Expanded Regulatory System', *Election Law Journal* 6(1): 38–55.

BBC Online News (2007) 'Slur Councillor Loses her Appeal', 30 November <http://news.bbc.co.uk/2/hi/uk_news/england/london/7122048.stm>.

Bennett, J. (2009) *Stifling Political Competition: How Government Has Rigged the System to Benefit Demopublicans and Exclude Third Parties* (New York: Springer).

Bennett, S. (2002) *Australia's Political Parties: More Regulation?* Parliamentary Library Research Paper No. 21 2001–02 (Canberra: Parliament of Australia).

Blackshield, T. and G. Williams (2002) *Australian Constitutional Law and Theory: Commentary and Materials* (Sydney: The Federation Press).

Blackstone, W. (2001) (1st edition 1830) *Blackstone's Commentaries on the Laws of England*, Volume 1 (London: Cavendish).

Blais, A. and L. Massicotte (2002) 'Electoral Systems', in L. LeDuc, R.G. Niemi and P. Norris (eds) *Comparing Democracies 2* (London: Sage).

Blondel, J. (1963) *Voters, Parties and Leaders: The Social Fabric of British Politics* (Harmondsworth: Penguin).

Blyth, M. and R. Katz (2005) 'From Catch-all Politics to Cartelisation: The Political Economy of the Cartel Party', *West European Politics* 28(1): 33–60.

Boatright, R. (2007) 'Situating the New 527 Organizations in Interest Group Theory', *The Forum* 5(2): 1–23.

Bogdanor, V. (2009) *The New British Constitution* (Oxford: Hart Publishing).

—— (2004) 'The Constitution and the Party System in the Twentieth Century', *Parliamentary Affairs* 57(4): 717–33.

Bradley, A.W. and K.D. Ewing (2003) *Constitutional and Administrative Law*, 13th edition (London: Longman).

Briffault, R. (2006) 'Soft Money, Congress and the Supreme Court', in K.D. Ewing and S. Issacharoff (eds) *Party Funding and Campaign Financing in International Perspective* (Oxford: Hart Publishing).

—— (2000) 'The Political Parties and Campaign Finance Reform', *Columbia Law Review* vol. 100: 620–66.

Brooks, S. (2009) *Canadian Democracy*, 6th edition (Don Mills, ON: Oxford University Press).

Busby, N. (2003) 'Sex Equality in Political Candidature: Supply and Demand Factors and the Role of the Law', *Modern Law Review* 66(1): 245–60.

Button, J. (2002) 'Beyond Belief: What Future for Labor?', *Quarterly Essay* 6: 1–79.

Carothers, T. (2006) *Confronting the Weakest Link: Aiding Political Parties in New Democracies* (Washington, DC: Carnegie Endowment for International Peace).

Carty, R.K. (2002) 'Canada's Nineteenth Century Cadre Parties at the Millennium', in P. Webb, D. Farrell and I. Holliday (eds) *Political Parties in Advanced Industrial Democracies* (Oxford: Oxford University Press).

Casas-Zamora, K. (2005) *Paying for Democracy: Political Finance and State Funding for Parties* (Colchester: ECPR Press).

Cass, D. and S. Burrows (2000) 'Commonwealth Regulation of Campaign Finance – Public Funding, Disclosure and Expenditure Limits', *The Sydney Law Review* 22: 447–96.

Catt, H. (2008) 'Administering the Electoral Finance Act', paper presented at the LexisNexis electoral law forum, Wellington, 2 September <http://www.elections.org.nz/administration/ec-corp-info/administering-efa.html>.

Chambers, W. (1963) *Political Parties in a New Nation: The American Experience, 1776–1809* (New York: Oxford University Press).

Christodoulis, E. and S. Tierney (2008) 'Public Law and Politics: Rethinking the Debate', in E. Christodoulis and S. Tierney (eds) *Public Law and Politics: The Scope and Limits of Constitutionalism* (Aldershot: Ashgate).

CSPL (Committee on Standards of Public Life) (1998) *The Funding of Political Parties in the United Kingdom* (Cmnd 4067) (London: HMSO).

Coghill, K. (2001) 'Let the People Decide: Primaries for Preselections', paper presented at the Good Governance: Fair Elections and Ethical Parties Conference, Monash University, Melbourne, 23 February 2001.

Committee on Election Expenses (Canada) (1966) *Report of the Committee on Election Expenses* (Ottawa: Queen's Printer).

Courtney, J. (1993) 'Discrimination in Canada's Electoral Law', in W. Tarnopolsky, J. Whitman and M. Owlette (eds) *Discrimination in the Law in the Administration of Justice* (Toronto: Carswell).

—— (1978) 'Recognition of Canadian Political Parties in Parliament and in Law', *Canadian Journal of Political Science* 11(1): 33–60.

Cowley, P. (1996) 'Crossing the Floor: Representative Theory and Practice in Britain', *Public Law* [1996]: 214–24.

Craig, P. (1990) *Public Law and Democracy in the United Kingdom* (Oxford: Clarendon Press).

Criminal Justice Commission (Queensland) (2001) *The Shepherdson Inquiry: An Investigation into Electoral Fraud* (Brisbane: Criminal Justice Commission).

Cross, W. (2004) *Political Parties* (Vancouver: UBC Press).

—— (1994) 'Regulating Independent Expenditures in Federal Elections', *Canadian Public Policy* 20(3): 253–64.

Crotty, W. (2006) 'Party Origins and Evolution in the United States', in R. Katz and W. Crotty (eds) *Handbook of Party Politics* (London: Sage).

CTV News Online (2005) 'Conservative MP Introduces Party Hopping Bill', CTV News Online, 17 June <http://edmonton.ctv.ca/servlet/an/local/CTVNews/20050617/party_hopping_050617?hub=TorontoHome>.

Dalton, R. (2000) 'The Decline of Party Identification', in R. Dalton and M. Wattenberg (eds) *Parties without Partisans: Political Change in Advanced Industrial Democracies* (Oxford: Oxford University Press).

Dalton, R. and S. Weldon (2005) 'Public Images of Political Parties: A Necessary Evil?', *Party Politics* 28(5): 931–51.

Duverger, M. (1954) *Political Parties* (London: Methuen).

ECQ (Electoral Commission of Queensland) (2008) 'Registration of Political Parties – Queensland', 8th edition (Brisbane: Electoral Commission of Queensland).

Elections Canada (2010) 'Political Parties – Political Financing and Other Information' <http://www.elections.ca/content.asp?section=fin&dir=pol&document=index&lang=e&textonly=false>.

Elections NZ (2009) 'Broadcast allocation to parties process report – Election '08' (Wellington: New Zealand Electoral Commission).

—— (2008) 'Party election guide 2008: Election advertising rules – Summary', published 9 July <http://www.elections.org.nz/rules/parties/partysub/e5-party-advertising-summary.html>.

—— (2006) 'National Front Logo Registered to Appear on Ballot Papers' <http://www.elections.org.nz/news/ec-media-nflogo-090206.html>.

Epperson, J. (1986) *The Changing Legal Status of Political Parties in the United States* (New York: Garland).

Epstein, L.D. (1989) 'Will American Political Parties be Privatized?', *Journal of Law and Politics* 5(2): 239–74.

—— (1986) *Political Parties in the American Mold* (Madison: University of Wisconsin Press).

—— (1980) *Political Parties in Western Democracies* (New Brunswick, NJ: Transaction Books).

Ewing, K. (2007) *The Cost of Democracy: Party Funding in Modern British Politics* (Oxford: Hart Publishing).

—— (1987) *The Funding of Political Parties in Britain* (Cambridge: Cambridge University Press).

—— and N.S. Ghaleigh (2007) 'The Cost of Giving and Receiving: Donations to Political Parties in the United Kingdom', *Election Law Journal* 6(1): 56–71.

Ewing, K.D. and S. Issacharoff (2006) 'Introduction', in K.D. Ewing and S. Issacharoff (eds) *Party Funding and Campaign Financing in International Perspective* (Oxford: Hart Publishing).

Fay, J. (1982) 'Legal Regulation of Political Parties', *Journal of Legislation* 9: 263–81.

Feasby, C. (2007) 'Constitutional Questions About Canada's New Political Finance Regime', *Osgoode Hall Law Journal* 45: 513–70.

—— (2006) 'Political Theory and the Constitutionality of the Political Finance Regime', in K.D. Ewing and S. Issacharoff (eds) *Party Funding and Campaign Financing in International Perspective* (Oxford: Hart Publishing).

—— (1999) '*Libman v. Quebec (AG)* and the Administration of the Process of Democracy under the *Charter*: The Emerging Egalitarian Model', *McGill Law Journal* 44: 5–38.

Finer, S.E., V. Bogdanor and B. Rudden (1995) *Comparing Constitutions* (Oxford: Clarendon Press).

Fisher, J. (1997) 'Donations to Political Parties', *Parliamentary Affairs* 50(2): 235–45.

Flew, T. (2008) 'Not Yet the Internet Election: Online Media, Political Commentary and the 2007 Australian Federal Election', *Media International Australia* 128.

Forbes, J. (1995) 'Judicial Review of Political Parties', Research Paper No. 21 (Canberra: Department of the Parliamentary Library).

Forcese, C. and A. Freeman (2005) *The Laws of Government: The Legal Foundations of Canadian Democracy* (Toronto: Irwin Law).

Franklin, M. (2004) *Voter Turnout and the Dynamics of Electoral Competition* (New York: Cambridge University Press).

Freeman, A. and E. Mensch (1987) 'The Public Private Distinction in American Law and Life', *Buffalo Law Review* 36: 237.

Gallagher, M. (1988) 'Introduction', in M. Gallagher and M. Marsh (eds) *Candidate Selection in Comparative Perspective* (London: Sage).

—— and P. Mitchell (eds) (2005) *The Politics of Electoral Systems* (Oxford: Oxford University Press).

Gardner, J. (2000) 'Symposium: Law and Political Parties: Can Party Politics be Virtuous?', *Columbia Law Review* 100: 667–701.

Garrett, E. (2005) 'Veiled Political Actors and Campaign Disclosure Laws in Direct Democracy', *Election Law Journal* 4: 295–328.

—— (2002) 'Is the Party Over? Courts and the Political Process', *The Supreme Court Review* [2002]: 95–152.

Gauja, A. (2010) 'Party Dimensions of Representation in Westminster Parliaments: Australia, New Zealand and the United Kingdom', in M. Blomgren and O. Rozenberg (eds) *Parliamentary Roles in Modern Legislatures* (London: Routledge).

—— (2008) 'State Regulation and the Internal Organisation of Political Parties: The Impact of Party Law in Australia, Canada, New Zealand and the United Kingdom', *Commonwealth and Comparative Politics* 46(2): 244–61.

—— (2006a) 'Enforcing Democracy? Towards a Regulatory Regime for the Implementation of Intra-party Democracy', Discussion Paper 16/06 (April), Democratic Audit of Australia, Political Science Program, Australian National University.

—— (2006b) 'From Hogan to Hanson: The Regulation and Changing Legal Status of Australian Political Parties', *Public Law Review* 17: 282–99.

—— (2005) 'Keeping the Party Under Control: The Legal Regulation of Australia's Political Parties', *Australian Review of Public Affairs*, 11 July.

Gay, O. (2001) 'What's in a Name? Political Parties, Lists and Candidates in the United Kingdom', *Public Law*, Summer: 245–55.

——, I. White and R. Kelly (2007) *The Funding of Political Parties*, House of Commons Research Paper 07/34 (10 April 2007) (London: Parliament and Constitution Centre, House of Commons Library).

Geddis, A. (2009) 'The Legal Status of Political Parties Under MMP', *New Zealand Journal of Public and International Law* 7: 21–38.

—— (2008) 'New Zealand's Electoral Finance Act 2007 and its Discontents', *Public Law Review* 19: 215–33.

—— (2007a) *Electoral Law in New Zealand: Practice and Policy* (Wellington: Lexis Nexis).

—— (2007b) 'Rethinking the Funding of New Zealand's Election Campaigns', *Policy Quarterly* 3(1): 3–10.

—— (2006a) 'Proportional Representation, "Party Hopping" and the Limits of Electoral Regulation: A Cautionary Tale from New Zealand', *Common Law World Review* 34(4): 24–50.

—— (2006b) 'The Regulation of Campaign Funding in New Zealand: Practices, Problems and Prospects for Change', in K.D. Ewing and S. Issacharoff (eds) *Party Funding and Campaign Financing in International Perspective* (Oxford: Hart Publishing).

—— (2005) 'The Unsettled Legal Status of Political Parties in New Zealand', *New Zealand Journal of Public and International Law* 3: 105.

—— (2004) 'Regulating the Funding of Election Campaigns in New Zealand: A Critical Overview', *Otago Law Review* 10(4): 575–97.

—— (2003) 'Three Conceptions of the Electoral Moment', *Australian Journal of Legal Philosophy* 28: 53–77.

—— (2002a) 'Towards a System of Taxpayer Funding for New Zealand Elections?', *Otago Law Review* 10: 181–212.

—— (2002b) 'Gang Aft A-Gley: New Zealand's Attempt To Combat "Party Hopping" By Elected Representatives', *Election Law Journal* 1(4): 557–71.

Ghaleigh, N.S. (2006) 'Expenditure, Donations and Public Funding under the United Kingdom's *Political Parties, Elections and Referendums Act 2000* – And Beyond?', in K.D. Ewing and S. Issacharoff (eds) *Party Funding and Campaign Financing in International Perspective* (Oxford: Hart Publishing).

Ghazarian, Z. (2006) 'State of Assistance? Political Parties and State Support in Australia', *Australian Review of Public Affairs* 7(1): 61–76.

Goldsworthy, J. (ed.) (2006) *Interpreting Constitutions: A Comparative Study* (Oxford: Oxford University Press).

Graber, M. (2008) 'Constitutional Law and American Politics', in K. Whittington, R.D. Kelemen and G. Caldeira (eds) *The Oxford Handbook of Law and Politics* (Oxford: Oxford University Press).

Grattan, M. and Murphy, D. (2000) 'ALP Frontbencher Stood Down in Poll Cash Row', *Sydney Morning Herald*, 2 December: 1.

Griffith, G. and T. Drabsch (2007) 'Election Finance Law: Recent Developments and Proposals for Reform', New South Wales Parliamentary Library Research Service, Briefing Paper No. 8/07 (Sydney: NSW Parliament).

Gunlicks, A. (1993) *Campaign and Party Finance in North America and Western Europe* (Boulder, CO: Westview Praeger).

Gunther, R. and L. Diamond (2001) 'Types and Functions of Parties', in R. Gunther and L. Diamond (eds) *Political Parties and Democracy* (Baltimore, MD: Johns Hopkins University Press).

Hager, N. (2006) *The Hollow Men: A Study in the Politics of Deception* (Nelson: Craig Potton Publishing).

Hall, P. and R. Taylor (1996) 'Political Science and the Three New Institutionalisms', *Political Studies* 44: 936–57.

Hasen, R. (2001) 'Do the Parties or the People Own the Electoral Process?', *University of Pennsylvania Law Review* 149: 815–41.

Hausegger, L., M. Hennigar and T. Riddell (2009) *Canadian Courts: Law, Politics, and Process* (Don Mills, ON: Oxford University Press).

Hazan, R. and G. Rahat (2006) 'Candidate Selection: Methods and Consequences', in R. Katz and W. Crotty (eds) *Handbook of Party Politics* (London: Sage).

Head, M. (2003) 'The Jailing of Pauline Hanson: A Victory for Democracy?', *Alternative Law Journal* 28(6): 264–8.

Hoadley, J. (1986) *Origins of American Political Parties 1789–1803* (Lexington: University Press of Kentucky).

Hofstadter, R. (1969) *The Idea of a Party System: The Rise of Legitimate Opposition in the United States, 1780–1840* (Berkeley: University of California Press).

Holland, I. (2002) 'Members of Parliament (Staff) Act: Background', Research Note 14 2002–03 (Canberra: Australian Parliamentary Library).

Houghton, Lord (1976) *Report of the Committee on Financial Aid to Political Parties* (London: HMSO).

Hughes, C. (1998) 'Electoral Bribery', *Griffith Law Review* 7: 209.

Ignazi, P. (2003) *Extreme Right Parties in Western Europe* (Oxford: Oxford University Press).

Issacharoff, S. (2001) 'Private Parties with Public Purposes: Political Parties, Associational Freedoms, and Partisan Competition', *Columbia Law Review* 101: 274–313.

—— (2000) 'Introduction: The Structures of Democratic Politics', *Columbia Law Review*, 'Symposium: Law and Political Parties', 100(3): 593–7.

—— and R.H. Pildes (1998) 'Politics as Markets: Partisan Lockups of the Democratic Process', *Stanford Law Review* 50: 643.

——, P. Karlan and R. Pildes (1998) *The Law of Democracy* (Westbury, NY: Foundation Press).

ITC (Independent Television Commission) (2001) *Election 2001: Viewers' Responses to the Television Coverage* (London: ITC).

Jackson, K. and A. McRobie (1998) *New Zealand Adopts Proportional Representation: Accident? Design? Evolution?* (Aldershot: Ashgate Press).

Jaensch, D., P. Brent and B. Bowden (2004) *Australian Political Parties in the Spotlight*, Report No. 4, Democratic Audit of Australia, Political Science Program, Research School of Social Sciences, (Canberra: Australian National University).

Janda, K. (2009) 'Laws Against Party Switching, Defecting, or Floor Crossing in National Parliaments', The Legal Regulation of Political Parties Working Paper 2, August <www.partylaw.bham.ac.uk/pdfs/wp0209>.

—— (2005) 'Adopting Party Law', Political Parties and Democracy in Theoretical and Practical Perspectives (Washington, DC: National Democratic Institute for International Affairs).

Jansen, H. and L. Young (2005) 'Solidarity Forever? The NDP, Organized Labour and the Changing Face of Party Finance in Canada', paper presented to the Canadian Political Science Association Annual Conference.

Jennings, I. (1961) *Party Politics II: The Growth of Parties* (Cambridge: Cambridge University Press).

Jenson, J. (1991) 'Innovation and Equity: The Impact of Public Funding', in F. Leslie Siedle (ed.) *Comparative Issues in Party and Election Finance* (Toronto: Dundurn).

Johns, G. (2000) 'Party Democracy: An Audit of Australian Parties', *Australian Journal of Political Science* 35: 401–25.

—— (1999) 'Political Parties: From Private to Public', *Commonwealth and Comparative Politics* 37(2): 89–113.

Johnson, J. (2008) 'Democracy and Disclosure: Electoral Systems and the Regulation of Political Finance', *Election Law Journal* 7(4): 325–41.

Jones, B., D. Kavanagh, M. Moran and P. Norton (eds) (2007) *Politics UK*, 6th edition (Harlow: Pearson).

Jones, R. (2001) 'Electoral Misconduct and the Regulation of Political Parties', Briefing Paper No. 05/2001 (New South Wales Parliament: Parliamentary Library).

Joseph, P. (2007) *Constitutional and Administrative Law in New Zealand*, 3rd edition (Wellington: Thomson).

JSCEM (Joint Standing Committee on Electoral Matters) (1989) *Who Pays the Piper Calls the Tune: Minimising the Risks of Funding Political Campaigns* (Canberra: Parliament of Australia).

JSCER (Joint Select Committee on Electoral Reform) (1983) *First Report* (Canberra: Parliament of the Commonwealth of Australia).

Jupp, J. (1968) *Political Parties* (London: Routledge).

Kam, C. (2009) *Party Discipline and Parliamentary Politics* (Cambridge: Cambridge University Press).

Kang, M. (2005) 'The Hydraulics and Politics of Party Regulation', *Iowa Law Review* 91: 131–87.

Karvonen, L. (2007) 'Legislation on Political Parties: A Global Comparison', *Party Politics* 13(4): 437–55.

Katz, R. (2007) *Political Institutions in the United States* (Oxford: Oxford University Press).

—— (2002) 'The Ascendancy of the Party in Public Office: Party Organizational Change in Twentieth-Century Democracies', in R. Gunther, J. Ramon-Montero and J. Linz (eds) *Political Parties: Old Concepts and New Challenges* (Oxford: Oxford University Press).

—— (2001) 'The Problem of Candidate Selection and Models of Party Democracy', *Party Politics* 7(3): 277–96.

—— (1993) 'The Evolution of Party Organizations in Europe: The Three Faces of Party Organization', in W. Crotty (ed.) *Political Parties in a Changing Age*, special issue of the *American Review of Politics* 14: 593–617.

—— (1987) 'Party Government and Its Alternatives', in R. Katz (ed.) *Party Governments: European and American Experiences* (Florence: EUI; Berlin: De Gruyter).

—— (1986) 'Party Government: A Rationalistic Conception', in F.G. Castles and R. Wildenmann (eds) *Visions and Realities of Party Government* (Berlin: De Gruyter).

—— and Mair, P. (1995) 'Changing Models of Party Organization and Party Democracy: the Emergence of the Cartel Party', *Party Politics* 1(1): 5–28.

—— (2009) 'The Cartel Party Thesis: A Restatement', *Perspectives on Politics* 7(4): 753–66.

Kelly, R. (2006) *Funding of Political Parties – A Brief Overview*, House of Commons Library Standard Note SN/PC/3138 (London: HMSO).

Kelsen, H. (1929) (1981 edition) *Vom Wessen und Wert der Democratie*, 'On the Essence and Value of Democracy' (Aalen: Scientia Verlag).

Key, V.O. (1964) *Politics, Parties and Pressure Groups* (New York: TY Crowell).

—— (1961) *Public Opinion and American Democracy* (New York: Albert A. Knopf).

King-Hall, S. (1954) 'The Duties of a Member of Parliament', *Parliamentary Affairs* 8(3): 302.

Kirchheimer, O. (1966) 'The Transformation of Western European Party Systems', in J. La Palombara and M. Weiner (eds) *Political Parties and Political Development* (Princeton, NJ: Princeton University Press).

Koole, R. (2001) 'Political Finance in Western Europe: Britain and France', in K.H. Nassmacher (ed.) *Foundations of Democracy: Approaches to Comparative Political Finance* (Baden Baden: Nomos).

Lambert, L.A. and H. Jansen (2007) 'Party Building by a State Dependent Party: The Case of the Green Party of Canada', paper presented to the Annual Meeting of the Canadian Political Science Association, Saskatoon, Sasketchewan, 30 May–1 June.

Lawrence, C. (2006) 'Political Corporations', in B. Jones (ed.) *Coming to the Party: Where to Next for Labor?* (Melbourne: Melbourne University Press).

Lawson, K. (1988) 'When Linkage Fails', in K. Lawson and P. Merkl (eds) *When Parties Fail: Emerging Alternative Organizations* (Princeton, NJ: Princeton University Press).

Loveday, P., A.W. Parker and R.S. Martin (eds) (1977) *The Emergence of the Australian Party System* (Sydney: Hale and Iremonger).

Loveland, I. (2006) *Constitutional Law, Administrative Law and Human Rights* (Oxford: Oxford University Press).

Lowenstein, D. (2006) 'Legal Regulation and Protection of American Parties', in R. Katz and W. Crotty (eds) *Handbook of Party Politics* (London: Sage).

—— (1993) 'Associational Rights of Major Political Parties: A Skeptical Inquiry', *Texas Law Review* 71: 1741–92.

—— and R. Hasen (2004) *Election Law*, 3rd edition (Durham, NC: Carolina Academic Press).

Lutz, D. (2006) *Principles of Constitutional Design* (New York: Cambridge University Press).

Macedo, S. et al. (2005) *Democracy at Risk: How Political Choices Undermine Citizen Participation in Politics and What We Can Do About It* (Washington, DC: Brookings Institution Press).

MacIvor, H. (2004) 'The Charter of Rights and Party Politics: The Impact of the Supreme Court Ruling in *Figueroa v. Canada (Attorney General)*', *Choices*, vol. 10 (Montreal: Institute for Research on Public Policy).

Magarian, G. (2003) 'Regulating Political Parties under a "Public Rights" First Amendment', *William and Mary Law Review* 44: 1942–2061.

Mair, P. (2005) 'Democracy Beyond Parties', discussion paper, Centre for the Study of Democracy (Irvine, CA: University of California).

—— and I. van Biezen (2001) 'Party Membership in Twenty European Democracies', *Party Politics* 7: 5–21.

Malbin, M.J. and T.L. Gais (1998) *The Day After Reform: Sobering Campaign Finance Lessons From the American States* (Albany, NY: Rockerfeller Institute Press).

Malone, R. (2008) *Rebalancing the Constitution: The Challenge of Government Law-Making under MMP* (Victoria: University of Wellington, IPS).

Manin, B. (1997) *The Principles of Representative Government* (Cambridge: Cambridge University Press).

Massicotte, L., A. Blais and A. Yoshinaka (2003) *Establishing the Rules of the Games: Election Laws in Democracies* (Toronto: University of Toronto Press).

McAllister, I. (2002) 'Political Parties in Australia: Party Stability in a Utilitarian Society', in P. Webb, D. Farrell and I. Holliday (eds) *Political Parties in Advanced Industrial Democracies* (Oxford: Oxford University Press).

McAuslan, P. (1983) 'Administrative Law, Collective Consumption and Judicial Policy', *The Modern Law Review* 46(1): 1–20.

McHarg, A. (2006) 'Quotas for Women! The Sex Discrimination (Election Candidates) Act 2002', *Journal of Law and Society* 33(1): 141–59.

McKenzie, R. (1982) 'Power in the Labour Party: The Issue of Intra-party Democracy', in D. Kavanagh (ed.) *The Politics of the Labour Party* (London: Macmillan).

—— (1963) *British Political Parties* (London: Mercury Books).

McLaughlin, A. (1912) *The Courts, The Constitution and Parties: Studies in Constitutional History and Politics* (Chicago, IL: Chicago University Press).

Mersel, Y. (2006a) 'Hans Kelsen and Political Parties', *Israel Law Review* 39: 158–81.

—— (2006b) 'The Dissolution of Political Parties: The Problem of Internal Democracy', *International Journal of Constitutional Law* 4: 84.

Michels, R. (1962) (1st edition 1915) *Political Parties* (New York: Collier Books).

Miller, R. (2005) *Party Politics in New Zealand* (Auckland: Oxford University Press).

—— (2004) 'Constitutionality of Voter Participation Provisions for Primary Elections', 120 *American Law Reports* ALR5th 125.

Miskin, S. (2003) 'Politician Overboard: Jumping the Party Ship', Research Paper No. 4 2002–03 (Department of the Parliamentary Library: Commonwealth of Australia).

Morris, C. (2008) 'Conceptualising Candidate Selection in the Courts: Where to After *Watt v. Ashan*?', *Public Law* [2008]: 415–29.

Moss, J. and J.C. Tham (2011) 'Freedom of Association, Political Parties and Party Funding', in J.C. Tham, B. Costar and G. Orr (eds) *Electoral Regulation and Prospects for Australian Democracy* (Melbourne: Melbourne University Press, forthcoming).

Müller, W. (2003) 'The relevance of the state for party system change', *Journal of Theoretical Politics* 5: 419–54.

—— and U. Sieberer (2006) 'Party Law', in R. Katz and W. Crotty (eds) *Handbook of Party Politics* (London: Sage).

Murray, A. and M. Rock (2000) 'The Dangerous Art of Giving, *Australian Quarterly* 72(3): 29.

Namier, L. (1952) *Monarchy and the Party System* (Oxford: Oxford University Press).

Nassmacher, K.H. (2006) 'Regulation of Party Finance', in R. Katz and W. Crotty (eds) *Handbook of Party Politics* (London: Sage).

—— (2001) *Foundations for Democracy: Approaches to Comparative Political Finance. Essays in Honour of Herbert E. Alexander* (Baden Baden: Nomos).

—— (1993) 'Comparing Party and Campaign Finance in Western Democracies', in A.B. Gunlicks (ed.) *Campaign and Party Finance in North America and Western Europe* (Boulder, CO: Westview Press).

—— (1989) 'Structure and Impact of Public Subsidies to Political Parties in Europe: The Examples of Austria, Italy, Sweden and West Germany', in H.E. Alexander (ed.) *Comparative Political Finance in the 1980s* (Cambridge: Cambridge University Press).

Nelson, R.L. (2005) 'The U.S. Supreme Court and the Institutional Role of Political Parties in the Political Process: What Tradition?', *Widener Law Journal* 15: 85–107.

Nokken. T. (2000) 'Dynamics of Congressional Loyalty: Party Defection and Roll-Call Behavior, 1947–97', *Legislative Studies Quarterly* 25(3): 417–44.

Norris, P. (2006) 'Recruitment', in R. Katz and W. Crotty (eds) *Handbook of Party Politics* (London: Sage).

—— (2004) *Electoral Engineering* (Cambridge: Cambridge University Press).

NZ Labour (New Zealand Labour Party) (2003) *Constitution and Rules* (Wellington: NZ Labour Party).

NZ Ministry of Justice (2009) *Electoral Finance Reform* (Wellington: NZ Ministry of Justice).

NZ Office of the Auditor-General (2006) *Advertising Expenditure Incurred by the Parliamentary Service in the Three Months before the 2005 General Election* (Wellington: Office of the Auditor-General).

Oliver, D. (2003) *Constitutional Reform in the United Kingdom* (Oxford: Oxford University Press).

Orr, G. (2011) 'Legal Conceptions of Political Parties through the Lens of Anti-Discrimination Law', in J.C. Tham, B. Costar and G. Orr (eds) *Electoral Regulation and Prospects for Australian Democracy* (Melbourne: Melbourne University Press).

—— (2007) 'Political Disclosure Regulation in Australia: Lackadaisical Law', *Election Law Journal* 6(1): 72–88.

—— (2006a) 'Supressing Vote-Buying: The "War" on Electoral Bribery from 1868', *The Journal of Legal History* 27(3): 289–314.

—— (2006b) 'Political Finance Law in Australia', in K.D. Ewing and S. Issacharoff (eds) *Party Funding and Campaign Financing in International Perspective* (Oxford: Hart Publishing).

—— (2003) 'The Currency of Democracy: Campaign Finance Law in Australia, *UNSW Law Journal* 26(1): 1–31.

—— (2002) 'A Politician's Word: The Legal (Un)Enforceability of Political Deals', *Constitutional Law and Policy Review* 5(1): 1–11.

—— (2001) 'Overseeing the Gatekeepers: Should the Preselection of Political Candidates be Regulated?', *Public Law Review* 12: 89–94.

—— (2000) 'The Law Comes to the Party: The Continuing Juridification of Political Parties in Australia', *Constitutional Law and Policy Review* 3(2): 41–9.

——, B. Mercurio and G. Williams (eds) (2003) *Realising Democracy: Electoral Law in Australia* (Sydney: Federation Press).

Ortiz, D. (2000) 'Duopoly Versus Autonomy: How the Two-party System Harms the Major Parties', *Columbia Law Review* 100: 753–74.

Osiatynski, W. (2003) 'Paradoxes of Constitutional Borrowing', *International Journal of Constitutional Law* 1(2): 244–68.

Page, B., R. Shapiro, P. Gronke and R. Rosenberg (1984) 'Constituency, Party, and Representation in Congress', *The Public Opinion Quarterly* 48(4): 741–56.

Palmer, G. and M. Palmer (2004) *Bridled Power: New Zealand's Constitution and Government*, 4th edition (Oxford: Oxford University Press).

Paltiel, K.Z. (1987) 'Canadian Election Expense Legislation, 1963–1985: A Critical Appraisal or Was the Effort Worth It?', in H.E. Alexander (ed.) *Comparative Political Finance in the 1980s* (Cambridge: Cambridge University Press).

Panebianco, A. (1988) *Political Parties: Organization and Power* (Cambridge: Cambridge University Press).

Persily, N. (2006) 'The Law of American Party Finance', in K.D. Ewing and S. Issacharoff (eds) *Party Funding and Campaign Financing in International Perspective* (Oxford: Hart Publishing).

—— (2001) 'Toward a Functional Defense of Political Party Autonomy', *New York University Law Review* 76: 750.

—— and B. Cain (2000) 'The Legal Status of Political Parties: A Reassessment of Competing Paradigms', *Columbia Law Review* 100(3): 775–812.

Peters, G. (1999) *Institutional Theory in Political Science: The New Institutionalism* (London: Pinter).

Petterson, P. (1995) 'The Supreme Court and the Legal Status of Political Parties', unpublished PhD thesis, University of Massachusetts.

Pildes, R.H. (2004) 'The Supreme Court, 2003 Term', *Harvard Law Review* 118(1): 25–154.

Pinto-Duschinsky, M. (2002) 'Financing Politics: A Global View', *Journal of Democracy* 13(4): 69–86.

Pomper, G. (1992) *Passions and Interests: Political Party Concepts of American Democracy* (Lawrence: University of Kansas Press).

Power Inquiry (2006) *Power to the People. The Report of Power: An Independent Inquiry into Britain's Democracy* (York: York Publishing Distribution).

Rae, D. (1967) *The Political Consequences of Electoral Laws* (New Haven, CT: Yale University Press).

Ranney, A. (1981) 'Candidate Selection', in D. Butler, H.R. Penniman and A. Ranney (eds) *Democracy at the Polls* (Washington, DC: American Enterprise Institute).

—— (1975) *Curing the Mischiefs of Faction: Party Reform in America* (Berkeley: University of California Press).

Rawlings, H.F. (1988) *Law and the Electoral Process* (London: Sweet and Maxwell).

Reid, G. and M. Forrest (1989) *Australia's Commonwealth Parliament 1901–1988: Ten Perspectives* (Melbourne: Melbourne University Press).

Risjord, N. and G. DenBoer (1974) 'The Evolution of Political Parties in Virginia', *Journal of American History* 60: 961.

Rose, R. (1969) 'The Variability of Party Government: A Theoretical and Empirical Critique', *Political Studies* 17(4): 413–45.

Rosenblum, N. (2000) 'Symposium: Law and Political Parties: Political Parties as Membership Groups', *Columbia Law Review* 100: 813–44.

Rossiter, C. (1961) *The Federalist Papers: Alexander Hamilton, James Madison and John Jay* (New York: New American Press).

Rowbottom, J. (2006) 'Access to the Airwaves and Equality: The Case against Political Advertising on the Broadcast Media', in K.D. Ewing and S. Issacharoff (eds) *Party Funding and Campaign Financing in International Perspective* (Oxford: Hart Publishing).

Royal Commission on Electoral Reform and Party Financing (Canada) (1991) *Reforming Electoral Democracy: Final Report* (Ottawa: Royal Commission on Electoral Reform and Party Financing).

Sajo, A. (1993) 'Preferred Generations: A Paradox of Restoration Constitutions', *Cardozo Law Review* 14: 847–63.

Sartori, G. (1968) 'Representational Systems', *International Encyclopaedia of the Social Sciences* 13: 470–75.

—— (1965) *Democratic Theory* (New York: Praeger).

Sawer, M., N. Abjorensen and P. Larkin (2009) *Australia: The State of Democracy* (Sydney: Federation Press).

Sayers, A. and L. Young (2004) 'Election Campaign and Party Financing in Canada', Democratic Audit of Australia, Political Science Program (Canberra: Australian National University).

Scalia, A. (1981) 'The Legal Framework for Reform', *Commonsense* 4(2): 40.

Scarrow, S. (2005) 'Implementing Intra-party Democracy', discussion paper (Washington, DC: National Democratic Institution for International Affairs).

—— (2000) 'Parties without Members? Party Organization in a Changing Electoral Environment', in R. Dalton and M. Wattenberg (eds) *Parties without Partisans* (Oxford: Oxford University Press).

—— (1996) *Parties and their Members: Organizing for Victory in Britain and Germany* (Oxford: Oxford University Press).

Schattschneider, E.E. (1942) *Party Government* (New York: Farrar and Rinehart).

Schlesinger, A.M. (1973) *History of U.S. Political Parties, Volume 1 1789–1860* (New York: Chelsea House Publishers).

Schmitter, P. and A. Trechsel (2004) *The Future of Democracy in Europe: Trends, Analyses and Reforms* (Strasbourg: Council of Europe).

Schultz, D. (2005) 'Disclosure is Not Enough: Empirical Lessons from State Experiences', *Election Law Journal* 4(4): 349–70.

Schumpeter, J. (1942) *Capitalism, Socialism and Democracy* (London: Allen and Unwin).

Schwartzberg, M. (2007) *Democracy and Legal Change* (New York: Cambridge University Press).

Smith, R. (1997) 'The Party System', in R. Smith (ed.) *Politics in Australia*, 3rd edition (Sydney: Allen and Unwin).

—— and A. Gauja (2010) 'Understanding Party Constitutions as Responses to Specific Challenges', *Party Politics*, 19 April <http://ppq.sagepub.com/content/early/2010/03/31/1354068809346076.abstract>.

Somes, T. (1996) 'The Legal Status of Political Parties', in M. Simms (ed.) *The Paradox of Parties: Australian Political Parties in the 1990s* (Sydney: Allen and Unwin).

Stockley, A. (2004) 'What Difference Does Proportional Representation Make?' *Public Law Review* 15: 121–36.

Sullivan, K.M. (1988) 'Rainbow Republicanism', *Yale Law Journal* 97: 1713–23.

Tardi, G. (2007) 'Change of Allegiance in Political Life', *Commonwealth Law Bulletin* 33(3): 429–41.

Taylor, M. (2010) 'BNP Given Last Chance to Make Equality Change', *The Guardian*, 28 January: 13.

Tennant-Wood, R. (2004) 'The Role of the Media in the Public Disclosure of Electoral Funding', discussion paper for the Democratic Audit of Australia (Canberra: Australian National University).

Tham, J.C. (2003) 'Campaign Finance Reform in Australia: Some Reasons for Reform', in G. Orr, B. Mercurio and G. Williams (eds) *Realising Democracy* (Sydney: Federation Press).

——, B. Costar and G. Orr (eds) (2011) *Electoral Regulation and Prospects for Australian Democracy* (Melbourne: Melbourne University Press).

Thomassen, J. (1994) 'Empirical Research into Political Representation: Failing Democracy or Failing Models?', in M.K. Jennings and T.E. Mann (eds) *Elections at Home and Abroad: Essays in Honor of Warren Miller* (Ann Arbor, MI: Michigan University Press).

Trevett, C. (2009) 'Wide Agreement on Dumping Electoral Act', *New Zealand Herald*, 11 February.

Tribe, Laurence (1988) *American Constitutional Law*, 2nd edition (Mineola, NY: Foundation Press).

Tully, S. (2003) 'Party Registration and Preselection: A Minefield for Electoral Administrators?', in G. Orr, B. Mercurio and G. Williams (eds) *Realising Democracy: Electoral Law in Australia* (Sydney: The Federation Press).

Turpin, C. (1999) *British Government and the Constitution: Text Cases and Materials*, 4th edition (London: Butterworths).

—— and A. Tomkins (2007) *British Government and the Constitution*, 6th edition (Cambridge: Cambridge University Press).

UK Electoral Commission (2009) 'Guidance on Preventing and Detecting Electoral Malpractice' (London: Electoral Commission).

—— (2006) 'Guidance on Registering as a Political Party' (London: Electoral Commission).

—— (2001) 'Party Political Broadcasting Review, 2001–02, Discussion Paper' (London: Electoral Commission).

UK Parliament (Department of Finance and Administration) (2007) 'The Communications Allowance and the Use of House Stationery' (London: HMSO).

van Biezen, I. (2008a) 'Party Regulation and Constitutionalization: A Comparative Overview', in P. Nordlund and B. Reilly (eds) *Political Parties and Democracy in Conflict-Prone Societies: Regulation, Engineering and Democratic Development* (Tokyo: UN University Press) <www.partylaw.bham.ac.uk/pdfs/vanBiezen2008.pdf>.

—— (2008b) 'State Intervention in Party Politics: The Public Funding and Regulation of Political Parties', *European Review* 16(3): 263–9.

—— (2004) 'Political Parties as Public Utilities', *Party Politics* 10(6): 701–22.

—— (2003) 'The Place of Parties in Contemporary Democracies', *West European Politics* 26(3): 171–84.

—— and G. Borz (2009) 'The Place of Political Parties in National Country Constitutions: A General Overview', The Legal Regulation of Political Parties Working Paper 01/09 <http://www.partylaw.bham.ac.uk>.

—— and P. Kopecky (2007) 'The State and the Parties: Public Funding, Public Regulation and Rent-seeking in Contemporary Democracies', *Party Politics* 13(2): 235–54.

Vowles, J. (2002) 'Parties and Society in New Zealand', in P. Webb, D. Farrell and I. Holliday (eds) *Political Parties in Advanced Industrial Democracies* (Oxford: Oxford University Press).

Wallace, Justice J. (1986) *Towards a Better Democracy*. Report of the Royal Commission on the Electoral System, Wellington.

Ward, I. and R. Stewart (2006) *Politics One*, 3rd edition (South Yarra: Palgrave Macmillan).

Ware, A. (1987) *Citizens, Parties and the State* (Princeton, NJ: Princeton University Press).

Watt, B. (2006) *UK Election Law: A Critical Examination* (London: Glass House Press).

Wattenberg, M. (2003) *Where Have all the Voters Gone?* (Cambridge, MA: Harvard University Press).

Williams, W. (1928) *Rogers on Elections, vol. II, Parliamentary Elections and Petitions*, 12th edition (London: Stevens and Sons Ltd).

Wilson, J. (1962) *The Amateur Democrat* (Chicago, IL: University of Chicago Press).

Wilson, M. (1998) 'Political Parties and Participation', in A. Simpson (ed.) *The Constitutional Implications of MMP*, Occasional Publication No. 9, School of Political Science and International Relations, Victoria University of Wellington.

Winkler, A. (2000) 'Voters' Rights and Parties' Wrongs: Early Political Party Regulation in the State Courts, 1886–1915', *Columbia Law Review* 100: 873.

Winterton, G. (2003) 'The *Communist Party* Case', in H.P. Lee and G. Winterton (eds) *Australian Constitutional Landmarks* (Cambridge: Cambridge University Press).

Young, L. (1998) 'Party, State and Political Competition in Canada: The Cartel Model Reconsidered', *Canadian Journal of Political Science* 31(2): 339–58.

Young, S. (2005) 'Theories for Understanding Government Advertising in Australia', discussion paper for the Democratic Audit of Australia, Australian National University, Canberra, August 2005.

—— (2004) *The Persuaders: Inside the Hidden Machine of Political Advertising* (North Melbourne: Pluto Press).

—— and J.C. Tham (2006) *Political Finance in Australia: A Skewed and Secret System*, Focused Audit No. 7 for the Democratic Audit of Australia (Canberra: Australian National University).

Index